According to TASTE

The purpose of the Lufkin Service League, Inc. is exclusively educational and charitable and is to promote voluntarism; to develop the potential of its members for voluntary participation in community affairs; and to demonstrate the effectiveness of trained volunteers. The profits from the sale of these cookbooks will be used strictly for educational and charitable endeavors.

Additional copies may be obtained from:
LUFKIN SERVICE LEAGUE PUBLICATIONS
P. O. Box 1311
Lufkin, Texas 75902-1311
Area Code (409) 639-6929

$11.95 per copy $0.61 *(Texas residents only)*
$2.00 shipping & handling $1.00 per copy for gift wrap

Make checks payable to:
LUFKIN SERVICE LEAGUE PUBLICATIONS

First Printing   September 1985   5,000 copies

Printed in the United States of America
Hart Graphics, Inc., 8000 Shoal Creek, Austin, Texas 78758

TABLE OF CONTENTS

Foreword

The Lufkin Service League presents *According to Taste* in appreciation for the gracious people and many natural resources of our beautiful East Texas area. This collection of delicious recipes has been compiled, tested and enthusiastically approved by the members of the Service League, by friends and supporters of the League and by our sustaining members. Our section entitled *According to Taste* gives you suggestions on cooking to please your own palate; cook according to our taste, or be creative and cook to yours. Our *Southern Hushpuppy Olympics* section spotlights winning recipes from the nationally famous Southern Hushpuppy Olympics which is held in Lufkin each spring. The Lufkin Service League dedicates the proceeds from the sale of *According to Taste* to the community services and projects which it sponsors.

Committee Members

Vickie Anders Haglund, Chairman
Len Arnett Medford, Co-Chairman
Susan Gissell Sumners, Co-Chairman

Marcia Stolnacke Griffin
Alys Frazier Ray
An Walker Sweeny
Libby Love Stapleton
Susan Rutherford Mathis

Debbie Moore Todd
Mary Jane Medford West
Sarah Zeagler Hunter
Bobbi Riassetto Robinson

Cover and Illustrations by Peter Lisieski

According to Taste

According to Taste

Our According to Taste section offers the opportunity to be creative. Each recipe includes variations which allow you to produce original dishes to suit your palate. The instructions were written so as to indicate at which points changes may be made and are indicated by the term "variation". We hope this special section will stimulate you to try all of our variations or create a few of your own.

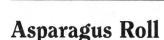

Asparagus Roll

350 degrees, preheated
Cookie sheet
Yield: Equal to number of spears

1   8-ounce package cream
    cheese, softened
1   4-ounce package Bleu
    Cheese Ranch Style
    Dressing Mix
Bread slices, trimmed of crust
    and rolled thin (number to
    equal number of
    asparagus spears)
1   14½-ounce can asparagus
    spears, well drained
½   cup butter, melted
1   teaspoon garlic powder

Mix cream cheese and dressing mix. Spread mixture on bread and roll each slice around an asparagus spear. Combine melted butter and garlic powder. Dip asparagus rolls in melted butter mixture. Place on cookie sheet and freeze or refrigerate until firm. Slice and bake 15 to 20 minutes (longer if frozen).

Variation I:
Omit cream cheese and dressing mix. Roll bread around asparagus. Dip in mixture of ½ cup melted butter and ¾ cup grated Parmesan cheese. Follow remaining directions.

Variation II:
Substitute 3-ounce crumbled bleu cheese for dressing mix.

Cheese Dreams

Yield: 144 to 180

1   loaf unsliced bread, crust removed, cut into 1 to 1½-inch cubes

Cheese Coating Variation I:
½   pound Old English cheese
1   cup cream
½   pound butter

Cheese Coating Variation I:
Melt cheese, cream and butter in the top of a double boiler. Dip bread cubes in cheese mixture and place on a wax paper covered cookie sheet. Refrigerate at least 6 hours. Remove wax paper and bake at 350 degrees for 10 minutes.

Cheese Coating Variation II:
2   3-ounce packages cream cheese
8   ounces sharp Cheddar cheese, grated
1   cup butter
4   egg whites, stiffly beaten

Cheese Coating Variation II:
Melt cheeses and butter in the top of a double boiler. Remove from heat. Fold a small amount of hot cheese mixture into the egg whites. Fold egg white mixture into remaining cheese mixture. Dip bread into cheese mixture. Place cubes 1 inch apart on a lightly greased baking sheet. Cover and refrigerate overnight. Bake uncovered at 400 degrees for 10 to 12 minutes.

Layered Mexican Dip

13-inch tray or platter
Yield: 20 to 30 servings

Layer 1:
2 10½-ounce cans bean dip
Or
1 16-ounce can refried
   beans
½ of a 1.25-ounce package
   taco seasoning

Layer 2:
3 avocados, mashed
2 Tablespoons lemon juice
3 Tablespoons mayonnaise
½ teaspoon salt
¼ teaspoon black pepper
Or
6 ounces avocado dip

Layer 3:
1 cup sour cream
½ cup mayonnaise
1 1.25-ounce package taco
   seasoning mix
Or
1 cup sour cream

Layers 4, 5, 6 and 7:
2 to 3 chopped tomatoes
½ cup chopped green or
   white onions
1 4½-ounce can chopped
   olives
8 ounces grated Cheddar
   cheese or grated Monterey
   Jack cheese

Mix together your choice of ingredients for first 3 layers. Spread layer 1 over 13-inch tray or platter. Top with remaining layers in the order listed. Serve with tostado chips.

Appetizer Meatballs

Yield: 48

Combine 1 of the meatball variations with 1 of the sauce variations. Serve warm in a chafing dish.

Meatballs Variation I:
1   pound ground beef
¾   cup seasoned bread crumbs
2   Tablespoons chopped onion
1   Tablespoon ketchup
4   drops Tabasco sauce
½   teaspoon horseradish
2   eggs, well beaten
½   teaspoon salt
½   teaspoon black pepper
½   teaspoon monosodium glutamate
1   Tablespoon grated Parmesan cheese
2 to 3 Tablespoons vegetable oil

Meatballs Variation I:
In a mixing bowl, combine first 11 ingredients, mixing well. Form meat mixture into 1-inch balls and fry in hot oil until lightly brown. Set aside.

Meatballs Variation II:
1½ pounds ground beef
1   small onion, finely chopped
1   cup uncooked oatmeal
1   cup milk
Salt and black pepper to taste
2 to 3 Tablespoons vegetable oil

Meatballs Variation II:
In a mixing bowl, combine first 5 ingredients, mixing well. Form meat mixture into 1-inch balls and fry in hot oil until lightly brown. Set aside.

Sauce Variation I:
1   cup ketchup or tomato juice
3   Tablespoons Worcestershire sauce
1   teaspoon chili powder
2½ teaspoons granulated sugar

Sauce Variation I:
Combine ingredients and pour over meatballs. Cover and bake at 350 degrees for 1 hour.

(continued on next page)

Sauce Variation II:
1   10-ounce jar grape jelly
1   10-ounce jar chili sauce
3   Tablespoons
     Worcestershire sauce

Sauce Variation III:
½ cup ketchup
½ cup chili sauce
1   teaspoon monosodium
     glutamate
¼ cup vinegar
½ cup packed brown sugar
2   Tablespoons chopped
     onion
1   Tablespoon
     Worcestershire sauce
4   teaspoons dry mustard
¼ teaspoon black pepper
1   teaspoon salt

Sauce Variation II:
Combine ingredients in a saucepan and simmer for 3 to 4 minutes. Add meatballs and continue simmering for at least 1 hour. You may substitute small smoked link sausages for meatballs.

Sauce Variation III:
Combine ingredients in a saucepan and simmer for 5 to 10 minutes. Add meatballs and continue simmering for 15 to 20 minutes.

Sangria

Yield: 16 to 18 cups

6   oranges, sliced
3   lemons, sliced
1   lime, sliced
1   apple, sliced (optional)

Liquor Variation I:
1   cup sugar
1   cup brandy or peach
     brandy
1   gallon dry red wine

Liquor Variation II:
1   quart burgundy wine
2   quarts limeade (diluted
     from concentrate)
1   cup brandy
1   cup triple sec

Liquor Variation I:
Place fruit in large pitcher or crock. Sprinkle sugar over fruit. Add brandy. Let mixture sit for 1 hour. Add wine and stir. Let sit for 30 minutes. Chill or serve over ice.

Liquor Variation II:
Mix ingredients together. Pour over fruits. Chill or serve over ice.

Stuffed Mushrooms

350 degrees, preheated
Large shallow pan
Yield: 25

25 large, fresh mushrooms, washed, stems removed, reserving stems

Stuffing Variation I (Sausage):
5   Tablespoons butter
¼   pound bulk sausage
2   stalks celery, chopped
Mushroom stems, finely chopped
1   teaspoon Worcestershire sauce
½   teaspoon lemon juice
Dash of monosodium glutamate
½   teaspoon dry mustard
2   Tablespoons finely minced parsley
1   cup herb stuffing mix
1   cup beef or chicken broth

Stuffing Variation II (Italian):
2   teaspoons butter
½   cup finely chopped onion
½   cup diced pepperoni
4   Tablespoons chopped bell pepper
1   small clove garlic, chopped
Chopped reserved mushroom stems
½   cup finely crushed Ritz crackers
3   Tablespoons Parmesan cheese
4   teaspoons chopped parsley
½   teaspoon seasoned salt
½   teaspoon oregano
Dash of black pepper

Stuffing Variation I:
In a large saucepan, melt 3 Tablespoons butter over low heat and gently sauté mushrooms. Remove from heat and drain mushrooms. Melt 2 Tablespoons butter in large saucepan. Add sausage. Cook until browned. Add celery and mushroom stems. Sauté until tender. Remove from heat. Add seasonings and stuffing mix. Slowly add broth to reach a moist stuffing consistency. Stuff mushroom cups and arrange in large shallow pan. May be frozen at this point. When ready to serve, bake for 10 to 15 minutes.

Stuffing Variation II :
In a large bowl, combine butter, onion, pepperoni, bell pepper, garlic and mushroom stems. Cook covered on high in microwave for 2 to 3 minutes or sauté in saucepan for 10 minutes. Stir in cracker crumbs, cheese, parsley, salt, oregano and pepper. Mix well. Fill mushrooms with mixture and place in shallow pan. Cook in oven for 10 to 15 minutes.

(continued on next page)

Stuffing Variation III (Crab):
1   8-ounce package cream
      cheese
1   Tablespoon milk
1   6½-ounce can crabmeat
2   Tablespoons minced onion
½   teaspoon horseradish
Dash of Worcestershire sauce
Salt to taste
1   cup bread crumbs

Stuffing Variation III:
Blend all ingredients except bread crumbs in large mixing bowl. Fill mushroom caps and place in shallow pan. Sprinkle top of mushrooms with bread crumbs and bake for 10 to 15 minutes.

**Stuffing Variation IV
      (Parmesan):**
Chopped reserved mushroom
      stems
½   cup chopped onion
6   Tablespoons butter
⅔   cup bread crumbs
6   Tablespoons Parmesan
      cheese
¼   teaspoon oregano
1   teaspoon salt
2   Tablespoons chopped
      parsley

Stuffing Variation IV:
In a bowl, combine chopped stems and onion. Sauté in the butter until tender. Add remaining ingredients and mix well. Stuff mushroom caps and place in shallow pan. Bake for 10 to 15 minutes.

Vegetable-Beef Soup

4- to 5-quart Dutch oven
Yield: 3 to 4 quarts soup

1 pound ground beef
1 onion, chopped
1 box (2 envelopes) dried
  vegetable beef soup mix
6 to 7 cups water
1 15-ounce can tomato
  sauce
5 potatoes, cut into large
  pieces
6 carrots, cut into large
  pieces
Salt and black pepper to taste

Brown beef and onion in a large Dutch oven. Add remainder of ingredients. Simmer slowly for 1 to 1½ hours. Serve hot.

Variation I:
Substitute 2 pounds of stew meat for ground beef; cook until meat is fork tender.

Variation II:
Add 4 stalks celery, chopped, 1 15-ounce can tomatoes and 4 ounces spaghetti, cooked.

Variation III:
Add 1 teaspoon chili powder and ½ teaspoon garlic powder to soup while it is cooking.

Variation IV:
Omit beef vegetable soup mix; substitute 3 beef bouillon cubes. Substitute 1 10-ounce package frozen mixed vegetables and 1 10-ounce package frozen cut okra for fresh vegetables.

Variation V:
Use ½ water and ½ V-8 Juice for the liquid.

Layered Salad

Yield: 10 to 12 servings

1 bunch fresh spinach, washed and torn in bite-sized pieces
½ to 1 head lettuce, torn in bite-sized pieces
1 bunch green onions
½ cup chopped celery
¾ cup chopped bell pepper
¾ cup chopped onion
½ pound bacon, fried and crumbled
1 10-ounce package frozen green peas, cooked and drained
6 hard-boiled eggs, chopped

Dressing Variation I:
¾ cup salad dressing
¾ cup sour cream

Dressing Variation II:
1½ cups mayonnaise
2 Tablespoons sugar
1 Tablespoon milk

Garnish:
Choose 1 or a combination of the following cheeses:
4 ounces grated Parmesan cheese
10 ounces grated Cheddar cheese
10 ounces grated Swiss cheese

Layer first 9 ingredients in a large bowl, according to the order listed. Top with dressing ingredients mixed together. Top with desired cheese. Cover tightly and refrigerate 24 hours or overnight.

Salad Bar Toppings

Yield: 6 to 8 servings

Suggested toppings for any
    salad greens:
Jalapeño pinto beans, drained
Chopped celery
Chopped tomato
Chopped green onions
Chopped avocados
Chopped purple or white
    onion
Chopped bell pepper
Crushed corn chips
Cheddar cheese
Mushroom Topping (recipe
    follows)
Olive Topping (recipe follows)
Taco Salad Topping (recipe
    follows)

Variation I (Mushroom
    Topping):
½   cup chopped onion
¼   cup chopped celery
½   cup sour cream
¼   cup mayonnaise
2   Tablespoons lemon juice
1   Tablespoon chopped
    parsley
1   teaspoon salt
1   teaspoon horseradish
1   teaspoon prepared
    mustard
¼   teaspoon leaf oregano
⅛   teaspoon black pepper
½   to 1 pound fresh
    mushrooms, thinly sliced

Variation I (Mushroom Topping):
Mix all ingredients well. Chill at least 2 hours.
Serve as a topping on salad greens.

(continued on next page)

Variation II (Olive Topping):
1   4¼-ounce can chopped
      ripe olives, drained, juice
      reserved
1   4-ounce jar green salad
      olives
1   large onion, chopped
1   large bell pepper, chopped
3   stalks of celery, chopped
3   cloves garlic, pressed
1   Tablespoon oregano
½   cup vegetable oil
½   cup vinegar
Salt and black pepper to taste

**Variation III (Taco Salad
      Topping):**
1   pound ground beef
½   teaspoon cumin
½   teaspoon oregano
½   teaspoon cayenne or red
      pepper (optional)
1   clove garlic, pressed
2   Tablespoons green chiles
      (optional)
1   8-ounce can tomato sauce

Variation II (Olive Topping):
Combine olives and ½ jar of juice from the green olives. Add onion, celery, bell pepper and garlic to olives and mix well. Add remaining ingredients and mix lightly. Marinate overnight in a jar or covered container. Does not have to be refrigerated. Serve as a topping for salad greens. Yield: 12 to 18 servings

Variation III (Taco Salad Topping):
Brown ground beef and drain. Add remaining ingredients and simmer 15 to 20 minutes. Serve hot with salad greens.

Marinated Vegetables

Advance preparation
time required
Large salad bowl
Yield: 15 servings

Fresh Vegetable Variations:
1   pound broccoli, cut in
    bite-sized pieces
1   head cauliflower, cut in
    bite-sized pieces
1   pound cherry tomatoes,
    halved
3   carrots, sliced
3   zucchini, sliced
2   small onions, sliced
1   bunch celery, sliced
2   bell peppers, sliced
4   ounces mushrooms
1   cucumber, sliced
1   6-ounce jar ripe olives,
    sliced
1   3-ounce jar green olives,
    sliced

Canned Vegetable Variations:
1   16-ounce can French style
    green beans
1   12-ounce can whole
    kernel corn
1   17-ounce can English peas
1   cup chopped celery
1   medium onion, sliced
½   cup chopped bell pepper
1   4-ounce jar pimiento
(Can substitute 3 16-ounce
    cans green beans for the
    corn and peas.)

Choose either the fresh vegetable combination or the canned vegetable variation or a combination of both and place in a large salad bowl. Choose 1 of the marinade variations, mixing the ingredients well and pouring over vegetables. Cover and refrigerate 24 hours.

(continued on next page)

Marinade Variation I:
½   cup vegetable oil
1½ cups white wine vinegar
2   cloves garlic, pressed
⅓   cup sugar
2   teaspoons prepared
    mustard
2   teaspoons salt
1   teaspoon oregano
Black pepper to taste

Marinade Variation II:
1   cup cider vinegar
1   Tablespoon sugar
1   Tablespoon dried dill
    weed
1   teaspoon salt
1   teaspoon garlic salt
2   teaspoons black pepper
1½ cups vegetable oil

Marinade Variation III:
½   cup mayonnaise
1   cup sour cream
1   Tablespoon sugar
1   Tablespoon white vinegar
Salt and black pepper to taste

Sour Cream Sauce Variation:
1   cup sour cream
½   cup mayonnaise
1   teaspoon lemon juice
¼   teaspoon garlic salt or ¼
    teaspoon dry mustard and
    1 Tablespoon horseradish
Sliced water chestnuts
    (optional)

Sour Cream Sauce Variation:
Combine sour cream, mayonnaise, lemon juice and either garlic salt or dry mustard and horseradish, mixing well. Pour over drained, marinated vegetables and serve. May garnish with water chestnuts.

Hot Baked Fruit

350 degrees, preheated
9 × 13 casserole
Yield: 8 to 10 servings

1   16-ounce can pears
1   16-ounce can peach or
    apricot halves
1   20-ounce can pineapple
    chunks
1   8-ounce can mandarin
    oranges
2 or 3 medium bananas, sliced
1   16-ounce can dark sweet
    pitted cherries or 8 to 10
    maraschino cherries

Open and drain the fruits, reserving, in all, 1¼ cups fruit juice. Cut larger fruits into bite-sized pieces; arrange first 4 fruits in 9 × 13 casserole. Reserve sliced bananas and cherries for use later.

Sauce:
½   cup butter
3   Tablespoons cornstarch
¼ to ½ cup packed brown
    sugar
1¼ cup reserved fruit juice

Spice Variation I:
¼   teaspoon cinnamon
2   teaspoons almond extract

Spice Variation II:
2 to 3 Tablespoons almond
    extract

Sauce:
Melt butter in a medium saucepan; stir in cornstarch and cook until smooth and bubbly. Add brown sugar and dissolve completely. Add fruit juices and stir constantly until thickened. Remove from heat and stir in one of the spice variations. Pour over fruit. Garnish with cherries. Bake for 20 minutes. Stir in bananas and bake for an additional 10 to 20 minutes, or until bubbly.

Mexican Casserole

350 degrees, preheated
2-quart casserole, buttered
Yield: 6 to 8 servings

2 Tablespoons bacon
drippings or vegetable oil
1 cup chopped onion
1 cup chopped bell pepper
2 cloves garlic, pressed
1½ pounds ground beef

Sauté onion, bell pepper and garlic in oil until tender. Add ground beef and cook until brown. Choose 1 of the variations to complete casserole.

Variation I:
12 flour tortillas, cut in 1-inch strips
1 15-ounce can Ranch Style beans
½ pound Cheddar cheese, grated
1 14½-ounce can Rotel tomatoes with green chiles
1 10¾-ounce can cream of chicken soup

Variation I:
Line a 2-quart buttered casserole with half of the tortilla strips. Top with meat mixture and beans. Sprinkle with grated cheese. Top with remaining tortillas. Combine Rotel tomatoes and soup. Pour over casserole. Bake covered for 30 to 45 minutes.

Variation II:
1 14-½-ounce can tomatoes
1 8-ounce can tomato sauce
2 4-ounce cans chopped green chiles (optional)
2 1½-ounce packages enchilada sauce mix
½ cup water
1 15-ounce can pinto beans
12 to 15 tortillas
¼ to ½ cup vegetable oil
1 cup grated Cheddar cheese
1 tomato, chopped
1 cup shredded lettuce

Variation II:
In a saucepan, add tomatoes, tomato sauce, green chiles, enchilada sauce mix, water and beans to meat mixture. Simmer uncovered for 10 minutes. Fry tortillas in oil until softened. Spoon 1 cup of meat sauce into a lightly greased 9 × 13 baking dish. Spread each tortilla with ¼ cup meat sauce, roll up and place, seam side down in the baking dish. Spoon remaining sauce over tortillas. Sprinkle with cheese and chopped tomato. Bake for 20 minutes. Before serving, arrange lettuce around edge of casserole.

Teriyaki Marinade

Yield: 1 to 2 cups

Choose 1 of the marinade variations, mixing all ingredients well.

Variation I:
¼ cup soy sauce
3 Tablespoons sesame oil
3 Tablespoons crushed sesame seeds
2 Tablespoons sugar
⅓ cup chopped onions
4 Tablespoons chopped green onions
1 clove garlic, pressed
1 teaspoon ground ginger
1 teaspoon monosodium glutamate

Variation II:
¾ cup vegetable oil
¼ cup soy sauce
¼ cup honey
2 Tablespoons cider vinegar
2 Tablespoons finely chopped green onions
1 clove garlic, pressed
1½ teaspoons ground ginger

Variation III:
1¼ cup vegetable oil
¾ cup soy sauce
¼ cup Worcestershire sauce
2 teaspoons dry mustard
1 teaspoon salt
1 Tablespoon black pepper
½ cup vinegar
1½ teaspoons parsley flakes
1½ teaspoons garlic powder
⅓ cup lemon juice

In a large bowl, combine one of the marinades with 1½ to 2 pounds round steak, flank steak or chicken breasts which have been cut into 1-inch strips. Chicken breasts may also be marinated whole. Cover and refrigerate for 3 hours. Meat may be grilled, fried in 2 to 3 Tablespoons of oil, or used as fondue meat.

Scalloped Duck or Chicken

350 degrees, preheated
Dutch oven and 2-quart casserole
Yield: 6 to 8 servings

2   large ducks, cleaned or 2 large chicken hens, cleaned
3   stalks celery, chopped
1   onion, sliced
1½   teaspoons salt
¼   teaspoon black pepper

In a large Dutch oven, combine the ingredients and cover with water. Bring to a boil over high heat, reduce heat and simmer 1 hour or until birds are tender. Remove birds from stock; strain stock and reserve until later. Cool birds, remove meat from bones and cut into bite-sized pieces. Add meat to either of the sauce variations.

Sauce Variation I:
6   slices bacon
2   Tablespoons butter
2   Tablespoons chopped onion
2   Tablespoons chopped green pepper
¼   cup flour
2   cups reserved stock
1   cup half and half
1   4-ounce can mushrooms
½   teaspoon salt
¼   teaspoon black pepper
⅓   cup white wine
2   Tablespoons chopped parsley (for garnish)

Sauce Variation I:
Cook bacon until crisp. Crumble bacon into pieces and set aside, leaving bacon drippings in skillet. To the bacon drippings add butter, onion and green pepper. Cook until tender. Blend in flour and cook until bubbly. Add stock and cream to the mixture stirring constantly. Cook until sauce thickens. Add duck or chicken, mushrooms, bacon, salt, pepper and wine. Garnish with parsley. Heat thoroughly at low temperature; do not boil.

Sauce Variation II:
1   6-ounce package long grain and wild rice mix
½   cup margarine or butter
½   cup chopped onion
1   4-ounce can mushrooms
¼   cup flour
1½   cups reserved stock
1½   cups half and half
1   Tablespoon chopped parsley
½   cup slivered almonds

Sauce Variation II:
Cook rice according to package directions and set aside. In a saucepan, combine margarine and onion. Sauté until onion is tender. Add flour and cook until brown and bubbly. Add mushrooms and cook 1 minute stirring constantly. Gradually add reserved stock and half and half. Stir constantly until sauce is thick. Add duck or chicken and parsley. Remove from heat. Put cooked rice into a greased 2-quart casserole. Pour sauce over rice. Garnish with slivered almonds. Cover and bake for 15 to 20 minutes or until thoroughly heated.

Baked Chicken and Sauce

Dutch oven
Yield: 4 to 6 servings

2½ to 3 pound fryer, cut up
Or
6 chicken breasts, boned
¼ cup flour
½ teaspoon salt
¼ teaspoon black pepper
½ teaspoon paprika
⅓ cup oil or butter, melted

Coat chicken with flour which has been seasoned with salt, pepper and paprika. Brown in oil or butter. Drain oil from skillet. Choose 1 of the sauce variations.

Sauce Variation I:
1 10-ounce jar peach preserves
½ cup barbeque sauce
½ cup chopped onion
2 Tablespoons soy sauce
1 6-ounce can water chestnuts, drained and sliced
1 green pepper, cut into strips

Sauce Variation I:
Combine preserves, barbeque sauce, onion and soy sauce. Pour over chicken. Cover and simmer 40 minutes. Add green pepper and water chestnuts during last 10 minutes. Serve over rice.

Sauce Variation II:
1 medium onion, sliced
1 to 2 cups water
4 teaspoons flour
½ cup warm water
1 cup sour cream

Sauce Variation II:
Pour water over chicken and onion so that it covers ½ to ¾ of the chicken. Cook covered for 45 minutes to 1 hour or until tender. Combine flour and warm water. Add to sour cream. Remove chicken and add sour cream mixture to the stock. Stir well to thicken and make gravy. Add chicken and cook 5 minutes more. Serve over rice.

Sauce Variation III:
⅓ to ½ cup hot water
2¼ ounces slivered almonds

Sauce Variation III:
Remove sautéed chicken from skillet and place in baking dish. Add water to skillet drippings and stir. Cook over medium heat for 3 to 4 minutes. Add almonds and cook for 10 to 15 minutes. Pour mixture over chicken. Bake in a 350-degree oven for 30 to 40 minutes.

Hot Chicken Casserole

375 degrees, preheated
3- to 4-quart casserole, greased
Yield: 6 to 8 servings

Chicken Mixture:
2   cups cooked and diced chicken
1   cup chopped celery
½   cup chopped onion
½   teaspoon salt
½   teaspoon black pepper

Seasoning Variation I:
5   Tablespoons butter
2   Tablespoons chopped bell pepper
6   Tablespoons flour
2½ cups milk
2   cups ham, cooked and diced
1   Tablespoon pimiento
1   10¾-ounce can cream of mushroom soup

Seasoning Variation II:
¼   cup sliced almonds, toasted
1   Tablespoon lemon juice
3   drops Tabasco sauce
½   cup mayonnaise
2½ ounces sliced water chestnuts

Seasoning Variation III:
2   cups slivered almonds, toasted
½   cup chicken stock
6   hard-boiled eggs, chopped
2   10¾-ounce cans cream of chicken soup
1   cup mayonnaise
4   Tablespoons lemon juice

Chicken Mixture:
Combine the ingredients and choose from the seasoning variations.

Seasoning Variation I:
In a skillet, sauté ½ cup chopped onion (from the chicken mixture) and bell pepper in butter until tender. Stir in flour. Gradually add milk, stirring constantly until mixture is smooth and thick. Add ham, pimiento, soup and the remaining ingredients from the chicken mixture.

Seasoning Variation II:
Combine ingredients with the chicken mixture ingredients.

Seasoning Variation III:
Combine all ingredients with chicken mixture ingredients.

Place any of the combinations in a greased 3- to 4-quart baking dish. Top with 1 cup cracker crumbs, grated Cheddar cheese, bread crumbs, or crushed potato chips. Bake for 35 to 45 minutes.

Barbecued Shrimp

350 degrees, preheated
9 × 13 baking dish or
Dutch oven
Yield: 4 to 6 servings

3 pounds fresh shrimp in
   shells

Place shrimp in a 9 × 13 baking dish for Variations I and II; for Variation III, follow directions. Choose from the sauce variations to pour over shrimp.

Sauce Variation I:
2 cups butter, melted
2 Tablespoons black pepper
½ of 0.62-ounce jar Italian
   seasoning
2 Tablespoons
   Worcestershire sauce
Juice of 2 lemons
1½ teaspoons salt
2 Tablespoons soy sauce

Sauce Variation I:
Combine sauce ingredients and pour over shrimp. Bake for 30 minutes.

Sauce Variation II:
1 cup Italian dressing
1½ Tablespoons butter,
   melted
1 Tablespoon black pepper
1 Tablespoon cayenne or
   red pepper (less for milder
   taste)
½ teaspoon salt
1 teaspoon garlic powder
1½ Tablespoons lemon juice

Sauce Variation II:
Combine ingredients and pour over shrimp. Bake for 45 minutes.

Sauce Variation III:
1½ cups water
1 teaspoon salt
1 Tablespoon cayenne or
   red pepper
4 thin slices of lemon
6 whole garlic cloves
1 onion, finely minced
½ of 0.62-ounce jar Italian
   seasoning
1 cup olive oil

Sauce Variation III:
In a large Dutch oven, combine water, salt, pepper, lemon and garlic. Bring to a boil. Add shrimp and cook covered for 10 minutes. Add onion, Italian seasoning and olive oil. Uncover and cook for 5 minutes. Turn heat off, cover pan and let stand for 15 to 20 minutes before serving.

Serve all variations with French bread.

Rice Casserole

350 degrees, preheated
Casserole, lightly greased
Yield: 6 to 8 servings

1   cup uncooked rice

Choose 1 of the Variations. Combine the ingredients with uncooked rice and place in a lightly greased casserole. Bake covered for 1 hour.

Variation I:
2   14½-ounce cans beef
    consommé
½   cup chopped onion
½   cup butter, melted
¼   cup slivered almonds

Variation II:
3   green onions
1   14½-ounce can beef
    consommé
14½-ounces water
½   teaspoon thyme
½   teaspoon oregano
½   cup butter, melted
Salt and black pepper to taste

Variation III:
1   10¾-ounce can cream of
    mushroom soup
1   14½-ounce can beef
    consommé
1   3-ounce can sliced
    mushrooms
1   onion, chopped and
    sautéed in 2 Tablespoons
    butter
¼   teaspoon mace
¼   teaspoon curry powder
Salt and black pepper to taste

Baked Tomato Casserole

350 degrees, preheated
2-quart baking dish,
lightly greased
Yield: 8 to 10 servings

1 7-ounce package herb
   stuffing mix
2 15-ounce cans tomatoes in
   juice, drained, juice
   reserved

Combine with 1 of the variations.

Variation I:
½ to ¾ cup reserved tomato
   juice
1 medium onion, sliced into
   rings
1 teaspoon oregano
1 teaspoon garlic salt
½ teaspoon black pepper
1 Tablespoon bacon
   drippings (optional)
10 ounces grated Cheddar
   cheese

Variation I:
Sprinkle stuffing mix into baking dish as first layer; then layer juice, then tomatoes, onion, seasonings, optional bacon drippings, and ending with cheese. Do not stir. Bake for 20 to 30 minutes, or until cheese melts and is bubbly.

Variation II:
2 large or 3 small zucchini,
   sliced
½ cup brown sugar
1½ teaspoons leaf basil
¼ cup melted butter

Variation II:
In a baking dish, begin layers with half of herb stuffing mix; then layer sliced zucchini, drained tomatoes, sugar, basil, reserved juice and remainder of stuffing mix with melted butter drizzled on top. Bake until stuffing mix topping is browned and most of the juice is evaporated.

Cheese Grits or Rice Casserole

350 degrees, preheated
9 × 13 baking dish, greased
Yield: 10 to 12 servings

2 cups uncooked grits or rice, cooked according to package directions

Add any 1 of the variations to cooked grits or rice. Pour into greased 9 × 13 baking pan. Bake for 45 minutes to 1 hour.

Variation I:
½ cup butter
8 ounces Cheeze Whiz
2 eggs, beaten
1 pound sharp Cheddar cheese, grated
1 small onion, finely chopped
⅛ teaspoon cayenne or red pepper
⅛ teaspoon garlic powder
Paprika for garnish

Variation II:
1 pound sharp Cheddar cheese, grated
½ cup butter
3 eggs, beaten
¾ teaspoon Tabasco sauce
½ teaspoon garlic powder

Variation III:
½ cup butter
3 eggs, beaten
1 pound Cheddar cheese, grated
1 4-ounce can chopped green chiles
1 cup sour cream

Variation IV:
½ cup butter
2 6-ounce rolls garlic cheese
1 pound sharp Cheddar cheese, grated

Potato Casserole

350 degrees, preheated
2-quart casserole or
9 × 13 casserole
Yield: 8 to 10 servings

3   pounds potatoes, cooked
    and peeled

Variation I:
¼   cup butter
1   10¾-ounce can cream of
    chicken soup
2   cups sour cream
⅓   cup finely chopped onion
1½ cups grated Cheddar
    cheese
1 to 2 cups crushed cornflakes
2 to 3 Tablespoons butter,
    melted

Variation II:
½   cup butter
½   cup flour
4   cups milk

Seasoning Variation I:
2   cloves garlic, pressed
1   teaspoon curry powder
1   Tablespoon prepared
    mustard
White pepper to taste
3   drops Tabasco sauce

Seasoning Variation II:
4   ounces mushrooms, sliced
    and sautéed
½   cup cream
5¼ ounces beef consommé
½   teaspoon Worcestershire
    sauce
½   Tablespoon salt
⅛   teaspoon black pepper

Choose 1 of the variations to combine with potatoes.

Variation I:
In a saucepan, heat ¼ cup butter and soup. Blend in sour cream, onion and cheese. Gently stir in cooked potatoes which have been cut into cubes. Place in a buttered 2-quart casserole. Combine cornflakes and melted butter. Sprinkle over potato mixture. Bake for 45 minutes.

Variation II:
In a saucepan, melt butter; then stir in flour. Gradually add milk, blending well with a wire whisk. Cook over medium heat until thickened and smooth. Choose 1 of the seasonings to add to the white sauce. Cook if necessary until seasoned sauce is thick.

Place a layer of thinly sliced, cooked potatoes in a buttered 9 × 13 baking dish. Add a layer of sauce, a layer of potatoes and a final layer of sauce. Choose 1 of the toppings and bake for 45 minutes.

(continued on next page)

Topping Variations:
⅔ cup grated Swiss cheese
6 Tablespoons Bleu cheese
1 cup bread crumbs
   combined with
   2 Tablespoons melted
   butter

Variation III:
½ cup butter
¼ cup chopped green onions
2 cups sour cream
Salt and black pepper to taste
8 ounces Cheddar cheese,
   grated
¾ pound bacon, cooked and
   crumbled
4 Tablespoons chopped
   green onions

Variation III:
Mash potatoes with butter, ¼ cup green onion and sour cream. Season with salt and pepper. In a buttered 9x13 baking dish, layer ½ potato mixture, ½ cheese, ½ bacon and 2 Tablespoons green onions. Repeat the layers. Bake for 30 minutes.

Mexican Cornbread

400 degrees, preheated
2-quart casserole,
lightly greased

1½ cups yellow cornmeal
1   cup milk
2   eggs, beaten
½   teaspoon baking soda
½   teaspoon salt
1   16-ounce can cream-style
    corn
¼   cup bacon drippings,
    melted or ¼ cup vegetable
    oil
2 to 4 jalapeños, diced
1   large onion, diced
2 to 4 cups grated sharp
    Cheddar cheese

Grease casserole dish; sprinkle lightly with cornmeal and heat in oven until hot. Mix all ingredients well and pour into prepared pan. Bake for 20 to 30 minutes, or until lightly browned.

Variation I:
Add 1 pound ground beef, sautéed with 1 large onion, diced. Either mix into cornbread or layer ½ of cornbread, then meat, then remainder of cornbread on top.

Variation II:
Substitute 1 or 2 4-ounce cans green chiles for jalapeños.

Variation III:
Substitute 1 cup sour cream for half of the can of cream-style corn.

Quiche

350 degrees, preheated
Yield: 8 servings

3   eggs, beaten
1   9-inch deep dish pie shell,
     unbaked

Liquid Variations:
Half and half
Sour cream
Whipping cream
Milk
½ cup milk and ½ cup
     mayonnaise

Cheese Variations:
Cheddar cheese, grated
Swiss cheese, grated
Gruyere cheese, grated

Meat Variations:
Hamburger, cooked
Ham, cooked
Turkey, cooked
Chicken, cooked
Crab, cooked
Shrimp, cooked
Bacon, fried and crumbled

Vegetable Variations:
Sautéed mushrooms
Spinach, cooked and drained
Bell pepper, chopped
Onion, chopped

Seasoning Variations:
⅛   teaspoon nutmeg
¼   teaspoon dry mustard
1   Tablespoon Dijon mustard
Salt and black pepper to taste
¼   teaspoon thyme
¼   teaspoon basil
¼   teaspoon marjoram

Combine eggs, 1 cup of desired liquid variations, ½ to 1 cup of desired cheese variations, 1½ cups desired cooked meat, 1½ cups of desired vegetable variations and desired seasonings. You may combine meats, cheeses, vegetables and seasonings according to taste, being sure to use correct measurements. Pour into unbaked deep dish pie shell and bake 35 to 40 minutes or until firm.

Dinner Breads

350 degrees, preheated
Yield: 8 to 10 servings

Choose 1 variety of the breads and spread with 1 of the spread variations. Bake for 30 to 40 minutes or until brown and bubbly.

Breads:
1   package of pita bread,
    each split into two rounds
1   loaf of Italian bread, sliced
1   loaf of French bread,
    sliced

Spread Variation I:
½   cup softened butter
½   cup Parmesan cheese
¼   cup chopped parsley
1   clove garlic, pressed
1   Tablespoon olive oil
¼   teaspoon basil
½   teaspoon oregano

Spread Variation II:
Soft margarine
Garlic Bread Sprinkle by
    McCormick, to taste

Spread Variation III:
1   cup soft margarine
1   clove garlic, pressed
½   teaspoon dried parsley
½   teaspoon dried chives
½   teaspoon dried marjoram
½   teaspoon dried thyme
    (or 1 Tablespoon each of
    fresh herbs)

Spread Variation IV:
½ to 1 cup softened butter or
    margarine
2 to 3 teaspoons of any dried
    herb or herb combination

Amaretto Pound Cake

300 degrees, preheated
Tube pan, greased and floured
Yield: 1 cake

Cake:
1   cup butter
2½ cups granulated sugar
6   eggs
1   cup sour cream
1   teaspoon vanilla extract
1   teaspoon almond extract
1   teaspoon orange extract
1   teaspoon lemon extract
¼   teaspoon baking soda
½   teaspoon salt
3   cups flour
½   cup Amaretto

Glaze Variation I:
1   10-ounce jar orange
    marmalade
2½ ounces apricot preserves
¼   cup Amaretto
½   cup sliced almonds,
    toasted

Glaze Variation II:
⅓   cup butter, melted
1½ cups powdered sugar,
    sifted
2   Tablespoons Amaretto

Cake:
Cream butter and sugar. Add eggs 1 at a time, mixing well after each addition. Add sour cream and extracts. In another bowl, sift soda, salt and flour together. Add to butter mixture, mixing well. Stir in Amaretto. Pour into a greased and floured tube pan. Bake for 1 hour 30 minutes. Cool cake slightly and remove from pan. Choose 1 of the glaze variations to top warm cake.

Method Variation:
For a higher, lighter cake, separate eggs. Add yolks to the cake mixture when adding sour cream. Beat egg whites with ¼ teaspoon cream of tartar and fold into the batter last.

Glaze Variation I:
In a saucepan, heat marmalade, preserves and Amaretto. Pour over warm cake and top with almonds.

Glaze Variation II:
Combine butter and sugar and beat until creamy. Add Amaretto. Pour over warm cake.

Chocolate Pound Cake

300 degrees, preheated
Tube or bundt pan,
greased and floured
Yield: 1 cake

1 cup butter OR margarine OR shortening
2½ cups granulated sugar OR 1 pound dark brown sugar
4 eggs
3 cups flour
½ teaspoon baking powder
½ teaspoon salt
1 cup milk OR 1 cup buttermilk plus ½ teaspoon baking soda
2 teaspoons vanilla
2 teaspoons butter extract

Choose 1 of the following chocolates:
½ cup cocoa (sift with dry ingredients)
1 bar German Sweet chocolate, melted with 2 Tablespoons water
2 squares unsweetened chocolate, melted with 2 Tablespoons water

Cream together the butter and sugar. Add the eggs 1 at a time, mixing well after each. Sift together the flour, baking powder and salt. If cocoa is used, it should be sifted in, and if buttermilk is used, the baking soda should be sifted in. Add the dry ingredients to the batter alternately with the milk or buttermilk. Blend well. Add the vanilla and butter extract. If German chocolate or unsweetened chocolate is used, it should be melted with 2 Tablespoons water and added to the batter at this point. Pour batter into a greased and floured tube or bundt pan and bake for 1½ hours. The cake may be topped with powdered sugar.

Method Variation:
For a lighter, fluffier cake, you may separate the eggs. Add the egg yolks after the butter and sugar are creamed. Beat the egg whites separately and fold them into the batter as a final step.

Layered Dessert

350 degrees, preheated
9 × 13 × 2 pan
Yield: approximately 16
to 20 servings

Crust (Layer 1):
½   cup margarine
1   cup flour
1   cup finely chopped pecans
2   Tablespoons granulated
    sugar (optional)
Or
1   baked, cooled pie shell in
    9x13x2 pan

Crust:
Combine all ingredients and press into pan. Bake for 20 minutes. Cool.

Cream Filling (Layer 2):
1   8-ounce package cream
    cheese
1 or 2 cups powdered sugar
½   12-ounce tub Cool Whip,
    thawed, OR ½ cup
    whipping cream, whipped,
    flavored and sweetened
Or
2   cups powdered sugar
½   cup butter, softened
1   large egg
¼   teaspoon salt
¼   teaspoon vanilla

Cream Filling:
Choose one of the mixtures. Cream all ingredients well. Spread on cooled crust.

**Pudding or Fruit Filling
    (Layer 3):**
1   6-ounce package chocolate
    or butterscotch pudding,
    prepared

Pudding or Fruit Filling:

Or
1   cup whipping cream,
    whipped
1   cup crushed pineapple,
    drained
½   cup chopped nuts

Fold pineapple and nuts into whipped cream. This layer may be doubled, if desired.

(continued on next page)

Or
3   large bananas, sliced
1   21-ounce can blueberry
    pie filling

Topping (Layer 4):
Additional whipped,
    sweetened, flavored
    whipping cream or thawed
    Cool Whip

Garnish (Layer 5):
Chocolate curls or sprinkles
Chopped nuts
Additional sliced bananas

Layer bananas, then pie filling upon Layer 2.

Garnish:
Choose one of the garnishes to go with the chosen filling. Chill well before serving. Store in refrigerator.

Cream Pie

9-inch pie pan

1   9-inch pie shell, baked
1   cup sugar
⅓   cup flour
Pinch of salt
2   cups milk (or 1 5-ounce
    can evaporated milk and
    milk to equal 2 cups)
3   eggs, separated
1 to 1½ teaspoons vanilla
¼   cup butter
1   cup whipping cream,
    whipped, flavored and
    sweetened (optional)

Mix sugar, flour and salt in a saucepan. Stir in ½ cup milk until smooth. Scald remaining 1½ cups milk. Combine scalded milk with sugar mixture and cook, stirring constantly, over low heat until thickened. Add small amount of hot mixture to beaten egg yolks, then add egg yolks to custard mixture. Cook for approximately 1 more minute. Remove from heat and add vanilla and butter. Pour into baked crust and chill. Top with meringue or whipped cream.

Variation I (Chocolate Pie with cocoa):
Add 2 Tablespoons cocoa to sugar mixture.

Variation II (Chocolate Pie with unsweetened chocolate):
Pour scalded milk over 2 1-ounce squares of unsweetened chocolate; stir to melt. Follow remainder of basic recipe.

Variation III (German Chocolate Pie):
Reduce sugar to ¾ cup. Pour scalded milk over 1 4-ounce package of German sweet chocolate; stir to melt. Follow remainder of basic recipe.

Variation IV (Coconut Cream Pie):
Add ¾ of a 4-ounce can of flaked coconut along with vanilla and butter to cooked custard; use remainder of coconut to garnish meringue or whipped cream topping.

Variation V (Lemon Cream Pie):
Substitute 5 Tablespoons cornstarch for flour in basic recipe. When custard is done, add 1 teaspoon grated lemon rind and ⅓ cup lemon juice along with specified butter. Vanilla may be omitted.

Pecan Pie

425 degrees, preheated
9-inch pie pan

1 to 1½ cups pecans, chopped
or in halves
1   9-inch unbaked pie shell
1   cup sugar (granulated or
brown)
1   cup corn syrup (white or
dark)
¼   cup butter, melted
3   eggs, well beaten
1   teaspoon vanilla
¼   teaspoon salt (optional)
½   teaspoon lemon juice
(optional)

Place pecans in bottom of unbaked pie shell. Mix remaining ingredients and pour over pecans in pie shell. Bake 10 minutes. Lower heat to 350 degrees and bake for an additional 35 to 40 minutes or until center is firm when pie is shaken.

Variation I:
Pecans may be dry-roasted at 350 degrees for 5 to 10 minutes or roasted with 1 Tablespoon butter and dash of salt at the same temperature for same time. Pecans should be cooled before being put into pie shell.

Variation II:
Use ½ cup butter instead of ¼ cup butter. Melt and brown butter in a saucepan over medium heat until it is golden brown. Let butter cool before adding to remainder of ingredients.

Pear Pie

400 degrees, preheated
9-inch pie pan

1   9-inch unbaked pie shell
4   cups peeled, sliced hard
    pears

Spice Variation I:
1   cup granulated sugar
1   teaspoon cinnamon

Spice Variation II:
½   cup sugar
⅓   cup flour
1   teaspoon mace
1   teaspoon lemon juice
Cinnamon to taste

Crumb topping:
1   cup flour
½   cup brown sugar
½   cup butter

Combine sliced pears with either spice variation. Pour into unbaked pie shell.

Mix flour and brown sugar for crumb topping; cut in butter until crumbly. Top pears in pie shell. Bake for 15 minutes, then reduce heat to 350 degrees for an additional 1 hour 15 minutes, or until pears are tender.

Baking Variation:
Place pie in large brown grocery sack and fold end to close. Remove from sack after 1 hour at 350 degrees and return to oven without sack for final 15 minutes.

Appetizers

Antipasto Dip

Yield: 10 to 12 cups

4   carrots, diced
2   bell peppers, diced
2   large onions, diced
2   stalks celery, diced
8   ounces mushrooms, diced
1   small head cauliflower, diced
1   cup vegetable oil
1   6½-ounce can tuna, drained
14 ounces ketchup
6   ounces chili sauce
6   green olives, chopped
6   ripe olives, chopped
1   teaspoon salt
1   teaspoon monosodium glutamate
2   cloves garlic, pressed
Juice of 2 lemons

Cook first 6 ingredients in oil until crisp tender, approximately 10 minutes. Simmer and add remaining ingredients. Simmer 10 more minutes. Refrigerate several hours. Serve on crackers or melba rounds.

Hot Artichoke Spread

350 degrees, preheated
3 cup casserole, lightly greased
Yield: 2½ cups

1   14-ounce can artichoke hearts, drained and chopped
1   cup mayonnaise (not salad dressing)
1   cup grated Parmesan or Romano cheese
½   teaspoon garlic powder

Combine all ingredients, mixing well. Spoon into lightly greased casserole. Bake for 20 minutes. Serve with crackers.

Avocado Log

Yield: 1 log

1 cup mashed avocado
1½ cups cashew nuts, chopped
1 8-ounce package cream cheese, softened
½ pound sharp Cheddar cheese, grated (2 cups)
2 Tablespoons lemon or lime juice
1 clove garlic, pressed
½ teaspoon Worcestershire sauce
½ teaspoon salt
½ teaspoon Tabasco sauce
Paprika

Mix all ingredients except paprika and shape into an oblong log. Sprinkle with paprika. Serve with crackers.

Appetizer Cheese Pie

Advance Preparation
Time Required
9-inch pie pan, well buttered
Yield: 3 cups

6 ounces Cheese Nips, crushed
2 cups sour cream
1 bell pepper, chopped
3 green onions, chopped
2 stalks celery, chopped
½ cup chopped olives, ripe or stuffed
2 teaspoons lemon juice
Dash of Tabasco sauce
1 teaspoon salt

Using half of the crushed Cheese Nips, cover bottom of well-buttered pie pan. Combine rest of the ingredients and pour into pie pan. Cover with remaining Cheese Nips. Refrigerate for 24 hours.

Boursin Cheese

Yield: 3 to 4 cups

2 8-ounce packages cream
   cheese, softened
½ pound unsalted whipped
   butter, softened
2 cloves garlic, pressed
½ teaspoon black pepper
½ teaspoon thyme
1 teaspoon dill weed

Combine cream cheese and butter. Add remaining
ingredients, mix well. Chill. Before serving, let
cheese soften. Serve with crackers.

This can easily be made in food processor.

Curry Chutney Cheese Ball

Yield: 1 ball

1 8-ounce cream cheese,
   softened
1 teaspoon curry powder, or
   to taste
1 9-ounce jar chutney,
   chopped and divided
½ cup chopped almonds

Mix cream cheese, curry powder, half of the
chutney and almonds. Form into ball and chill 2
hours. Pour remaining chutney over ball before
serving. Serve with crackers.

Delicious Cheese Ball

Yield: 1 large or 2 small balls

2 8-ounce packages cream
   cheese, softened
1½ cups sharp Cheddar
   cheese, grated
2 teaspoons grated onion
1½ cups sweet pickles,
   chopped
1 3½-ounce can macadamia
   nuts, finely chopped

Combine first 4 ingredients until well blended.
Remove and shape into 1 large or 2 small balls.
Chill. This can be made in food processor. Before
serving roll in macadamia nuts.

Variation:
Pecans can be used instead of macadamia nuts.

Cheese Loaf

Yield: 1 large or 2 small loaves

1   pound sharp Cheddar
    cheese, grated
    (approximately 4 cups)
1   8-ounce package cream
    cheese, softened
2   5-ounce jars pimiento
    cheese spread
1   teaspoon cayenne or red
    pepper
1   medium onion, grated
1   teaspoon garlic powder
¼   teaspoon salt
1   Tablespoon
    Worcestershire sauce
1   Tablespoon prepared
    mustard
3   Tablespoons margarine,
    softened

Combine all the ingredients. Shape into ball or loaf. Chill.

Cream Cheese Rolls

400 degrees, preheated
Cookie sheet
Yield: 50 to 60 rolls

1   1-pound loaf white thin
    sliced bread, crust
    removed
1   8-ounce package cream
    cheese, softened
½   cup sugar
1   egg yolk
1   cup sugar
1   Tablespoon cinnamon
½   cup melted butter

Using a rolling pin, roll each slice of bread very thin. Combine cream cheese, ½ cup sugar and egg yolk. Spread approximately 1 Tablespoon of cheese mixture on each bread slice. Roll each slice as a jelly roll. Combine 1 cup sugar and cinnamon. Dip roll in melted butter and then dip in sugar mixture. Freeze. Cut into 1-inch slices and bake for 15 minutes.

Blackeyed Pea Dip

Double boiler
Yield: 5 to 6 cups

4   cups blackeyed peas,
    cooked and drained
5   jalapeños, seeded
1   Tablespoon jalapeño juice
½   medium onion, chopped
1   4-ounce can green chiles
1   clove garlic
½   pound Old English sharp
    cheese
1   cup butter

In blender, mix first 6 ingredients. Heat cheese and butter in double boiler. Add the blended ingredients to cheese mixture. Serve in chafing dish with potato chips or corn chips.

Great for New Years!

Hot Broccoli Dip

Yield: 3 to 4 cups

1   10-ounce package frozen
    chopped broccoli
⅓   cup finely chopped onion
⅓   cup finely chopped celery
8   fresh mushrooms,
    chopped
3   Tablespoons butter
1   10¾-ounce can cream of
    mushroom soup
1   6-ounce package garlic
    cheese
Juice of ½ lemon

Cook broccoli and drain well. Sauté onion, celery and mushrooms in butter until tender. Add broccoli, soup, cheese and lemon juice. Warm until cheese is melted. Serve warm.

Clam Dip

Yield: 2½ cups

1 8-ounce package cream
cheese, softened
1 6-ounce can clams,
drained
½ cup mayonnaise
2 Tablespoons lemon juice
1 Tablespoon minced onion
1 teaspoon garlic salt
1 Tablespoon
Worcestershire sauce
Tabasco sauce to taste
¼ teaspoon parsley flakes
Chili sauce
Lettuce

Combine cream cheese, clams and mayonnaise. Add remaining ingredients, except chili sauce. Chill. Place lettuce in a shallow dish. Shape dip with a 2-inch thickness over lettuce. Cover with chili sauce. Serve with crackers or chips.

Crab Spread Or Dip

Yield: 2½ to 3 cups

1 8-ounce package cream
cheese, softened
½ cup mayonnaise
½ cup grated Cheddar
cheese
1 teaspoon garlic salt
1¼ teaspoons Worcestershire
sauce
¼ teaspoon white pepper
1 6½-ounce can white
crabmeat, rinsed and
drained

Using mixer, beat cream cheese and mayonnaise until creamy. Stir in remaining ingredients in order given. Refrigerate at least 8 hours before serving. Serve with crackers or fresh vegetables.

Guacamole

Yield: 1½ to 2 cups

2   ripe medium avocados
1½ Tablespoons lemon juice
¼   teaspoon garlic powder
2   Tablespoons grated onion
½   teaspoon salt
¼   teaspoon black pepper
2   dashes Tabasco sauce
½   teaspoon horseradish
⅓   cup mayonnaise
3 to 6 slices of bacon

In a food processor, put peeled avocados; whip until smooth. Add lemon juice, garlic powder, onion, salt, pepper, Tabasco and horseradish; blend well. Put into small bowl and completely cover with mayonnaise. Do not stir until ready to serve. When ready to serve, fry bacon and crumble. Add to avocado mixture after it has been stirred.

Great with chips for a dip!

Shrimp Dip

Yield: 4 to 5 cups

1   8-ounce package cream
     cheese, softened
Juice of 1 lemon
2   pounds boiled shrimp,
     shelled, veined and
     chopped
1   small bunch green onions,
     chopped
15 to 20 drops Tabasco sauce
¼   teaspoon Worcestershire
     sauce
Salt and black pepper to taste
Mayonnaise
Milk (optional)

Mix cream cheese and lemon juice. Stir in shrimp, onions and remaining ingredients. Add mayonnaise to desired consistency. Refrigerate at least 8 hours before serving. When ready to serve, thin with small amount of milk or mayonnaise. May also thin with juice of olives or pickles.

Spinach Dip

Yield: 4 cups

1   10-ounce package frozen
    chopped spinach
1   teaspoon salt
1   teaspoon black pepper
½   cup chopped green onion
½   cup chopped parsley
2   cups mayonnaise

Cook spinach and drain. Combine all the ingredients and mix. Chill. Serve with fresh vegetables.

Vegetable Dip

Yield: 1½ cups

1   cup salad dressing
2   teaspoons tarragon
    vinegar
Dash of black pepper
½   teaspoon salt
⅛   teaspoon thyme
½   teaspoon curry powder
2   teaspoons chili sauce
2   teaspoons parsley

Combine all of the ingredients and mix. Serve as a dip for favorite vegetables.

Caviar Pie

9 × 13 baking dish
Yield: 16 to 24 servings

2   8-ounce packages cream
    cheese, softened
1   cup mayonnaise
9   green onions, chopped
Minced parsley
3   4-ounce jars whitefish
    caviar, rinsed in lukewarm
    water and drained
5   hard-boiled eggs, chopped
Chopped parsley

Cream together cheese, mayonnaise, onions and minced parsley. Spread in 9 × 13 baking dish. Cover and chill. Layer rinsed caviar on top. Add chopped eggs and top with parsley.

Crab Appetizers

Yield: 48 pieces

½ cup butter, softened
1½ teaspoons garlic salt
1 5-ounce jar Old English Cheese Spread
1 7-ounce can crabmeat
1½ teaspoons mayonnaise
6 English muffins, split

Blend first 5 ingredients and spread on muffins. Freeze on a cookie sheet until hard. Cut into quarters while frozen and put into a plastic bag. Keep frozen until ready to serve. Brown muffin quarters under broiler for a few minutes before serving.

Crabmeat Canapé

325 degrees, preheated
Cookie sheet
Yield: 20 canapés

Melted butter
1 1-pound loaf bread, crust removed and sliced horizontally or cut into shapes with cookie cutters
½ cup finely chopped shallots or green onions
2 Tablespoons olive oil
1 cup medium white sauce
1 pound crabmeat, flaked
2 ounces white wine
Salt and white pepper to taste
2 teaspoons chopped parsley

Brush melted butter on both sides of bread before cutting into shapes. Toast under broiler on one side only. Sauté shallots in oil until tender. Blend in white sauce. Add crabmeat, wine, salt and white pepper. Cook 8 minutes over low heat. Sprinkle on parsley and allow to cool. Spread on untoasted side of bread. Bake for 5 minutes.

Bread slices may be made several days ahead and frozen.

Crab Swiss Puffs

400 degrees, preheated
Cookie sheet, lightly greased
Yield: 30 puffs

1   6½-ounce can crabmeat
1   8-ounce can water
    chestnuts, slivered
½   cup mayonnaise
½   teaspoon lemon juice
¼   teaspoon curry powder
4   ounces Swiss cheese,
    grated
2   5-ounce cans flaky
    biscuits

Mix first 6 ingredients. Separate each biscuit into 3 separate layers. Put teaspoonful of crab mixture on each biscuit layer. Bake on lightly greased cookie sheet for 10 to 12 minutes.

Shrimp Mousse

Yield: 1 mold

1   10¾-ounce can tomato
    soup
1   8-ounce package cream
    cheese, softened
1   cup mayonnaise
¾   cup finely chopped celery
¾   cup finely chopped
    shallots or green onions
1½ cups canned shrimp,
    drained, liquid reserved
1½ Tablespoons unflavored
    gelatin (2 packages)
1   6½-ounce can crabmeat,
    drained
¼   teaspoon salt
¼   teaspoon black pepper
Dash of Tabasco sauce
Dash of horseradish

Heat soup and blend with cream cheese until smooth. Add mayonnaise and vegetables; mix. Add shrimp and gelatin dissolved in ¼ cup shrimp liquid. Blend. Add remaining ingredients. Pour into greased mold and chill. Unmold to serve.

Tuna Pâté

Yield: 2 to 2½ cups

1   8-ounce package cream
    cheese, softened
2   Tablespoons chili sauce
¼   teaspoon Tabasco sauce
2   Tablespoons parsley
    flakes
1   teaspoon minced onion
2   6½-ounce cans tuna

Combine first 5 ingredients, blend well. Add tuna.
Refrigerate.

Bacon And Apple Hors d'Oeuvres

Yield: 4 to 5 dozen

3   cups peeled and finely
    chopped apples
8   cups bread crumbs
4   Tablespoons minced onion
4   teaspoons minced parsley
4   teaspoons salt
4   teaspoons black pepper
4   eggs, well beaten
1   cup milk
3 to 4 pounds bacon

Combine apples, bread crumbs, onion and
parsley. Add seasonings, eggs, milk and stir.
Unwrap packages of bacon and cut bacon in half.
Separate into strips. Place about 1 Tablespoon of
mixture on the end of a bacon strip and roll up.
Place the bacon rolls on a broiler pan with the
outside end on the bottom. Broil approximately
30 minutes turning once. Serve warm. Recipe can
be refrigerated up to 24 hours before cooking.

Anchovy Dip

Yield: 1½ cups

1   8-ounce package cream
    cheese, softened
1 to 2 Tablespoons milk
1   teaspoon grated onion
1   teaspoon anchovy paste
½   teaspoon lemon juice
½   teaspoon Worcestershire
    sauce
¼   teaspoon Tabasco sauce
Salt to taste
Cayenne or red pepper to taste

Combine cream cheese and milk until smooth and
creamy. Add remaining ingredients, mix well.
Chill.

Good with corn chips or potato chips.

Water Chestnuts and Bacon
Yield: 6 to 8 servings

2   8-ounce cans whole water
     chestnuts
Thin sliced bacon
⅓   cup white vinegar
1   cup sugar
½   cup water
1   teaspoon black pepper
1   teaspoon paprika
1   teaspoon salt
1   Tablespoon cornstarch
1   Tablespoon water

Wrap chestnuts with ½ piece of bacon. Secure with toothpick. Be sure ends of bacon overlap to allow for shrinkage during cooking. Broil on lowest shelf until bacon is crisp. Combine vinegar, sugar, water, pepper, paprika and salt. Mix cornstarch with water and add to sauce. Cook until thickened. Pour over chestnuts. Serve warm.

Bacon Rollups
350 degrees, preheated
Broiler pan
Yield: 50 rollups

2   3-ounce packages cream
     cheese with chives,
     softened
1   Tablespoon milk
25   slices mixed grain
     sandwich bread, crust
     removed and cut in half
25   slices bacon, cut in half
Parsley sprigs (optional)

Combine cream cheese and milk, stirring until spreading consistency. Spread 1 scant teaspoon of cream cheese mixture on each slice of bread and roll tightly. Wrap each rollup with bacon; securing with a toothpick. Place rollups on a broiler pan and bake for 30 minutes; turn if necessary to prevent over-browning. Garnish with parsley if desired.

Sausage Rolls
400 degrees, preheated
Cookie sheet, ungreased
Yield: 50 rolls

2   cups flour
½   teaspoon salt
3   teaspoons baking powder
5   Tablespoons shortening
⅔   cup milk
1   pound well-seasoned or
     hot sausage

Blend flour, salt and baking powder. Cut in shortening and add milk. Divide dough in half and roll paper thin as for a pie crust. Divide sausage in half and spread thinly over dough, patting out with hand. Roll like a jelly roll. Wrap in wax paper or foil. Chill until firm. Slice ¼-inch thick and bake 15 to 20 minutes, or until golden brown. Can be frozen after wrapping in foil.

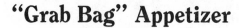

"Grab Bag" Appetizer

Chafing dish
Yield: 20 to 30 servings

2   cups mayonnaise
½   cup horseradish, drained
2   Tablespoons lemon juice
2   teaspoons dry mustard
½   teaspoon salt
Dash of cayenne or red pepper
1   cup whole mushrooms
1   12-ounce package boiled
     shrimp
2   cups ripe olives, pitted
Marble-sized Korean meatballs

Mix first 6 ingredients and heat, but do not boil. Add remaining ingredients. Serve with toothpicks for surprise in "grabbing".

Meatballs:
1   pound ground beef
1   egg
2   slices bread, made into
     crumbs
½   teaspoon black pepper
½   teaspoon monosodium
     glutamate
2   Tablespoons soy sauce
1   clove garlic, pressed
¼   cup chopped onion
⅓   teaspoon salt

Meatballs:
Mix all ingredients and shape into tiny balls. Bake at 350 degrees for 30 minutes.

Ham Roll-Ups

Yield: 8 to 10 servings

1   12-ounce package cream
     cheese, softened
1   7-ounce can jalapeño
     peppers, chopped (or less
     for taste)
¼   teaspoon garlic powder
¼   teaspoon onion powder
1   Tablespoon mayonnaise
½   teaspoon lemon juice
2   4-ounce packages ham
     luncheon meat

Combine first 6 ingredients; mix well. Spread thin layer of cheese mixture on a slice of ham. Roll ham jelly-roll style. Slice in bite-sized pieces and serve.

Curried Chicken Balls

Yield: 48 balls

1   3-ounce package cream cheese, softened
3   Tablespoons half and half or mayonnaise
1   cup finely chopped cooked chicken
2   cups finely chopped dry-roasted peanuts, divided
1   Tablespoon chopped chutney
½   teaspoon salt
3 to 4 teaspoons curry powder

Beat cream cheese and cream until smooth. Stir in chicken and 1 cup peanuts. Add remaining ingredients; mix. Shape into small balls. Roll in remaining cup of peanuts.

May be frozen 3 months. To serve, defrost for 3 to 4 hours.

Picadillo

Yield: 5 to 6 cups

1   pound ground beef
Salt and black pepper to taste
2   large tomatoes, peeled and diced
½   teaspoon cumin
½   teaspoon oregano
¼   teaspoon sugar
1   clove garlic, pressed
1   6-ounce can tomato paste
2   jalapeños, chopped
½   cup seedless raisins
½   cup diced pimientos
½   cup toasted almonds

Brown beef; drain. Stir in remaining ingredients and cook 15 to 20 minutes longer over low heat. Serve warm with nacho chips.

Variation:
May substitute 1 pound boiled and chopped chicken for beef.

Crab Stuffed Mushrooms

375 degrees, preheated
8-inch square baking
dish, ungreased
Yield: 20 to 24 mushrooms

20 to 24 large fresh
   mushrooms (about 1
   pound)
1   cup Italian salad dressing
¾   cup soft bread crumbs
1   6½-ounce can crabmeat,
   drained and flaked
2   eggs, beaten
¼   cup mayonnaise
¼   cup minced onion
1   teaspoon lemon juice

Clean mushrooms and remove stems. Combine mushroom caps and Italian dressing; cover and refrigerate 1 to 2 hours. Drain well. Combine ½ cup bread crumbs and remaining ingredients; mix well. Spoon crabmeat mixture into caps and sprinkle with remaining bread crumbs. Place in 8-inch square baking dish. Bake for 15 minutes.

Mushroom Appetizers

Cookie sheet, ungreased
Yield: 2 dozen

5 to 8 ounces mushrooms,
   chopped
½   small onion, finely
   chopped
3   Tablespoons butter
3   Tablespoons flour
¼   teaspoon salt
⅛   teaspoon black pepper
⅛   teaspoon garlic powder
Milk
Butter
24 bread rounds
¼   cup salad dressing
¼   cup parsley flakes

Sauté mushrooms and onion in butter. Add flour and seasonings. Add milk to make a thick paste. Cool. Cut bread rounds and brown in butter on one side. On untoasted side, spread salad dressing lightly. Spread generous amount of mushroom paste and sprinkle with parsley flakes. Broil until brown and bubbly. Paste may be prepared day before. (Melba rounds may be substituted for bread rounds.)

Mushroom Powder Puffs

Yield: 24 servings

¼ cup chopped shallots or
  green onions
2 Tablespoons butter
4 egg whites
6 ounces fresh mushrooms,
  chopped (2 cups)
½ cup grated Parmesan
  cheese
2 Tablespoons flour
½ teaspoon salt
Dash to ¼ teaspoon cayenne
  or red pepper
¼ teaspoon black pepper
Vegetable oil
Parsley sprigs
Fresh mushrooms

Cook shallots in butter until tender. Cool. Beat egg whites until stiff but not dry. Fold shallots mixture, mushrooms, cheese, flour, salt and peppers into egg whites. Blend. Heat 3 to 4 inches of oil in heavy pan to 375 degrees. Fry mushrooms mixture by rounded teaspoonfuls until brown and crisp, about 1 minute on each side. Drain on paper towel. Garnish with parsley and fresh mushrooms. Serve warm with toothpicks.

Spinach Balls

350 degrees, preheated
Cookie sheet, greased
Yield: 80 to 90 balls

2 10-ounce packages frozen
  chopped spinach
4 cups herb stuffing mix
6 beaten eggs
2 small onions, chopped
1 Tablespoon black pepper
1 Tablespoon monosodium
  glutamate
½ teaspoon thyme
1 Tablespoon garlic powder
½ cup Parmesan cheese
¾ cup butter, melted

Cook spinach; drain well. Add remaining ingredients and shape into balls. Bake for 20 minutes.

May freeze balls before cooking. Defrost 2 hours and bake as above.

Spinach Tarts

350 degrees, preheated
1¾-inch muffin pans, ungreased
Yield: 30 servings

Filling:
1   10-ounce package frozen
    spinach, thawed and
    drained
1   egg, beaten
¼   teaspoon salt
⅛   teaspoon black pepper
2   Tablespoons finely
    chopped onion
1   cup crumbled feta or
    grated Romano cheese
¼   cup butter, melted
Cream Cheese Pastry Shells
2   Tablespoons Romano
    cheese
Diced pimientos to garnish

Shells:
1   3-ounce package cream
    cheese, softened
½   cup butter, softened
1½ cups flour

Filling:
Combine well-drained spinach with next 6
ingredients; mix well. Fill each pastry shell with 1
heaping teaspoon of spinach mixture. Sprinkle
with Romano cheese and top with pimiento. Bake
for 30 to 35 minutes.

Shells:
Combine cream cheese, butter and flour, blend
well. Shape into 1-inch balls and place into
ungreased 1¾-inch muffin pans. Form dough
into thin shells.

*May be made in larger muffin tins as a
vegetable quiche dish.*

Chinese Fried Walnuts

Yield: 4 cups

6   cups water
4   cups walnuts
½   cup sugar
Vegetable oil
Salt

In a 4-quart saucepan heat water to boiling. Add nuts to water. Cook for 1 minute. Rinse nuts under running hot water; drain. In a large bowl with rubber spatula, gently stir warm nuts with sugar until sugar is dissolved. Heat approximately 1 inch oil over medium heat to 350 degrees. Using slotted spoon, add about half of the walnuts to the oil. Fry 5 minutes or until golden, stirring often. Drain walnuts in coarse sieve. Sprinkle lightly with salt and toss. Cool on paper towels. Repeat with remaining walnuts. Store in tightly covered container.

Variation:
Pecans may be substituted. Shorten frying time to approximately 3½ minutes.

Barbecued Pecans

400 degrees, preheated
11 × 15 baking dish, ungreased
Yield: 4 cups

2   Tablespoons butter
¼   cup Worcestershire sauce
1   Tablespoon ketchup
2   drops Tabasco sauce
4   cups pecan halves
Salt

Melt butter in saucepan. Add Worcestershire sauce, ketchup, and Tabasco. Spoon evenly over pecans in baking dish. Toast in oven for 20 minutes; stirring often. Turn out on paper towel and sprinkle with salt.

Sweet and Spicy Nuts

300 degrees, preheated
Jelly roll pan, greased
Yield: 2 cups

1   egg white
1   Tablespoon water
2   cups shelled walnuts or
      pecans
½   cup sugar
1   teaspoon cinnamon
¾   teaspoon salt
¼   teaspoon ground cloves
¼   teaspoon nutmeg

In a medium-sized bowl, beat egg white with water until foamy and double in volume. Stir in nuts. In a small bowl, combine remaining ingredients. Sprinkle over nuts. Mix well. Spread on greased jelly roll pan. Bake for 30 minutes. Cool and break apart. Store in jar.

Goopies

225 degrees, preheated
Large roaster
Yield: 3 to 4 pounds

½   cup margarine
1½   cups bacon drippings
4   Tablespoons
      Worcestershire sauce
4   Tablespoons seasoned salt
2 to 4 Tablespoons Tabasco
      sauce
4   Tablespoons liquid smoke
4   Tablespoons garlic
      powder
1   12-ounce box Corn Chex
1   12-ounce box Rice Chex
1   pound nuts (peanuts and/
      or pecan halves)
1   10-ounce box stick
      pretzels

Combine first 7 ingredients and boil for one minute. Put cereals, nuts and pretzels in roaster. Pour liquid mixture over the dry mixture and stir. Bake in an uncovered roaster for 1 hour, stirring often.

Beverages

Champagne Cocktail

Sugar cubes (1 per glass)
Bitters
Lemon rind, cut into strips
Champagne, chilled

Soak 1 sugar cube per glass in bitters for a minute or two while peeling and cutting lemon rind strips. Place 1 soaked sugar cube in each glass. Twist a lemon rind strip in center and place on sugar cube. Fill glass with chilled champagne.

Brandy Slush

*Advance Preparation
Time Required
Yield: 24 servings*

6   cups water
1½ cups sugar
1   cup water
4   tea bags
1   12-ounce can frozen
     lemonade
1   12-ounce can frozen
     orange juice
2½ cups brandy
7-up
Maraschino cherries

Boil 6 cups water and add sugar. Cool in refrigerator or freezer for 10 minutes. Boil 1 cup water and add tea bags. Combine with water and sugar mixture and add lemonade and orange juice. Stir in brandy and pour into a gallon container. Freeze overnight. Fill glass ¾ full with mixture and finish filling with 7-up. Add a cherry. This may be stored in the freezer and served one glass at a time.

Snowcap Brandied Coffee

Yield: 6 to 7 servings

4   ounces brandy
3   Tablespoons instant coffee
     granules
3   Tablespoons sugar
½   teaspoon cinnamon
⅛   teaspoon cardamon
27   ounces boiling water
     (approximately)
Whipped cream, flavored with
     sugar and vanilla

Stir brandy, coffee granules, sugar and spices together. Cover and let stand for 1 hour. Can be prepared ahead up to this point. Combine 27 ounces of boiling water with brandy and coffee mixture. Keep warm and pour into cups as needed. Stir well and top with whipped cream.

Fluffy Eggnog

Yield: 25 servings

14 eggs, separated
1¼ cups granulated sugar
1 to 1¾ cups bourbon
¾ to 1½ cups rum, brandy or
   a combination
1 pint vanilla ice cream,
   softened
2 cups milk
3 cups whipping cream
½ cup powdered sugar,
   divided
4 to 5 Tablespoons vanilla,
   divided
Cinnamon and nutmeg for
   garnish
Additional liquor, optional

Beat egg yolks well; add granulated sugar and beat well again. Gradually beat in liquors. Chill for several hours. Approximately 2 hours before serving, add softened ice cream and milk to mixture. Beat egg whites until soft peaks form, adding 1 Tablespoon powdered sugar and 1 Tablespoon vanilla while beating. Whip cream until fairly stiff, adding remainder of powdered sugar and vanilla while whipping. Fold whipped cream and egg whites into egg yolks. Chill well before serving. Additional liquor may be added or more sugar may be added if you like it very sweet.

Glugg

Yield: 30 to 40 servings

1 gallon Port wine
12 cloves
6 cardamon seeds, shelled
3 sticks cinnamon
½ pound raisins
3 cups sugar
⅓ cup whole almonds
1 fifth brandy

Combine all the above ingredients except the brandy and cook until white on top. Skim the liquid. Remove from heat and add brandy. Cover and let cool. Store in refrigerator. Serve hot.

To serve: leave solid ingredients in punch, straining out solids when serving.

Whiskey Sour Punch

Advance Preparation
Time Required
Yield: 20 servings

2½ cups Southern Comfort
1   12-ounce can frozen
    orange juice, undiluted
2   6-ounce cans frozen
    lemonade, undiluted
6   ounces lemon juice
4   32-ounce bottles 7-up,
    chilled

Combine Southern Comfort, orange juice, lemonade and lemon juice. Refrigerate for 24 hours. Mix with 7-up and serve in a punch bowl, pouring it over an ice mold.

Banana Punch

Advance Preparation
Time Required
Yield: 30 to 40 servings

4   cups sugar
16 cups water
1   12-ounce can frozen
    orange juice
1   46-ounce can pineapple
    juice
5   bananas, mashed
2   32-ounce bottles ginger
    ale

Boil sugar in 4 cups of the water for approximately 15 minutes to make sugar syrup. Add remaining ingredients except for ginger ale. Freeze. Take out 3 hours before serving and mash. Add ginger ale and stir well.

Frozen Margaritas

Blender
Yield: 6 to 8 servings

1   can frozen limeade
    concentrate
1   can full of tequila
1   jigger Orange Curaçao
2   Tablespoons fresh lime
    juice
Ice
Lime juice (optional)
Coarse salt (optional)

Place limeade, tequila, Curaçao, and lime juice in blender container. Fill container approximately ¾ full with ice cubes. Blend until ice is pureed. Serve; glass rims may be first dipped in lime juice, then in coarse salt before glass is filled.

Variation: Substitute ½ can full of Triple Sec for Orange Curaçao and omit lime juice.

Slushy Gelatin Punch

Advance Preparation
Time Required
Yield: 45 to 50 servings

1   6-ounce package gelatin
    (any flavor)
1½ cups hot water
1   12-ounce can frozen
    orange juice, mixed by
    directions on can
1   46-ounce can pineapple
    juice
1   6-ounce can lemonade,
    mixed by directions on can
1   cup sugar
Ginger ale

Dissolve gelatin in hot water. Add remaining ingredients except for ginger ale and mix thoroughly. Freeze overnight. About 2 hours before serving, remove punch from freezer and let thaw. Add ginger ale immediately before serving. Stir to make slushy.

Orange Julius

Yield: 4 to 6 servings

1   6-ounce can frozen orange
    juice
1½ cups water
½   cup milk
½   cup sugar
1   teaspoon vanilla
14 ice cubes

Mix together above ingredients in a blender until ice is crushed. Serve immediately.

Almond Tea

Yield: 6 to 7 servings

1½ cups water
1¼ cups sugar
½   cup lemon juice
1   Tablespoon almond
    extract
1   Tablespoon vanilla extract
1   quart strong tea

Boil water and sugar together for 4 minutes. Add lemon juice, almond extract and vanilla extract. Boil another 3 to 4 minutes. Add tea and heat. Serve warm.

Famous Spiced Tea

Yield: 12 to 15 servings

1   6-ounce can frozen
    lemonade
1   12-ounce can frozen
    orange juice
1   46-ounce can pineapple
    juice
2½ cups very strong tea
⅔   cup sugar
1½ quarts water
1   heaping Tablespoon
    cloves
5   cinnamon sticks

Mix all ingredients together and simmer for 1
hour. Do not boil! Serve warm. To serve later,
remove cinnamon sticks and cloves as they will
make tea too strong.

Hot Spiced Cider

Yield: 6 servings

1   cup sugar
6   cups apple juice
10 whole cloves
4   2-inch sticks cinnamon
Juice of 1 lemon
1   cup strong hot instant tea

Boil together sugar, 3 cups apple juice, cloves
and cinnamon. Turn off flame and add the rest of
the apple juice. Let cool 1 hour, then add lemon
juice. Reheat. When hot, add tea. Strain spices
and serve hot. Lace with rum for special flavor.

Makes your house smell wonderful!

Spiced Wassail

Yield: 8 to 9 servings

1   6-inch stick cinnamon
3   oranges
16 whole cloves
1   teaspoon whole allspice
6   cups apple cider
1   16-ounce bottle cranberry
    juice
¼   cup sugar
1   cup rum (optional)

Break cinnamon in pieces. Stud oranges with
whole cloves. Combine all ingredients except rum
and boil for about 10 minutes, covered. Add rum
and serve warm.

Soups and Sandwiches

Broaddus Stew

Yield: 3 to 4 quarts

2½ to 3 pounds stew meat
Meat tenderizer
Garlic powder to taste
Salt and black pepper to taste
4   bay leaves
4 to 5 onions, chopped
6   cloves garlic, chopped
1   Tablespoon oregano
1   Tablespoon marjoram
1   Tablespoon chili powder
1   Tablespoon parsley flakes
1   Tablespoon thyme
1   Tablespoon paprika
1 to 2 teaspoons cayenne or
     red pepper (optional)
2   Tablespoons
     Worcestershire sauce
1   14½-ounce can Rotel
     tomatoes with green
     chiles
2   15-ounce cans tomatoes
1   8-ounce can tomato sauce
1 to 2 packages frozen stew
     vegetables
2   Tablespoons sugar
Water

Tenderize meat, dusting with garlic powder, salt and pepper. Put all ingredients except stew vegetables in enough water to cover. Cook 2 to 3 hours adding vegetables the last hour. (Rotel tomatoes make this dish very hot.)

Shrimp Tomato Soup

Yield: 4 servings

1   10¾-ounce can cream of
     shrimp soup
1   8¼-ounce can tomatoes
¼   cup sherry
½   cup evaporated milk
2   drops Tabasco sauce
¼   cup shrimp pieces
Parsley to garnish

In medium saucepan, combine shrimp soup, undrained tomatoes, sherry and evaporated milk. Place over low heat, stirring occasionally. Add Tabasco sauce and shrimp pieces. Heat 1 minute more. When serving, sprinkle with parsley or garnish with sprig of parsley.

Mexican Carrot Soup

Yield: 4 servings

4   medium carrots, cut up (2
     cups)
½   cup water
2   teaspoons instant chicken
     bouillon granules
½   teaspoon sugar
¼   teaspoon dried mint,
     crushed
¼   cup chopped onion
1   Tablespoon butter
1   Tablespoon flour
2½   cups milk
1   3-ounce package cream
     cheese, cubed
½   teaspoon salt
Dash of black pepper

In covered saucepan, cook carrots in water with bouillon, sugar and mint 25 minutes or until tender. Cook onion in butter until tender, not brown and stir in flour. Add milk all at once. Cook, while stirring, until thick and bubbly. Gradually add about 1 cup of hot milk mixture to the cream cheese and beat until smooth. Return to saucepan and mix well. In blender, place carrots and their liquid. Cover and blend until smooth. Add carrot mixture to milk mixture. Cook and stir until soup comes to a boil. Stir in salt and pepper.

Cheese Soup for 12

Yield: 12 servings

½   cup butter
½   cup diced onion
½   cup diced carrots
½   cup diced celery
¼   cup flour
1½   Tablespoons cornstarch
4   cups chicken stock
4   cups half and half
⅛   teaspoon baking soda
1   cup sherry
1   pound Velveeta cheese,
     cut in pieces
½   pound black rind Cheddar
     cheese, grated
1   teaspoon salt
Black pepper to taste
Paprika for garnish
Parsley for garnish

In butter, sauté onion, carrots and celery until tender. Stir in flour and cornstarch and cook until bubbly. Add chicken stock and half and half, and heat until smooth and steaming. Add baking soda, sherry and both cheeses; stir until cheeses melt and mixture is smooth. Season to taste with salt and pepper. Serve with paprika and parsley for garnish.

Cheese Soup for 200

Yield: 200 servings

5   pounds butter
10 medium onions, diced
5   bunches celery, diced
12 pounds carrots, diced
10 cups flour
2   cups cornstarch
5   gallons chicken stock
5   gallons half and half
2½ teaspoons baking soda
1   gallon sherry to taste
20 pounds Velveeta cheese,
    cut in chunks
5   pounds black rind
    Cheddar cheese, grated
⅓   cup salt
Black pepper to taste
Paprika for garnish
Parsley for garnish

In butter, sauté vegetables. (May be handled more easily if divided into 5 or 6 batches.) Add flour and cornstarch and cook until bubbly. (May be easily frozen at this point if desired for early preparation.) Add stock and half and half and heat until smooth and steaming. Add baking soda, sherry and cheeses. Stir until cheese melts. Season with salt and pepper. Serve garnished with parsley and paprika.

Chili Soup

Dutch oven
Yield: 10 to 12 servings

3   onions, chopped
2   cloves garlic, pressed
2   Tablespoons vegetable oil
2   pounds ground beef
1   28-ounce can tomatoes,
    pureéd in blender
1   6-ounce can tomato paste
1   4-ounce can chopped
    green chiles
3   Tablespoons chili powder
1   Tablespoon ground cumin
1   bay leaf
2½ teaspoons salt
6   whole cloves
¼   teaspoon cayenne or red
    pepper

In a heavy Dutch oven, sauté onions and garlic in oil. Add ground beef and brown. Drain off any grease. Add pureéd tomatoes, tomato paste, green chiles and seasonings. Stir well. Cover and simmer for 2 hours.

Cold Weather Corn Chowder

Yield: 4 servings

1 large potato, peeled and diced
2 cups boiling salted water
1 bay leaf
¼ teaspoon sage
½ teaspoon cumin
3 Tablespoons butter
1 onion, chopped
3 Tablespoons flour
1¼ cups whipping cream or half and half
Kernels from 3 ears of corn
½ teaspoon yeast
Chopped chives and parsley to taste
¼ teaspoon nutmeg
Salt and black pepper to taste
1½ cups sharp Cheddar cheese, grated
4 to 6 Tablespoons white wine

Boil peeled and diced potato in salted water with bay leaf, sage and cumin for 15 to 20 minutes. Melt butter in a saucepan and sauté onion until tender. Add flour to the onion mixture and cook until bubbly. Add cream, stirring with a whisk for smoothness. Pour this cream sauce into the potatoes and their water, adding the fresh corn kernels. Add yeast, herbs and rest of spices. Simmer for 10 to 15 minutes. Add cheese and wine. Stir well and cook until cheese melts.

Zucchini Soup

Yield: 8 to 10 servings

5 zucchini, sliced
1 onion, sliced
1 potato, peeled and sliced
4 Tablespoons butter
1½ teaspoons salt
White pepper to taste
½ teaspoon soy sauce
1 teaspoon sugar
½ teaspoon sage (optional)
1 cup milk
3 cups chicken stock
1 13-ounce can evaporated milk or equal amount of cream

Sauté vegetables in butter until tender but not browned. Add salt, pepper, soy sauce, sugar and sage. Puree above with ¼ cup milk in a blender. Return to saucepan. Add stock. Bring to a boil then add remaining milk and canned milk. Heat until hot. Correct seasonings if necessary. Serve hot or cold with dash of nutmeg. Freezes well.

Blender Gazpacho

Blender
Yield: 4 to 6 servings

2   cups hot spicy tomato
    juice
1   cup chopped tomatoes
½   cup chopped green onions
½   cup chopped cucumbers
½   cup chopped celery
¼   cup chopped onion
2   teaspoons parsley
1   teaspoon chopped chives
1   clove garlic, pressed
1   Tablespoon garlic vinegar
1   Tablespoon salad vinegar
2   Tablespoons olive oil
1   teaspoon salt
1   teaspoon black pepper
1½ teaspoons Worcestershire
    sauce

Mix all ingredients in a blender and blend well.
Serve chilled.

Gazpacho

Yield: 12 servings

1   small clove garlic, pressed
1   Tablespoon sugar
1½ teaspoons salt
1   46-ounce can tomato juice
¼   cup olive oil
2   Tablespoons lemon juice
1   teaspoon Worcestershire
    sauce
3   whole tomatoes, chopped
1   whole cucumber, chopped
1   large bell pepper, chopped
1   cup grated carrots
1   cup chopped celery
¼   cup finely chopped green
    onion

Mix first 7 ingredients well in large container.
Add all other ingredients (finely chopped). Chill
overnight and serve garnished with croutons.

Fresh Mushroom Soup

Yield: 4 servings

1   cup sliced fresh
    mushrooms
⅓   cup chopped onion
¼   cup chopped bell pepper
¼   teaspoon minced garlic
2   Tablespoons butter,
    melted
½   teaspoon salt
⅛   teaspoon black pepper
⅛   teaspoon tarragon,
    crumbled
1   14½-ounce can chicken
    broth
1   8-ounce can tomatoes,
    drained
¾ to 1 cup water
Grated Parmesan cheese

Sauté mushrooms, onion, bell pepper and garlic in butter until onion is transparent. Add salt, pepper, tarragon, chicken broth, tomatoes and water; heat to simmer. Cover and simmer 10 minutes. Top each serving with Parmesan cheese.

A thick robust soup!

Baked French Onion Soup

325 degrees, preheated
6 ovenproof individual crocks
Yield: 6 servings

3 to 6 yellow onions, thinly
    sliced
¼   teaspoon sugar
1   clove garlic, pressed
½   cup butter
2   10½-ounce cans beef
    broth
½   cup white wine or sherry
    (optional)
1¼ cups water
3   slices French bread,
    toasted and cut in half
2   cups grated Swiss cheese

Sauté onions, sugar and garlic in butter until lightly brown. Add broth, sherry and water. Simmer until onions are tender. Ladle soup into individual ovenproof crocks. Top each serving with a half slice of bread. Sprinkle with cheese and bake until cheese melts.

Onion Potato Soup

Yield: 6 servings

3   slices bacon
4   medium onions, chopped
2   large potatoes, pared and
    diced
1   14½-ounce can chicken
    broth
½   cup water
1   teaspoon salt
¼   teaspoon curry powder
1   13-ounce can evaporated
    milk
2   Tablespoons parsley

In large saucepan, cook bacon until crisp. Reserve 2 Tablespoons of drippings. Drain and crumble bacon. Cook onions in drippings until tender, not brown. Add diced potatoes, chicken broth, water, salt and curry. Cover and cook about 10 minutes or until potatoes are tender. Slightly mash potatoes. Stir in evaporated milk, parsley and crumbled bacon. Heat and serve.

Potage Portugaise

Yield: 10 to 12 servings

6   Tablespoons butter
2   Tablespoons olive oil
2   large onions, thinly sliced
    (about 2 cups)
1   teaspoon leaf thyme
2   teaspoons leaf basil
Salt and black pepper to taste
2   14½-ounce cans Italian-
    style tomatoes
3   Tablespoons tomato paste
½   cup flour
2   14½-ounce cans chicken
    broth
2   soup cans water
1   teaspoon sugar
Fresh parsley, chopped

Sauté in butter with olive oil the onions, thyme, basil, salt and pepper to taste, until onions are soft but not browned. Add tomatoes and tomato paste. Blend well and simmer 10 minutes. Put flour into small bowl and add one can of chicken broth, stirring so there are no lumps. Add to tomato mix in saucepan, along with remaining broth, water and sugar. Bring to a boil, simmer 30 minutes, stirring frequently. Remove from heat and cool. Put soup through blender or food processor, a bit at a time. Reheat and serve, garnished with parsley.

Split Pea Soup

Yield: 6 to 10 servings

1   pound dry green split
     peas
2   quarts water
1   onion, sliced
2   stalks celery and tops,
     chopped
1   clove garlic, minced
2   sprigs parsley
1   bay leaf
Ham hock
Salt and black pepper to taste

Wash peas and put them in a large pot. Add water and all other ingredients. Bring to a boil. Reduce heat and simmer for 2 hours.

Cream of Shrimp Soup

Yield: 4 servings

1   pound raw shrimp, shelled
     and veined
6   Tablespoons butter
2   Tablespoons finely
     chopped onion
2   Tablespoons flour
1   teaspoon salt
½   teaspoon monosodium
     glutamate
Black pepper to taste
Pinch of dried thyme leaves
¼   teaspoon celery seed
3   cups milk or cream
1   teaspoon lemon juice
Paprika to garnish
Chopped fresh parsley to
     garnish

Coarsely chop shrimp. Melt 4 Tablespoons butter in saucepan. Add shrimp and cook until it turns pink. Remove shrimp. Add remaining butter and onion. Cook slowly until browned. Stir in flour, salt, monosodium glutamate, pepper, thyme and celery seed. Blend. Gradually stir in milk and bring to boil. Boil 1 minute stirring constantly. Add shrimp and heat. Stir in lemon juice. Put into cups. Sprinkle with paprika and parsley.

Hot Browns

Yield: 4 to 6 servings

⅓ cup butter
1 medium onion, chopped
⅓ cup flour
3 cups hot milk
1 teaspoon salt
½ teaspoon crushed red
    pepper
¼ pound processed cheese,
    cut in chunks
2 eggs, well beaten
1 Tablespoon butter
4 strips bacon
8 slices bread
Sliced chicken
Parmesan cheese
Paprika
4 sautéed mushrooms for
    garnish (optional)

Melt butter in heavy saucepan over medium heat; add onion and cook until clear. Add flour and blend to make a smooth paste; add milk, salt and red pepper. Stir and cook until thick and smooth. Stir in cheese, eggs and remaining Tablespoon butter. Continue to cook, stirring, until mixture almost reaches boiling point, but do not boil. Remove from heat. Fry bacon crisp; crumble if desired. To assemble, toast 8 slices bread. On 4 oven-proof plates, arrange toast and lay sliced chicken over it. Cover with sauce. Add bacon, Parmesan cheese and paprika. Place under broiler until sauce begins to bubble. Garnish and serve at once.

Spinach Sandwich Filling

Yield: 2 to 3 dozen tea sandwiches

1 10-ounce bunch of fresh
    spinach
1 8-ounce package cream
    cheese, softened
Juice of 1 lemon
Salt to taste
Garlic powder to taste

Wash, drain and pat spinach dry. Remove stems and finely chop leaves. Blend the chopped spinach with the softened cream cheese. Season to taste with lemon juice, salt and garlic powder.

Salads and Dressings

Avocado Salad

Bundt pan
Yield: 14 to 18 servings

2   3-ounce packages lime
    gelatin
2   cups boiling water
4   3-ounce packages cream
    cheese, softened
2   avocados, mashed
1   4-ounce jar pimientos,
    chopped
1   bell pepper, chopped
1   small onion, chopped
2   cups chopped celery
1   cup mayonnaise
Salt and black pepper to taste

In a saucepan, heat gelatin with water until dissolved. Add softened cream cheese to hot mixture and let cool slightly. Stir in remaining ingredients and pour into a large bundt pan. Chill until firm. Unmold on platter to serve.

Stuffed Avocados

Yield: 6 to 8 servings

½   cup chopped onion
¼   cup chopped green onion
¼   cup olive oil
2   chopped tomatoes
4   Tablespoons soft bread
    crumbs, divided
⅛   teaspoon Italian seasoning
Salt and black pepper to taste
3 or 4 avocados, cut in halves
    and peeled
¼   cup grated Parmesan
    cheese

Sauté onions and green onions in oil until tender. Add tomatoes and sauté a little longer. Add 3 Tablespoons bread crumbs and seasonings. Fill peeled avocado halves. Sprinkle with remaining bread crumbs and cheese. Broil until golden.

Aspic Salad

4 to 6 cup mold
Yield: 8 servings

1 envelope unflavored
    gelatin
¼ cup cold water
1 10¾-ounce can tomato
    soup
1 8-ounce package cream
    cheese, softened
1 Tablespoon grated onion
½ cup finely chopped
    avocado
½ cup mayonnaise
½ teaspoon salt
⅛ teaspoon (or less) cayenne
    or red pepper
1 teaspoon Worcestershire
    sauce
½ cup chopped celery

Dissolve gelatin in cold water. Heat soup to boiling. Add gelatin and stir until dissolved. Add cream cheese. Stir until smooth. Add remaining ingredients and pour into mold.

Variation:
Shrimp or crabmeat may be added to make an entree.

Chicken Salad

9 × 13 dish
Yield: 20 to 30 servings

3 3-ounce packages lemon
    gelatin
3 cups boiling water
Juice of 1 lemon
1½ cups salad dressing
3 cups evaporated milk
1 bell pepper, finely
    chopped
2 cups finely chopped celery
1 4-ounce jar pimientos
¼ teaspoon salt
2 cups cottage cheese,
    drained
2 cups boiled chicken (4
    breasts)

Dissolve gelatin in boiling water. Add lemon juice and let cool. Add salad dressing and milk, mixing well. Refrigerate until partially set. Stir in remaining ingredients. Pour into 9 × 13 dish and refrigerate until set. Cut into squares and serve on a lettuce leaf.

Turkey or Chicken Salad

Yield: 4 to 6 servings

2 cans turkey or chicken
1½ cups chopped celery
1 cup seedless green grapes
½ cup cashew nuts
½ cup mayonnaise
½ teaspoon curry powder

Dice turkey or chicken and toss with celery, grapes and cashews. Mix mayonnaise with curry powder. Add to salad and toss gently to bind together. Serve on toasted buns. Good served in small individually-sized French bread buns that have been heated and halved with middle of bread scooped out.

Apricot Gelatin Salad

Yield: 8 to 10 servings

1 3-ounce box of apricot
gelatin
2 cups boiling water
2 bananas, sliced
1 8-ounce can crushed
pineapple (juice reserved)
1 cup miniature
marshmallows

Mix apricot gelatin with boiling water. Add the fruit and marshmallows and refrigerate until congealed.

Topping:
2 Tablespoons margarine
2 Tablespoons flour
½ cup sugar
1 egg, well beaten
½ cup reserved pineapple
juice (add orange juice to
make ½ cup)
1 3-ounce package cream
cheese
Mandarin orange slices
Pecan halves

Topping:
Melt margarine over low heat. Add flour, sugar, egg and juice. Mix and cook until it thickens. Let cool. Add cream cheese and mix with electric mixer until smooth. Pour on top of gelatin and refrigerate. Garnish top with mandarin orange sections and pecan halves.

Congealed Cranberry Salad

12-cup mold or large casserole
Yield: 12 to 15 servings

1   3-ounce package lemon gelatin
1   3-ounce package cherry gelatin
1   cup sugar
3   cups boiling water
1   Tablespoon lemon juice
1   orange, quartered and peeled
3   cups or ½ pound fresh cranberries
1   8¾-ounce can crushed pineapple, drained
1   cup diced celery
1   cup chopped pecans

Mix gelatins together and stir in sugar. Add boiling water and lemon juice. Stir until dissolved. Refrigerate until slightly firm. In food processor (or blender), chop together cranberries and orange. Add cranberry mixture, pineapple, celery and pecans to gelatin mixture. Fold thoroughly and pour into a 12-cup mold or large casserole dish. Refrigerate until firm.

Pineapple Delight

Large mold
Yield: 6 servings

1   3-ounce package lime-flavored gelatin
1   cup boiling water
¾   cup pineapple juice
1   20-ounce can chunk pineapple
½ to 1 cup chopped pecans
1   cup grated Cheddar cheese
1   cup whipping cream, whipped, or 2 cups whipped topping

Dissolve the lime gelatin in the boiling water. Add the pineapple juice and pineapple chunks. Refrigerate. When mixture begins to congeal, add the pecans and cheese, and fold in the whipped cream or whipped topping. Pour into a mold or pretty glass dish. Chill until firm.

Congealed Spinach Salad

9 × 9 glass dish or 2-quart mold
Yield: 8 servings

Salad:
1   package lemon gelatin
1   cup boiling water
½   cup mayonnaise
½   teaspoon salt
1   cup small curd cottage cheese
1   cup chopped celery
2   Tablespoons lemon juice
1   10-ounce package frozen chopped spinach, thawed and drained
1   small onion, grated

Salad:
Dissolve gelatin in boiling water and allow to cool. Combine all other salad ingredients and pour into cooled gelatin. Pour into 9 × 9 glass dish or 2-quart mold. Chill.

Dressing:
3   Tablespoons mayonnaise
2   Tablespoons sour cream
½   teaspoon vinegar
½   teaspoon Worcestershire sauce
Dash of salt
Dash of paprika

Dressing:
Mix dressing ingredients together and put on salad when serving.

Confetti Gelatin Salad

12-cup mold or 9 × 13 dish
Yield: 15 to 20 servings

2   envelopes unflavored gelatin
1   cup water
1   cup chopped broccoli
1   cup grated carrots
1   cup grated cabbage
¼   cup chopped bell pepper
1   cup mayonnaise
2   cups cottage cheese
¼   teaspoon salt
¼   cup vinegar
¼   Tablespoon Tabasco sauce

Place gelatin and water over low heat until dissolved. Set aside. Mix mayonnaise, cottage cheese, salt, vinegar and Tabasco. Add to gelatin mixture and mix well. Add vegetables and mix well. Pour into a 12-cup mold or a 9 × 13 dish. Chill.

Garnish with parsley, fresh broccoli, radishes and cherry tomatoes. Salad will keep in refrigerator for 1 week.

Cucumber Salad

Yield: 4 to 6 servings

3   medium cucumbers, sliced
2   teaspoons salt

Vinegar Dressing:
3   Tablespoons vegetable oil
3   Tablespoons vinegar
3   Tablespoons water
1   teaspoon sugar
¼   teaspoon salt
¼   teaspoon black pepper
1   onion, chopped or 6 green
     onions, chopped

Sprinkle salt over cucumber slices.

Vinegar Dressing:
Mix dressing ingredients well. Pour over cucumbers. Cover and refrigerate for at least 1 hour before serving.

Frozen Fruitcake Salad

4½-cup ring mold
Yield: 8 servings

1   cup sour cream
1   cup whipping cream,
     whipped and sweetened
½   cup sugar
2   Tablespoons lemon juice
1   teaspoon vanilla
1   13-ounce can crushed
     pineapple, drained
2   bananas, diced
½   cup sliced red candied
     cherries
½   cup sliced green candied
     cherries
½   cup chopped walnuts
8 to 12 lettuce leaves

In a mixing bowl, combine sour cream, whipped cream, sugar, lemon juice and vanilla. Fold in fruits and nuts. Pour into a 4½ cup ring and freeze several hours or overnight. Unmold onto a plate lined with lettuce leaves. Garnish with additional cherries and nuts. Let stand 10 minutes before serving.

New Year's Eve Caesar Salad

Yield: 3 to 5 servings

1   head romaine lettuce
½ teaspoon salt (or garlic salt)
½ teaspoon freshly ground black pepper
¼ teaspoon dry mustard
¼ cup olive oil (or vegetable oil)
1   teaspoon fresh lemon juice
2   Tablespoons red wine vinegar
½ cup croutons
3   slices bacon, fried crisp and broken into small pieces
¼ cup Parmesan cheese
1   egg, beaten (mixed with rotary beater)

Tear leaves of lettuce from the head and wash. Drain. Place in refrigerator to crisp for 2 hours. Shake to dry. Tear leaf from stalk (on outside leaves) into bite-sized pieces. Retain stalks of center leaves and tear whole leaf into bite-sized pieces. Place lettuce in salad bowl and add salt and pepper. Toss. Sprinkle with dry mustard. Toss again. Pour in olive oil and toss, making sure each leaf is coated. Add lemon juice and vinegar. Toss. Add croutons, bacon and Parmesan cheese. Toss. Pour in egg and toss. Serve immediately.

Fruit Boats

Yield: 8 servings

1   8-ounce package cream cheese, softened
1   7-ounce jar marshmallow creme
1   Tablespoon grated orange rind
1   Tablespoon orange juice
Dash of ground ginger
1   cup seedless green grapes
1   cup halved fresh strawberries
¾ cup mandarin oranges
1¼ cup watermelon balls
2   large honeydew melons or cantaloupe, quartered and seeded
Orange rind curls (optional)

Beat cream cheese until smooth. Add marshmallow creme slowly, beating at medium speed, until well blended. Add orange rind, orange juice and ginger. Beat until mixture is light and fluffy. Fold in grapes, strawberries, mandarin oranges and watermelon, mixing well. Fill each melon quarter with fruit mixture. Garnish with orange curls if desired.

Orange Almond Salad

Yield: 4 to 6 servings

½ cup slivered almonds
3 Tablespoons sugar
½ head iceberg lettuce, torn
½ head romaine lettuce, torn
1 cup sliced celery
2 whole green onions, chopped
1 11-ounce can mandarin oranges, drained

Dressing:
½ teaspoon salt
Dash of black pepper
¼ cup vegetable oil
1 Tablespoon chopped parsley
2 Tablespoons sugar
2 Tablespoons vinegar
2 Tablespoons ketchup
Dash of Tabasco sauce

In a small pan, over medium heat, cook almonds and sugar, stirring constantly until almonds are coated and sugar is dissolved. Cool.

Mix lettuces, celery and onions. Just before serving, add almonds and oranges. Toss with dressing.

Dressing:
Mix dressing ingredients.

The coating will melt off almonds if tossed more than 5 to 10 minutes before serving. Coated almonds will keep indefinitely in an air-tight container, so they can be done ahead of time.

Sherry Baked Fruit

350 degrees, preheated
9-inch round casserole
Yield: 8 servings

1 16-ounce package pitted prunes
5½ ounces dried apricots
1 13-ounce can pineapple chunks, drained
1 16-ounce can cherry pie filling
1½ cups water
¼ cup dry sherry
⅓ cup slivered almonds

Put prunes, apricots and pineapple in a deep 9-inch round casserole. Combine cherries, water and sherry. Pour over the fruit, mixing well. Stir in almonds. Cover and bake for 1¼ hours.

Spinach Mushroom Orange Salad

Yield: 6 to 8 servings

1   pound spinach, washed
    and cut into bite-sized
    pieces
¾   pound mushrooms, thinly
    sliced
1 to 2 large naval oranges,
    peeled, sectioned and
    cubed or sliced

Place spinach, mushrooms and orange sections in bowl. Toss with dressing to coat each leaf lightly. Let set 10 to 15 minutes before serving.

Dressing:
½   cup olive oil
⅓   cup red wine vinegar
2   Tablespoons honey
1   Tablespoon finely grated
    onion
½   teaspoon salt
½   teaspoon dry mustard
⅛   teaspoon black pepper

Dressing:
Prepare dressing early in the day. Place all ingredients in a jar and shake well to blend. Let set several hours. Shake well before serving.

Spinach Salad

*Advance Preparation
Time Required*
Yield: 4 to 8 servings

8   slices bacon, cooked and
    crumbled
2   hard-boiled eggs, chopped
Fresh spinach
Fresh mushrooms, chopped

Prepare bacon and eggs. At serving time pour dressing through a strainer over the spinach and mushrooms. Add bacon and eggs and toss lightly.

Dressing:
1   cup vegetable oil
⅓   cup red wine vinegar
¼   cup sour cream
½   teaspoon dry mustard
2   Tablespoons sugar
¼   cup chopped, fresh
    parsley
2   cloves garlic, chopped
1½ teaspoons salt

Dressing:
Combine all the dressing ingredients in a container and mix well. Let stand in the refrigerator, covered, for at least 24 hours.

German Potato Salad

3-quart baking dish
Yield: 10 to 12 servings

½ pound smoked bacon
2 onions, chopped
1 cup sour cream
½ cup sugar
¼ cup vinegar
½ teaspoon salt
½ teaspoon black pepper
2 Tablespoons parsley, chopped
4 to 6 medium potatoes, cooked, peeled and diced

Fry bacon until crisp and drain. Sauté onions in bacon grease until tender. Add sour cream, sugar, vinegar, salt, pepper and parsley, mixing well. Place cooked and diced potatoes in a 3-quart baking dish. Pour sauce over potatoes. Crumble bacon and fold into potato mixture. Serve warm.

Ham and Potato Salad Loaf

10 × 5 loaf pan
Yield: 12 to 16 servings

6 cups cooked, peeled and sliced potatoes
1 onion, chopped
½ cup chopped celery
1½ teaspoons salt
¼ teaspoon black pepper
2 envelopes unflavored gelatin
½ cup water
8 to 10 slices of ham, divided
1½ cups salad dressing
¼ cup mustard (optional)

In a large bowl, combine potatoes, onion, celery, salt and pepper and mix well. In a small bowl, dissolve gelatin in water. Coarsely chop 4 to 5 pieces of ham and combine with salad dressing and mustard. Stir dissolved gelatin into ham mixture. Combine ham and potatoes mixtures and mix well. Line a 10 × 5-inch loaf pan with foil, extending 3 inches over all edges. Line pan with remaining ham slices. Spread potato salad in pan. Refrigerate overnight. Slice to serve.

Italian Potato Salad

Yield: 8 to 12 servings

5   cups sliced cooked
    potatoes
1   cup chopped celery
1   cup (4 ounces) provolone
    or Cheddar cheese, diced
½   cup chopped bell pepper
½   cup sliced cotto salami
¼   cup minced onion
2   Tablespoons chopped
    Peperoncini (Italian
    pickled peppers)
1   cup sour cream
¼   cup brine from
    Peperoncini
12 cherry tomatoes, cut in
    half
Parsley

In a large bowl, toss potatoes, celery, cheese, bell pepper, salami, onion and Peperoncini. In a small bowl, blend sour cream and brine. Add to potato mixture and toss to blend. Fold in ½ of cherry tomatoes. Cover and chill. Before serving, top with remaining tomato halves and parsley.

A spicy and unusual recipe.

Artichoke Rice Salad

Yield: 8 servings

2   cups chicken broth
1   cup uncooked rice
⅓   cup chopped green onion
⅓   cup chopped bell pepper
⅓   cup sliced stuffed olives
1   7-ounce jar marinated
    artichoke hearts, drained
    and chopped
⅓   cup chopped celery
½   cup mayonnaise
1   4-ounce can chopped
    mushrooms
1   teaspoon dill weed
Salt and black pepper to taste
Lettuce
Sliced stuffed olives for
    garnish

Bring chicken broth to a boil and add rice. Cook over low heat for 20 minutes or until rice is tender and broth is absorbed. Remove from heat and cool. Combine rice and next 9 ingredients. Chill well. Serve on lettuce and garnish with sliced olives.

Virginia's Potato Salad

Yield: 8 to 12 servings

6   large red potatoes, boiled, peeled and sliced
12 hard-boiled eggs, peeled and sliced
Salt to taste
Lemon pepper to taste
Paprika to taste
¾   cup drained olives, divided

Layer 2 sliced potatoes and 4 hard-boiled eggs in a large bowl. Sprinkle with salt, lemon pepper, and paprika. Top with ¼ cup olives. Pour on ⅓ of dressing. Repeat the layers 2 more times. Refrigerate overnight or several hours before serving.

Dressing:
1¼ cup mayonnaise
¼   cup prepared Thousand Island Dressing
2   Tablespoons lemon juice
1   Tablespoon Worcestershire sauce
1   Tablespoon dried minced onion
1   Tablespoon ketchup
½   cup salad olives
1   3-ounce bottle capers, drained (optional)

Dressing:
Mix dressing ingredients and set aside.

Curried Rice Salad

Yield: 8 to 10 servings

2   cups cooked rice, cooled
1   cup mayonnaise
1   Tablespoon curry powder
1   teaspoon salt
1   teaspoon black pepper
½   cup chopped onion
1   cup chopped bell pepper
1   6-ounce jar marinated artichokes, drained and chopped
1   cup chopped, cooked ham, chicken or shrimp
½ to 1 cup prepared French Dressing

Mix first 9 ingredients together. Add dressing and mix well. This is better if refrigerated several hours before serving.

Sauerkraut Salad

Yield: 8 servings

1 32-ounce jar sauerkraut, drained
1 onion, chopped
1 bell pepper, chopped
1 4-ounce jar chopped pimientos
1 cup sugar
½ cup vinegar
¼ cup vegetable oil

Combine sauerkraut, onion, bell pepper and pimientos in a bowl. In a small bowl, combine sugar, vinegar and oil and mix well. Pour dressing over sauerkraut mixture, stirring well. Refrigerate overnight in a tightly covered bowl.

Shrimp and Apple Salad

Yield: 6 to 8 servings

4 large Delicious apples, peeled and cored
2 pounds shrimp, boiled, shelled and veined
2 cups diced celery
1¼ cup mayonnaise
1 Tablespoon finely minced chives
2 Tablespoons lemon juice
2 teaspoons sugar
4 ounces cashews, divided
Salt and black pepper to taste
Lettuce leaves

Cut apples into ½-inch cubes. Combine shrimp, apples, celery, mayonnaise, chives, lemon juice, sugar, half of cashews, salt and pepper. Add more mayonnaise if desired. Chill several hours. Serve on lettuce leaves and top with remaining cashews.

Garnish with wedges of hard-boiled eggs and tomatoes.

Apple Slaw

Yield: 8 servings

1 8-ounce carton sour cream
3 Tablespoons lemon juice
1 Tablespoon sugar
1 Tablespoon poppy seeds
¾ teaspoon salt
⅛ teaspoon black pepper
4 cups finely grated cabbage
4½ cups thinly sliced apple wedges

Combine first 6 ingredients and mix well. Pour over cabbage and apples and stir well. Refrigerate at least 1 hour before serving.

Cauliflower Slaw

Yield: 4 to 6 servings

1   head cauliflower, finely
     chopped
1   bunch green onions,
     finely chopped
1   cup finely chopped celery
     leaves
1   avocado, finely chopped
1   cup sour cream
½   cup Italian dressing
1¼   teaspoon dill weed
Salt and black pepper to taste

Combine cauliflower, green onions, celery leaves and avocado. Add sour cream, Italian dressing and dill weed. Mix well. Salt and pepper to taste.

Sweet and Sour Coleslaw

Yield: 20 to 25 servings

1   small to medium head of
     cabbage, coarsely chopped
1   bell pepper, finely
     chopped
¼   cup grated carrot
1   medium onion, finely
     chopped
¼   cup finely chopped celery
1   cup sugar
2   Tablespoons honey
1   teaspoon salt
¼   cup vegetable oil
½   cup vinegar (white or
     cider)
¼   teaspoon dry mustard

Place chopped cabbage in a sealable bowl. Add pepper, carrot, onion and celery. Pour sugar over vegetables. Mix honey, salt, oil, vinegar and mustard in a small saucepan. Bring to a boil. Pour over vegetables and mix well. Seal and refrigerate for at least 6 hours before serving.

Keeps well for several days in refrigerator.

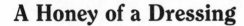

A Honey of a Dressing

Yield: 2 cups

1 cup vegetable oil
⅔ cup honey
½ teaspoon dry mustard
½ teaspoon onion juice
½ teaspoon salt
⅓ cup white vinegar

Blend all ingredients except vinegar. Add vinegar slowly. Chill and let set before serving.

Dijon Mustard Dressing

Yield: ½ cup

2 Tablespoons red wine
   vinegar
½ teaspoon salt
White or black pepper to taste
⅓ to ½ cup olive oil
1 teaspoon Dijon mustard
½ teaspoon sugar (optional)

Combine all ingredients and stir briskly with a wire whip. Refrigerate until ready to serve. Dash of sugar may be added if too tart. Serve over a Bibb lettuce or spinach salad.

French Dressing

Yield: 2½ cups

½ cup cider vinegar
1 cup olive oil
1 cup ketchup
2 Tablespoons sugar
1 Tablespoon
   Worcestershire sauce
½ teaspoon salt
1 or 2 whole cloves garlic
1 teaspoon paprika
   (optional)

Add ingredients in order listed to blender. Blend until thick.

Mayonnaise

Yield: 2 cups

2 egg yolks
1 Tablespoon vinegar
1 Tablespoon lemon juice
1 Tablespoon Worcestershire sauce
1 teaspoon salt
½ teaspoon black pepper
1 Tablespoon dry mustard
2 cloves garlic, pressed (garlic powder may be substituted)
1 teaspoon coarsely ground cayenne or red pepper
2 cups vegetable oil
1 Tablespoon very hot water

Mix all ingredients but oil and water in an electric mixer on medium speed until slightly thickened. Add first cup of oil by Tablespoons, mixing on medium high speed. As it begins to thicken, the second cup of oil can be added faster, mixing well after each addition. Mix until all oil is incorporated, then add very hot water. Chill at least one hour before serving.

Variation:
Add 4 ounces crumbled bleu cheese to finished mayonnaise.

Onion Salad Dressing (or Raw Vegetable Dip)

Yield: 2 ½ cups

2 teaspoons dry mustard
1 raw egg
1 teaspoon salt
¼ teaspoon black pepper
2 Tablespoons apple cider vinegar
1 cup vegetable oil
1 bunch small green onions

In the blender mix mustard, egg, salt, pepper and vinegar with ¼ cup of the vegetable oil. Turn blender on high and slowly pour in the remaining oil. With the blender still on high, add the green onions. Continue blending until smooth.

Spinach Salad Dressing

Yield: 2 cups

¾ cup soy sauce
3   Tablespoons lemon juice
1   teaspoon sugar
1   teaspoon toasted sesame
    seeds
1   teaspoon chopped onion
1½ cups peanut oil

Combine all ingredients, except oil, in blender on low speed or in a food processor with steel knife. Blend until onion is minced. With machine running, add oil in a thin stream. Blend until oil is thoroughly incorporated. For the salad, mix raw spinach with sliced raw mushrooms. Top with bean sprouts. Drizzle dressing over top.

Entrées

Sautéed Tenderloin

Heavy skillet
Yield: 4 to 6 servings

8   1-inch thick slices of beef
    tenderloin
3   Tablespoons butter
8   ounces fresh mushrooms,
    sliced
2   tomatoes, peeled and
    coarsely chopped
2   teaspoons arrowroot
1   Tablespoon powdered beef
    stock base
1   cup hot water
⅔   cup dry red wine
Chopped parsley

Sauté meat slices in butter in a heavy skillet for 3 to 4 minutes on each side. Remove meat to a warm platter. Sauté mushrooms and tomatoes, adding more butter if needed. Combine arrowroot, beef stock base and water; add to sautéed vegetables in skillet. Add wine and stir over low heat. Pour sauce over beef slices and sprinkle with parsley. Serve immediately.

Spicy Pot Roast

300 degrees, preheated
Dutch oven
Yield: 8 to 10 servings

2   Tablespoons olive or
    peanut oil
4   to 5 pounds pot roast
2   onions, quartered
1   8-ounce can tomato sauce
1   cup red wine or sherry
3   to 4 pieces dried orange
    peel, each about 1 × 2
    inches
1   teaspoon cinnamon
½   teaspoon ground cloves
½   teaspoon allspice
1   clove garlic, pressed

Heat oil in a large Dutch oven. Add pot roast and onions and brown thoroughly. Add remaining ingredients, stirring well. Cover pan and bake for 3 hours 30 minutes or until roast is tender.

Fajitas

Grill
Yield: 10 to 12 servings

2	cups dry or cream sherry
⅓	cup soy sauce
⅓	cup Worcestershire sauce
⅓	cup brown sugar
1	cup vegetable oil
1	teaspoon coarsely ground black pepper
1	clove garlic, pressed or
½	teaspoon garlic powder
1	teaspoon dry mustard
½	teaspoon basil leaves
½	teaspoon oregano leaves
1	onion, chopped
8	pounds beef skirt or flank steak

Flour tortillas

Mix all ingredients except beef in a large stainless steel or glass baking dish. Marinate steak in the sauce for 5 to 6 hours. Cook quickly over a hot charcoal fire until desired degree of doneness is reached. Remove meat and slice thinly across the grain. Serve rolled in warm flour tortillas. Serve with Pinto Beans for Mexican Dinner, page 159 and Mocajéte, page 114.

California Beef Stew

Dutch oven
Yield: 6 to 8 servings

2	pounds stew meat
2	Tablespoons vegetable oil
1	Tablespoon salt
½	teaspoon black pepper
1	bay leaf
2	cups water
1	cup dry red wine
1	bunch carrots, peeled and sliced
12	small boiling onions, peeled and pierced at each end
3	zucchini, cut diagonally into 4 or 5 pieces
2	large tomatoes, chopped
2	Tablespoons flour
¼	cup water

Brown meat in oil. Add salt, pepper and bay leaf. Stir in water and wine. Bring to a boil, then reduce heat, cover and simmer 1 hour 15 minutes. Add carrots and cook for 10 minutes. Add onions and zucchini and cook until tender. Add tomatoes and flour which has been mixed with ¼ cup water. Stir in slowly. Bring to a boil and serve immediately.

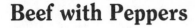

Beef with Peppers

Wok
Yield: 6 to 8 servings

Beef Marinade:
1   Tablespoon soy sauce
2   teaspoons brown sugar
Pinch of black pepper
2   teaspoons sesame seed oil
1   Tablespoon cornstarch
1   pound flank steak, cut
    against the grain into
    slices ⅛-inch thick and 2
    inches long
2   cups vegetable oil
½   pound bell peppers, cut
    into ½-inch strips
1   teaspoon minced fresh
    ginger root
1   clove garlic, pressed
2   scallions or green onions,
    cut into 1½-inch lengths

Sauce:
2   Tablespoons soy sauce
2   teaspoons brown sugar
2   Tablespoons dry sherry
1   teaspoon cornstarch
1   Tablespoon water
¼   teaspoon monosodium
    glutamate (optional)

Beef Marinade:
Mix soy sauce, brown sugar, pepper, oil and cornstarch in a sealable bowl. Place meat in mixture. Cover and marinate 30 minutes to 1 hour. Heat vegetable oil in wok over high heat until hot but not smoking. Add marinated beef mixture and stir quickly to separate pieces. Cook briskly until beef loses its pink color. Remove beef from wok and set aside. Remove all but 3 Tablespoons of oil. Heat oil and add peppers. Stir fry for 1 minute. Remove peppers and set aside with beef. Add garlic, ginger and onions to wok. Stir fry. Return beef and peppers. Add prepared sauce. Cook until sauce is thickened, adding water if needed.

Sauce:
Combine all ingredients in a small bowl and mix well.

Serve hot over rice or fried Chinese noodles.

Beer Brisket

300 degrees, preheated
9 × 13 baking dish
6 to 8 servings

4   pounds beef brisket,
     trimmed
Salt and black pepper to taste
½   onion, sliced
2   teaspoons Tabasco sauce
2   Tablespoons brown sugar
1   clove garlic, pressed
1   12-ounce can beer

Season brisket with salt and pepper. Place in 9 × 13 inch baking pan. Cover with onion slices. Combine remaining ingredients and mix well. Pour sauce over meat. Cover with foil. Bake for 3 hours 30 minutes. Uncover and bake an additional 30 minutes, basting occasionally.

Beef and Rice Dinner

Dutch oven
Yield: 4 to 6 servings

1½   pounds round steak,
     cubed
2   Tablespoons vegetable oil
1   onion, chopped
2   bell peppers, chopped
1   10½-ounce can beef
     bouillon
1¼   cups water
1   2-ounce jar pimientos
1   cup uncooked rice
3   Tablespoons soy sauce
½   teaspoon salt
½   teaspoon curry powder

Brown meat in oil. Add onion and bell pepper and cook on low heat until tender. Add remaining ingredients. Cook over medium heat until liquid is absorbed and meat is tender.

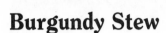

Burgundy Stew

300 degrees, preheated
Dutch oven
Yield: 6 to 8 servings

6   slices bacon
1   Tablespoon bacon
    drippings
2   to 3 pounds round steak,
    cubed
1   Tablespoon salt
Black pepper to taste
12 to 15 small onions
2   green onions, chopped
6   carrots, peeled and sliced
⅛   teaspoon garlic salt
2   Tablespoons flour
2   cups burgundy wine
1   10½-ounce can beef broth
    or consommé
2   teaspoons parsley
2   stalks celery, chopped
Pinch of thyme
3   medium potatoes, peeled
    and chopped
8   ounces fresh mushrooms
¼   cup butter

Fry bacon. Drain and crumble it then set aside. Reserve 1 Tablespoon bacon grease. Season beef with salt and pepper and brown in bacon drippings. Add onions, carrots, green onions, garlic salt and flour, mixing well. Add wine, broth, parsley, celery and thyme. Cover pan and place in oven for 45 minutes. Add potatoes and cook for an additional 1 hour. Sauté mushrooms in butter. Just before serving, add mushrooms and bacon.

Wild Rice Casserole

350 degrees, preheated
3-quart ovenproof casserole
Yield: 10 to 12 servings

1½ onions, chopped
2 cups chopped celery
1 clove garlic, pressed
½ cup butter
1 pound beef, cubed
1 pound pork, cubed
½ cup wild rice
½ cup white rice
2 10½-ounce cans beef consommé, divided
4 teaspoons soy sauce
1 8-ounce can mushrooms
1 8-ounce can water chestnuts, chopped
2 teaspoons salt
½ cup slivered almonds, toasted

Sauté onions, celery and garlic in butter. Add meats and brown lightly. Add rices, 1 can beef consommé, soy sauce, mushrooms, water chestnuts and salt. Pour into a 3-quart casserole dish, cover and bake for 2 hours. Then add remaining can of consommé which has been heated. Stir well and bake an additional 30 minutes. The last 5 minutes of baking, top with almonds.

Variation:
Substitute 2 cups cooked chicken for the beef and pork. Add chicken when adding second can of consommé. Add 1 cup chicken broth when adding chicken.

Hot Meat Loaf

350 degrees, preheated
10 × 5 loaf pan
Yield: 6 servings

1½ pounds ground beef
1 4-ounce can chopped green chiles
1 egg, beaten
1 cup crushed crackers
1¼ cups evaporated milk
½ teaspoon dry mustard or 2 teaspoons prepared mustard
1 onion, chopped
Salt and black pepper to taste

Combine all ingredients. Shape into a loaf and place in a greased 10 × 5 inch loaf pan. Bake for 1 hour 30 minutes.

Variation:
15 ounces ricotta cheese
3 eggs, beaten

Variation:
Combine cheese and eggs and mix well. Layer ½ of the above meat mixture in a greased 10 × 5-inch loaf pan. Add ricotta mixture and top with remaining mixture. Bake as directed.

Cornbread Tacos

Yield: 6 to 8 servings

1   pan cornbread, cooked

Meat mixture:
1   pound ground beef
½   teaspoon ground cumin
½   teaspoon ground oregano
½   teaspooon cayenne or red
    pepper (optional)
1   clove garlic, pressed
2   Tablespoons green chiles
    (optional)
1   8-ounce can tomato sauce

Toppings:
Grated cheese
Chopped lettuce
Chopped tomatoes
Chopped onion
Chopped ripe olives
Chopped avocado

Meat mixture:
Brown ground beef and drain. Add remaining mixture ingredients and simmer 15 to 20 minutes. Slice cornbread into pie-shaped pieces. Split each slice open and top with meat sauce. Add any of the listed toppings.

Chili

Dutch oven
Yield: 10 to 12 servings

3   pounds ground meat
1   onion, chopped
4   cloves garlic, pressed
1   28-ounce can tomatoes
½   cup chili sauce
1   8-ounce can tomato sauce
4   Tablespoons chili powder
4   Tablespoons cumin
Salt and black pepper to taste
1   16-ounce can refried
    beans
1   pound dry pinto beans,
    cooked with 1 10-ounce
    can Rotel tomatoes with
    green chiles

Brown meat. Add all ingredients except refried and pinto beans. Cook for 2 to 3 hours. Add beans 1 hour before serving.

Baked Spaghetti

325 degrees, preheated
2-quart casserole, greased
Yield: 6 to 8 servings

3 Tablespoons bacon
   drippings or vegetable oil
2 onions, chopped
1 clove garlic (optional)
1 pound ground beef
1½ teaspoons salt
⅛ teaspoon pepper
1 28-ounce can tomatoes
1 teaspoon chili powder
1 cup water
1 8-ounce package
   spaghetti, uncooked and
   broken in half
1 cup grated Cheddar
   cheese

Put bacon drippings or oil in a large skillet and slowly cook onions and garlic for about 5 minutes. Add meat and brown. Add salt, pepper, tomatoes, chili powder and water. Simmer, covered, for 30 minutes. Remove garlic clove. In a 2-quart greased casserole, place ½ of the broken spaghetti. Pour ½ of meat sauce over spaghetti. Layer the remaining spaghetti and meat sauce. Top with cheese. Bake, covered, for 35 minutes. Uncover and bake for an additional 15 minutes.

West Texas Spaghetti

350 degrees, preheated
9 × 13 baking dish
Yield: 8 to 10 servings

1 onion, chopped
1 bell pepper, chopped
1 pound ground beef
1 Tablespoon vegetable oil
1 16-ounce package
   spaghetti, cooked and
   drained
Salt and black pepper to taste
1 10¾-ounce can tomato
   soup
¾ cup water
1 12-ounce can whole
   kernel corn
1 4-ounce bottle Spanish
   olives, sliced
½ pound Cheddar cheese,
   grated and divided

Sauté onions, bell pepper and meat in oil until meat is brown. Add cooked spaghetti, salt and pepper to meat mixture. Add soup, water, corn, olives and ¼ pound cheese and mix well. Place in a 9 × 13 inch baking dish and top with remaining cheese. Bake for 20 to 25 minutes.

Lasagna

350 degrees, preheated
12 × 8 × 2 baking pan
Yield: 10 servings

½ cup chopped onions
1½ pounds ground beef
2 Tablespoons vegetable oil
2 cloves garlic, pressed
1½ teaspoons salt
¼ teaspoon pepper
¼ teaspoon oregano
3 Tablespoons parsley
2 14½-ounce cans tomatoes, chopped
1 8-ounce can tomato sauce or 1 6-ounce can tomato paste
2 Tablespoons Parmesan cheese
1 8-ounce package lasagna noodles, cooked according to package directions
1 12-ounce package sliced Mozarella cheese
1 16-ounce carton ricotta or cottage cheese
Grated Parmesan cheese

In a large saucepan, sauté onions and ground beef in oil until brown. Add the next 8 ingredients, cover and simmer for 30 minutes. In a 12 × 8 × 2 baking pan, layer ⅓ of meat sauce, 4 cooked lasagna noodles, 2 slices Mozarella cheese, ½ of the ricotta cheese and sprinkle with Parmesan cheese. Repeat layers and top with remaining ⅓ of meat sauce. Sprinkle with Parmesan cheese. Bake for 30 minutes.

Beef Manicotti

350 degrees, preheated
9 × 13 baking dish
Yield: 6 servings

½ pound ground beef
1 clove garlic, pressed
1 cup small curd cottage
   cheese
4 ounces shreeded
   mozzarella cheese
¼ teaspoon salt
½ cup mayonnaise
10 to 12 manicotti noodles,
   cooked and drained
1 16-ounce jar spaghetti
   sauce
½ teaspoon oregano
Parmesan cheese

Brown beef and garlic; drain. Combine next 4 ingredients in a bowl. Stir in beef. Fill manicotti noodles with about ¼ cup filling. Place in 9 × 13 inch baking dish and cover with spaghetti sauce. Sprinkle with oregano and Parmesan cheese. Cover with foil. Bake for 15 minutes. Remove foil and bake another 10 minutes.

Snow Casserole

375 degrees, preheated
9 × 13 baking dish
Yield: 6 to 8 servings

1 pound ground beef
2 8-ounce cans tomato sauce
¼ cup chopped onion
1 teaspoon basil
1 teaspoon parsley
½ teaspoon salt
½ teaspoon oregano
¼ teaspoon black pepper
2 10-ounce packages
   chopped spinach, cooked
   and drained
2 cups cottage cheese
¼ teaspoon salt
1 8-ounce package
   mozzarella cheese, sliced

Brown beef. Add tomato sauce, onion and seasonings. Simmer uncovered for 10 minutes. Combine spinach, cottage cheese and ¼ teaspoon salt. In a 9 × 13 inch baking dish, spoon spinach mixture around edges. Pour beef mixture into center of dish. Cut cheese slices into thirds and arrange in lattice fashion on top of casserole. Bake for 20 to 25 minutes.

Stuffed Turk's Turban

350 degrees, preheated
Baking pan, ungreased
Yield: 6 to 8 servings

1   turban squash (a fall
    vegetable)
2   Tablespoons butter or
    vegetable oil
¼   cup finely chopped green
    onions
1   pound mushrooms, sliced
1   pound bell peppers, sliced
    in strips
1½ pounds ground beef
½   teaspoon paprika or chili
    powder
1   teaspoon marjoram
1   teaspoon parsley
1   teaspoon salt
¾   teaspoon black pepper
½   cup toasted bread crumbs

Bake turban squash in an ungreased baking pan
for 1 hour or until soft. Sauté onions and
mushrooms in butter for 3 to 4 minutes or until
lightly brown. Add peppers and cook until soft.
Remove vegetables from skillet. Brown meat,
then add seasonings and cook for 5 minutes over
low heat. Add meat mixture to vegetables. Add
bread crumbs and mix well. Cut the top off the
turban squash and remove seeds and string. Fill
cavity with stuffing mixture. May keep warm in a
300 degree oven. Scoop out some squash with
each serving of meat mixture.

Blackberry Beef

350 degrees, preheated
2-quart baking dish, greased
Yield: 12 to 15 servings

1   fresh beef tongue
Salted water
1   Tablespoon pickling spice
2   bay leaves
1   teaspoon dried celery
    leaves or 2 stalks celery,
    chopped
6   whole cloves
Salt to taste
1   16-ounce jar blackberry
    jelly
1   cup raisins, cooked until
    tender in 1 cup water
Juice of 1 lemon

Cook tongue until very tender in salted water,
pickling spice, bay leaves and celery. When
tender, remove skin, trim root end and stud solid
meat with cloves. Place in a greased 2-quart
baking dish and sprinkle with salt. Beat jelly with
a fork, add cooked raisins and lemon juice and
mix well. Pour over tongue and bake for 20
minutes, basting often. Serve hot or at room
temperature.

Sicilian Meat Roll

350 degrees, preheated
9 × 13 baking dish
Yield: 8 servings

2   eggs, beaten
1   slice of soft bread, made
    into crumbs
½   cup tomato juice or
    tomato sauce
1   Tablespoon chopped
    parsley
½   teaspoon oregano
¼   teaspoon salt
¼   teaspoon black pepper
1   clove garlic, pressed
2   pounds ground beef
8   thin slices boiled ham
6   ounces mozzarella cheese,
    grated
3   slices mozzarella cheese,
    halved diagonally

Combine eggs, crumbs, tomato juice, parsley, oregano, salt, pepper and garlic. Add beef and mix well. On wax paper, pat meat into a 12 × 10 inch rectangle. Place ham on top of meat, leaving small margin around edges. Sprinkle grated cheese on ham. Starting from the short end, carefully roll up meat using paper to lift. Seal edges and ends. Place roll, seam side down in a 9 × 13 inch baking dish. Bake for 1 hour 15 minutes. Place cheese wedges over top of roll and return to oven for 5 minutes.

A really good and different meat loaf.

Spicy Meat Loaf

400 degrees, preheated
10 × 5 loaf pan
Yield: 8 servings

½   onion, chopped
¼   cup finely chopped bell
    pepper
¼   cup butter
2   pounds ground beef
1   cup rolled oats, uncooked
2   eggs, beaten
¾   cup ketchup
3   teaspoons salt
2   teaspoons paprika
1   teaspoons dry mustard
¼   cup horseradish

Topping:
½   cup ketchup
½   cup brown sugar

Sauté onion and bell pepper in melted butter for about 10 minutes. Combine remaining ingredients except for topping in a large bowl. Add onions and green pepper, mixing well. Place in a 10 × 5-inch loaf pan. Combine topping ingredients and spread on meat loaf. Bake for 1 hour.

Veal or Beef Parmesan

350 degrees, preheated
Shallow baking dish
Yield: 6 to 8 servings

2 eggs, well beaten
½ teaspoon black pepper
½ teaspoon salt
½ teaspoon oregano
½ teaspoon sweet basil
1½ cups bread crumbs
½ cup grated Parmesan
    cheese
6 to 8 veal or beef cutlets,
    pounded thin
½ cup butter
2 8-ounce cans tomato sauce
8 slices mozzarella cheese

Combine eggs, pepper, salt, oregano and basil. Combine breadcrumbs and cheese. Dip cutlets into egg mixture and then in crumb mixture. Refrigerate prepared cutlets for 30 minutes. Brown cutlets on both sides in butter. Place cutlets in a shallow dish and top with tomato sauce and slices of mozzarella cheese. May sprinkle with additional Parmesan cheese. Bake for 30 minutes or until cheese is melted.

Veal Chops with Artichokes and Mushrooms

Large skillet
Yield: 4 servings

4 thick loin veal chops
Salt and black pepper to taste
¼ cup flour
3 Tablespoons butter,
    divided
2 teaspoons finely chopped
    shallots
1 clove garlic, pressed
    (optional)
1 9-ounce package frozen
    artichoke hearts, broken
    apart
1 Tablespoon crushed green
    peppercorns
1 cup champagne or dry
    vermouth
1 cup whipping cream
3 large mushrooms, sliced

Season chops with salt and pepper, then dredge in flour. Melt 2 Tablespoons butter in a skillet and brown chops on both sides. Browning should take 12 to 15 minutes. Remove chops and keep warm. Drain skillet and add remaining butter, shallots and garlic. Cook briefly and add artichoke hearts. Cook, stirring for 1 to 2 minutes. Add peppercorns, champagne, and cook over high heat until liquid is reduced to about ⅓ cup, stirring as necessary. Add cream and mushrooms. Cook over high heat for about 5 minutes. Pour sauce over chops and serve immediately.

Sausage Filled Crepes

375 degrees, preheated
11¾ × 7½ inch baking dish
Yield: 16 crepes

1   recipe of basic crepes
     (Page 183)

Filling:
1   pound bulk sausage
¼   cup chopped onion
½   cup grated cheese
3   ounces cream cheese
¼   teaspoon marjoram

Filling:
Brown sausage and onion, then drain. Add cheeses and marjoram. Cook on low heat until cheese melts.

Topping:
½   cup sour cream
¼   cup butter, softened

Topping:
Combine sour cream and butter, stirring well.

Place 2 Tablespoons of filling in each crepe. Roll them up and place them in a 11¾ × 7½ × 1¾-inch baking dish. Bake for 20 minutes. Spoon topping over crepes and bake uncovered for an additional 5 minutes.

Chinese Spareribs

300 degrees, preheated
Baking dish
Yield: 4 to 6 servings

4   to 5 pounds pork ribs
1   4-ounce bottle soy sauce
1   12-ounce jar apricot
     preserves

Arrange ribs in a baking dish. Pour soy sauce and preserves over ribs. Bake at 300 degrees for 2 hours 30 minutes, basting frequently.

Sweet and Sour Pork

Wok or large skillet
Yield: 4 to 6 servings

1   egg, slightly beaten
1   teaspoon salt
¼   cup cornstarch
¼   cup flour
¼   cup chicken broth
2   pounds lean boneless
    pork, trimmed and cut
    into bite-sized pieces
1½ cups peanut or vegetable
    oil

In a medium bowl, mix first five ingredients. Place pork in mixture and set aside. Heat oil and add pork cubes. Fry for about 6 minutes, until pork is golden brown and completely done. Drain pork on a paper towel and keep warm.

Sauce:
2   Tablespoons vegetable oil
1   clove garlic, pressed
2   large bell peppers, sliced
    in strips
3   carrots, sliced
1   cup chicken broth
8   Tablespoons sugar
8   Tablespoons cider vinegar
2   teaspoons soy sauce
2   Tablespoons cornstarch
    dissolved in
4   Tablespoons cold water

Sauce:
Heat oil. Add vegetables and stir fry 3 to 4 minutes. Add broth, sugar, vinegar and soy sauce. Bring to a boil and boil 1 minute. Add cornstarch and water mixture and cook 1 minute longer. Stir in pork. Serve immediately over rice.

Cranberry Pork Chops

Large covered skillet
Yield: 4 servings

4   pork chops, ¾-inch thick
Salt and black pepper to taste
1   8½-ounce can pineapple
    slices, drained, reserve
    juice
½   cup whole cranberry sauce
1   chicken bouillon cube
½   cup boiling water
2   Tablespoons brown sugar
2   Tablespoons vinegar
1   bell pepper, cut into 1-
    inch pieces
2   Tablespoons cornstarch
2   Tablespoons water

Trim fat from chops. In a large skillet, cook trimmings until 1 Tablespoon of fat accumulates. Discard trimmings and brown chops in fat. Season with salt and pepper. Add pineapple juice and cranberry sauce to chops. Dissolve bouillon cube in boiling water and then add to chops. Add brown sugar and vinegar. Cover and simmer 40 minutes or until chops are tender. Add drained pineapple and bell pepper. Cover and cook 10 minutes. Remove chops and pineapple to a serving plate. Combine cornstarch and water and stir into cranberry mixture and cook until thickened. Pour over chops.

Pork Chops

350 degrees, preheated
Ovenproof dish

Extra thick pork chops
Salt and black pepper to taste
Sage (optional)
Bacon slices (2 per pork chop)
Onion, sliced
Tomato, sliced

Season chops with salt, pepper and sage. Top each chop with 1 slice of onion and 1 slice of tomato. Criss-cross 2 strips of bacon and place chops on bacon. Bring bacon ends around chops and secure with a toothpick. Repeat procedure with each chop. Place in an ovenproof dish and bake for 1 hour.

Barbecue Sauce

Medium saucepan
Yield: 1 pint

½ cup ketchup
¼ cup Worcestershire sauce
¼ cup white vinegar
1 teaspoon salt
1 teaspoon prepared
   mustard
2 drops Tabasco sauce
¼ cup butter
¼ cup sugar
1 onion, very finely chopped
1 clove garlic, very finely
   chopped

Heat all ingredients to boiling; reduce heat and simmer for 15 minutes.

Spicy Barbecue Sauce

Large saucepan
Yield: 3 cups

1 cup ketchup
½ cup cider vinegar
1 teaspoon sugar
1 teaspoon chili powder
⅛ teaspoon salt
1½ cups water
3 stalks celery, chopped
3 bay leaves
1 clove garlic, minced
2 Tablespoons chopped
   onion
4 Tablespoons butter
4 Tablespoons
   Worcestershire sauce
1 teaspoon paprika
Dash of black pepper

Combine all ingredients and bring to a boil. Lower heat and simmer 15 minutes. Sauce may be strained before serving. Serve warm.

Blender Hollandaise Sauce

Yield: ⅔ cup

3 egg yolks
1 Tablespoon lemon juice
⅛ teaspoon salt
Dash of black pepper
½ cup butter, melted

Blend first four ingredients until thick and lemon colored. Add butter in a slow, steady stream; continue to blend until thick. Serve over vegetables, seafood or chicken.

Fluffy Mustard Sauce

Double Boiler
Yield: 1 to 1½ cups

2 egg yolks, slightly beaten
2 Tablespoons sugar
3 Tablespoons prepared
   mustard
2 Tablespoons cider vinegar
1 Tablespoon water
½ teaspoon salt
1 Tablespoon butter
2 teaspoons prepared
   horseradish
⅓ cup whipping cream,
   whipped

Beat egg yolks slightly in the top of a double boiler. Add next 5 ingredients and mix well. Cook egg mixture over barely simmering water until smooth and thickened, about 5 minutes. Remove from heat and add butter and horseradish. Let cool, then fold in whipped cream.

Mocajéte (Mexican Hot Sauce)

Large skillet
Yield: 10 to 12 servings

4   to 5 slices of bacon,
    chopped
2   large bell peppers,
    chopped
2   10-ounce cans Rotel
    tomatoes with green
    chiles
2   4-ounce cans chopped
    green chiles
½   teaspoon salt
1   Tablespoon sugar
¼   teaspoon cayenne or red
    pepper
1   clove garlic, pressed

Brown bacon in large skillet. Add bell pepper and sauté until lightly brown. Add remaining ingredients and simmer for 1 hour or until bell pepper is very soft.

Microwave Roux

Microwave dish

Flour
Vegetable oil

Use equal parts of flour and oil in a microwave dish. Microwave on high for 6 to 7 minutes. Stir at the end of 6 minutes. Let stand. Microwave 1 minute longer and stir. Repeat until desired brownness. Add vegetables and cook until soft and clear. Pour off excess oil.

Chicken Rollups

350 degrees, preheated
9 × 13 baking dish, greased
Yield: 8 servings

¾ cup butter, melted
2 cloves garlic, pressed
1 cup fine dry bread crumbs
⅔ cup grated Parmesan cheese
¼ cup minced fresh parsley
1 teaspoon salt
¼ teaspoon black pepper
4 whole chicken breasts, split, skinned and boned
Juice of 1 lemon
Paprika to garnish

Combine butter and garlic, stir well and set aside. Combine bread crumbs, cheese, parsley, salt and pepper and stir well. Dip chicken in butter mixture and coat with bread crumb mixture. Fold long sides of chicken together. Bring short ends over and secure with a toothpick. Place chicken rolls seam side down in a greased pan. Sprinkle with lemon juice and paprika. Bake for 1 hour or until done.

Chicken Parmesan

350 degrees, preheated
Baking dish
Yield: 4 servings

4 chicken breasts, boned and skinned
2 Tablespoons vegetable oil
Salt and black pepper to taste
1½ cups chicken stock
1½ cups dry white wine
2 cloves garlic, pressed
1 bay leaf, crumbled
1 pound mushrooms
3 Tablespoons butter
3 Tablespoons flour
½ cup cream
1 cup grated Parmesan cheese

Brown chicken breasts in oil. When browned, remove to a baking dish and add salt and pepper to taste. Add chicken stock, wine, garlic, bay leaf and mushrooms. Cover and bake for 30 minutes. While chicken is baking, melt butter in a saucepan and add flour. Cook until mixture thickens and slowly add cream. When chicken is done, remove chicken and mushrooms to another plate and strain liquid into saucepan of flour, butter and cream. Cook the mixture until it bubbles and thickens. Add Parmesan cheese. Return chicken to the baking dish and cover it with the cheese mixture. Return it to the oven for approximately 5 minutes. Serve over rice or English muffin.

Broiled Chicken Breasts Sesame

Yield: 4 to 6 servings

¼ cup butter, melted
¼ cup soy sauce
¼ cup dry white wine
1 teaspoon dried tarragon
1 teaspoon dry mustard
6 chicken breasts, boned
Sesame seeds

Mix together first 5 ingredients. Marinate chicken in sauce mixture for at least 3 hours. Broil breasts over a medium charcoal fire for 4 or 5 minutes on each side, starting with the skin side up and basting with the marinade 2 or 3 times. Remove the chicken from fire when done and brush with marinade. Roll in sesame seeds until well coated. Return to fire for a minute to brown seeds.

Chicken Supreme

Advance Preparation
Time Required
350 degrees, preheated
9 × 13 baking dish, greased
Yield: 6 to 8 servings

2 cups sour cream
¼ cup lemon juice
4 teaspoons Worcestershire
   sauce
¼ teaspoon celery salt
¼ teaspoon garlic salt
¼ teaspoon salt
½ teaspoon black pepper
2 teaspoons paprika
12 chicken breasts, boned
   and skinned
1¼ cups herb stuffing mix
¼ cup butter
¼ cup shortening
½ cup sherry

Combine sour cream and seasonings in a bowl, add chicken. Stir and refrigerate overnight. Before baking, remove chicken from sauce and arrange in shallow greased baking dish. Pour sauce over chicken. Sprinkle with herb stuffing mix. Melt butter and shortening and pour over top of chicken. Bake covered for 45 minutes. Uncover and pour sherry over chicken. Bake uncovered for additional 15 minutes or until brown and tender.

Chicken in Tarragon Sauce

Large skillet
Yield: 8 servings

Chicken:
8   chicken breasts
½   lemon
1   cup flour
1   teaspoon salt
¼   teaspoon white pepper
2   Tablespoons butter
2   Tablespoons vegetable oil

Sauce:
2   Tablespoons flour
½   teaspoon salt
½   cup dry white wine
½   cup condensed chicken
     broth
½   teaspoon tarragon
1   cup whipping cream

Chicken:
Bone and flatten chicken breast. Rub each with cut side of a lemon. Dip breasts into flour seasoned with salt and white pepper. Shake off excess flour. Set aside until flour no longer looks dry (about 20 minutes). Twenty minutes prior to serving, heat butter and oil in a large skillet; sauté chicken over medium heat for 8 to 10 minutes on each side, until golden brown. Remove to heated serving platter.

Sauce:
Add flour and ½ teaspoon salt to pan drippings. Cook 1 minute over medium heat without browning. Stir in white wine and whisk until smooth. Whisk in chicken broth and tarragon. When smooth, whisk in cream. Adjust seasonings. Spoon over chicken breasts and serve.

Chicken and Wild Rice Casserole

350 degrees, preheated
2-quart casserole
Yield: 8 to 10 servings

1   cup wild rice
½   cup chopped onion
½   cup margarine
½   cup flour
1   6-ounce can mushrooms
Chicken broth
½   cup evaporated milk
3   cups chopped, cooked
       chicken
¼   cup pimiento
2   Tablespoons parsley
1½   teaspoons salt
¼   teaspoon black pepper
½   cup slivered almonds

Prepare rice according to package directions. Sauté the onion in margarine. Add flour. Drain mushrooms, reserve liquid and add enough chicken broth to mushroom liquid to make 1½ cups. Stir into flour mixture. Add milk. Cook and stir until it thickens. Add the wild rice, mushrooms, chicken, pimiento, parsley, salt and black pepper. Place in a 2-quart casserole. Sprinkle with almonds. Bake for 25 to 30 minutes.

Basil Chicken

350 degrees, preheated
9 × 13 baking dish
Yield: 6 servings

6   chicken breasts
2   Tablespoons butter
1   teaspoon salt
1   teaspoon basil, divided
¼   teaspoon cayenne or red pepper
2   medium onions, chopped
10   cherry tomatoes
1   Tablespoon butter
1½   cups half and half
1   Tablespoon cornstarch
2   cups Danish Havarti cheese or other mild, white cheese

Brown chicken breasts in 2 Tablespoons butter. Season with salt, ½ teaspoon basil and cayenne pepper. Put the browned chicken into a baking dish. Sauté onions in the same butter and pour over the chicken. Slice tomatoes on top of chicken. Bake for 45 minutes. While chicken is baking, melt remaining butter in skillet. Add remaining basil. Mix in half and half and cornstarch. Stir over high heat until thickened. Add cheese and stir until well melted. Spoon over chicken as it comes from the oven and serve hot.

Golden Brown Baked Chicken

350 degrees, preheated
Shallow roasting pan
Yield: 6 to 8 servings

2   chickens, quartered
Seasoned salt
Black pepper
Garlic powder
1   cup pineapple juice
½   cup sherry
1   package dry onion soup mix
2   Tablespoons Kitchen Bouquet

Season quartered chickens with seasoned salt, black pepper and a little garlic powder. Mix remaining ingredients and pour over seasoned chickens which have been put in a shallow roasting pan. Cook covered for 1 hour 30 minutes. Uncover and baste. Continue cooking for 45 minutes at 400 degrees.

Chicken, Broccoli and Peaches

350 degrees, preheated
9 × 13 baking dish
Yield: 4 to 6 servings

½ cup butter
5 to 6 green onions, chopped
3 teaspoons paprika
6 boneless chicken breasts
1 16-ounce can peach halves
2 10-ounce packages frozen broccoli, cooked
1 cup sour cream
½ cup mayonnaise
Grated Parmesan cheese

Melt butter in skillet. Sauté green onions. Remove from heat and add paprika. Roll chicken in onion mixture. Place chicken in shallow baking dish, cover with foil and bake for 40 to 50 minutes. Place peaches and cooked broccoli around chicken. Mix sour cream and mayonnaise. Spread over chicken. Sprinkle with Parmesan cheese and broil 1 to 2 minutes to warm the sauce.

Sour Cream Enchiladas

325 degrees, preheated
9 × 13 baking dish
Yield: 6 to 8 servings

Filling:
3 cups cubed chicken (cooked)
1 cup chopped ripe olives
½ cup blanched, chopped almonds
½ cup minced green onion

Filling:
Mix together ingredients. Set aside.

Enchiladas:
3 cups vegetable oil
12 large corn tortillas
1 quart Old El Paso Red Enchilada Sauce, mild, heated
2 cups sour cream
1 cups grated Parmesan cheese

Enchiladas:
Heat vegetable oil and lightly fry one tortilla at a time. Dry on paper towel. Make sure tortillas can still bend easily. Then dip into Red Enchilada Sauce. Place good amount of filling in tortilla with 2 Tablespoons sour cream. Fold tortilla in tube with crease down. When finished, complete with sauce, rest of sour cream and cheese. May be served now or heated for about 20 minutes.

Chicken Delights

350 degrees, preheated
Baking pan
Yield: 24 delights

1   8-ounce package cream
    cheese
6   Tablespoons butter,
    melted
½   teaspoon salt
¼   teaspoon black pepper
¼   cup milk
2   Tablespoons chopped
    chives
4   cups cooked chicken
3   8-ounce cans refrigerated
    crescent rolls
Melted butter

Blend first six ingredients. Stir in chicken. Set aside. Separate rolls into rectangles and cut each rectangle in half. Flatten each rectangle. Spoon 2 to 3 Tablespoons of chicken mixture in center of each rectangle. Pull corners to center and seal well. Brush each with butter. Bake for about 20 minutes or until brown.

Indian Chicken Curry

Advance Preparation
Time Required
Yield: 6 servings

2   2½ pound chickens, cut
    up
½   cup vegetable oil
1   cup chopped onion
1   teaspoon chopped garlic
1   to 2 Tablespoons curry
    powder
1   cup chopped, peeled
    tomato
¼   cup finely chopped celery
    leaves
1   10-ounce can chicken
    bouillon
¾   cup water
Juice and grated rind of 1 lime
3   apples (about 1 pound),
    peeled, cored and chopped
½   cup chutney, cut in large
    pieces
2   teaspoons salt
½   teaspoon freshly ground
    black pepper

Sauté chicken in oil until golden, about 10 minutes. Remove chicken from pan. Set aside. In remaining oil, sauté onion, garlic and curry powder for 5 minutes, stirring constantly. Add chicken, tomato, celery leaves, bouillon and water. Bring to a boil, reduce heat, then cover and simmer for 30 minutes. Cool and refrigerate. An hour before serving, remove mixture from refrigerator and let stand at room temperature for 20 minutes. Stir in lime juice and rind, apples, chutney, salt and pepper. Bring to a boil, reduce heat and simmer, uncovered, for 30 minutes.

India Rice Curry

Large skillet
Yield: 8 servings

2 Tablespoons chopped
    onion
½ cup butter
½ teaspoon salt
1 Tablespoon curry powder
½ cup flour
3 cups milk or 1½ cups half
    and half and 1½ cups
    chicken stock
1 cup half and half
2 Tablespoons sherry
3 cups cooked chopped
    chicken
1½ cups cooked rice

Condiments:
Hard-boiled eggs, separated
    and chopped
Chopped salted peanuts
Toasted coconut
Chutney
Grated Cheddar cheese
Fried bacon, crumbled
French-fried onion rings,
    chopped
Chopped sweet pickles
Ripe or stuffed olives,
    chopped
Chopped bell pepper

Sauté onion in butter; add salt and curry and mix thoroughly. Add flour and cook until bubbly. Add milk and half and half, stirring constantly until smooth and thick. Stir in sherry and chicken. Heat to serve. Serve with rice with suggested condiments.

Variation:
May substitute cooked beef, pork, shrimp or crabmeat for the chicken.

Sukiyaki

Wok
Yield: 12 servings

½ cup chicken broth
1 Tablespoon brown sugar
1 teaspoon salt
¼ cup soy sauce
1½ Tablespoons cornstarch
½ cup lemon juice
¼ cup vegetable oil
1 1-pound chicken, skinned,
    boned and sliced into bite-
    sized pieces
1 cup sliced carrots
1 cup chopped onion
1 cup chopped celery
1 cup chopped bell pepper
Broccoli, cut into bite-sized
    pieces
1 cup bean sprouts
1 8-ounce can water
    chestnuts, sliced
1 cup sliced mushrooms
Almonds (optional)

Mix first 6 ingredients and set aside. Heat oil in a 375 degree wok for 4 minutes. Place meat in wok and stir fry for 2 minutes. Add carrots, onion, celery and bell pepper for 2 minutes. Add broccoli and stir fry for 1 minute. Add bean sprouts, water chestnuts and mushrooms. Add broth mixture and toss well. Serve over white rice.

Slivered almonds add a gourmet touch.

Creamed Chicken

Large heavy skillet
Yield: 8 to 10 servings

2 Tablespoons vegetable oil
2 Tablespoons flour
1 onion, chopped
1 bell pepper, chopped
1 cup chopped celery
2 cloves garlic, pressed
1 10¾-ounce can cream of
    mushroom soup
2 cups cooked chicken
Salt and cayenne or red
    pepper to taste

To make a roux, in a heavy skillet, brown oil and flour until deep brown, stirring constantly. Sauté onion, bell pepper, celery and garlic in the roux until tender. Add soup and simmer 15 minutes. Add water if mixture is too thick. Stir in chicken and simmer 20 minutes. Season to taste. Serve in patty shells, over rice or toasted bread.

Prize Winning Chicken Crepes

325 degrees, preheated
Baking dish, lightly greased
Yield: 6 to 8 servings

Crepes:
1   cup sifted flour
3   eggs
1½ cups milk
½   teaspoon salt
1   Tablespoon butter, melted

Filling:
1   stewing chicken (3 to 4
    pounds), cooked and
    boned
1¼ pounds Swiss cheese,
    grated
2   (or more) jalapeño
    peppers, seeded and finely
    chopped
1   teaspoon salt
1   teaspoon black pepper
2   cups whipping cream

Crepes:
Put all ingredients into a blender and blend until smooth. Heat a crepe skillet (or large slightly-rounded shallow skillet). Brush skillet with butter and pour in enough batter to cover bottom (approximately 1½ to 2 Tablespoons). Tip and roll pan to spread batter thin and evenly. Brown lightly on one side and turn, browning other side. Repeat with all remaining batter. Set crepes aside.

Filling:
Dice chicken. Combine chicken and all but 1 cup of grated cheese, jalapeños, salt and pepper and mix well. Place a large spoonful of filling in each crepe and roll up. Arrange filled, rolled crepes in shallow greased baking dish. Top with remaining cheese. Pour cream over crepes. Bake for 20 to 30 minutes or until thoroughly heated.

Chicken and Dumplings

Dutch oven
Yield: 8 servings

1 large chicken
3 quarts water or enough to cover chicken
3 cups sifted flour
1½ teaspoons baking powder
1 teaspoon salt
1 Tablespoon shortening
1 cup milk
1 egg, beaten
½ cup butter, melted
½ cup butter to add to broth
3 heaping Tablespoons flour
2 cups milk
Salt and black pepper to taste

Boil chicken. Remove chicken from broth and bone it. To make dumplings, combine flour, baking powder and salt. Cut in shortening. Add milk, egg and melted butter. Mix until all turns loose from bowl. Refrigerate for at least 15 minutes. Add butter to broth and boil slowly. Roll out dumplings on floured surface as thin as possible and cut into 3-inch strips. Drop into boiling broth. Cook about 10 to 15 minutes. Mix together flour with milk and add to dumplings. Gently stir in the chicken. Add salt and pepper to taste. Cook another 10 minutes or until hot through.

Short-Cut Chicken and Dumplings

6-quart Dutch oven
Yield: 8 to 10 servings

1 large chicken, cut up
1 quart chicken broth
1 to 1½ quarts water
1 package of 10 large flour tortillas
2 teaspoons salt
2 teaspoons black pepper
1 teaspoon poultry seasoning
1 teaspoon curry powder
1 bay leaf
½ cup milk

Cook chicken and bone it. Reserve broth. Put chicken broth and water into a 4 to 6-quart Dutch oven. Bring to a boil. While broth is cooking, cut tortillas into 1-inch squares and add to boiling broth and lower heat. Add seasoning. Cook covered until tender (about 1 hour to 1½ hours). Remove from heat and let set for about 30 minutes to 1 hour. Return to heat and add chicken and milk. Adjust seasonings to taste.

Chicken Spaghetti for a Crowd

350 degrees, preheated
3   9 × 13 casseroles
Yield: 3 large casseroles

2   to 3 chickens (6 to 8
     pounds)
2   10¾-ounce cans cream of
     mushroom soup
1   cup chopped onion
2   Tablespoons butter
2   4-ounce cans sliced
     mushrooms
2   teaspoons paprika
2   4-ounce jars chopped
     pimientos
2   cups chopped ripe olives
Salt and black pepper to taste
4   cups grated American
     cheese
16   ounces cooked spaghetti
Paprika to garnish

Cook chicken in salted water with a little pepper, until tender, making a rich stock. Bone chicken and cut into large chunks. Put chicken back in stock and add soup. Stir until smooth. Add onion that has been cooked in butter until wilted. Add mushrooms, paprika, pimiento, ripe olives, salt and pepper. Add 2 cups grated cheese and stir until melted. Add spaghetti. Pour into casseroles and top with remaining cheese. Sprinkle with paprika. Heat until it bubbles.

Chicken and Spinach Noodles

Dutch oven
Yield: 8 servings

2   whole chicken breasts,
     skinned and cooked in
     water
8   ounces spinach noodles
¾   cup green peas, cooked
1   2½-ounce jar sliced
     mushrooms, drained
1   4-ounce jar sliced
     pimiento, drained
2   egg yolks
1   cup milk or lowfat milk
½   cup grated Parmesan
     cheese

Bone chicken and cut into strips, set aside. Cook noodles in 3 quarts of water in a Dutch oven. Boil 14 to 15 minutes. Drain and return to Dutch oven. Add chicken, peas, mushrooms and pimiento. Beat egg yolks and milk with a fork until foamy; gradually add to mixture in Dutch oven, stirring well. Add Parmesan cheese and cook over medium heat, stirring gently until mixture thickens.

Spinach Chicken

350 degrees, preheated
3-quart casserole
Yield: 10 to 12 servings

1   5 to 6-pound hen
5   ounces very thin noodles
1   bunch fresh spinach
¼   cup margarine
8   ounces fresh mushrooms,
    sliced
½   cup chopped onions
½   cup chopped celery
¼   cup flour
1   cup milk
1   cup reserved chicken
    broth
2   cups sour cream
⅓   cup lemon juice
1   8-ounce can water
    chestnuts, diced
1   2-ounce jar chopped
    pimientos
2   teaspoons seasoned salt
¼   teaspoon monosodium
    glutamate
¼   teaspoon cayenne or red
    pepper
1   teaspoon paprika
2   teaspoons black pepper
2   cups grated Monterey
    Jack cheese

Cook chicken in seasoned water, cool and bone. Reserve 1 cup broth. Boil noodles according to package directions. Cook spinach until crisp-tender and set aside. Melt margarine in large saucepan and sauté mushrooms, onions and celery. Add flour. Stir until smooth; then add milk, reserved chicken broth, sour cream and lemon juice. Add all remaining ingredients, except chicken and cheese. In a 3-quart casserole, pour in half of sauce, add chicken and top with remaining sauce. Top with grated cheese. Bake for 1 hour.

Artichoke and Chicken Casserole

375 degrees, preheated
Covered casserole
Yield: 4 servings

1   16-ounce can artichoke
    hearts, drained
1   2½ to 3-pound frying
    chicken, cut-up
Salt and black pepper to taste
Paprika
6   Tablespoons butter
4   Tablespoons minced
    onions
6   ounces fresh mushrooms,
    sliced
2   Tablespoons flour
⅔   cup chicken broth
¼   cup dry white wine
¼   cup sherry
¾   teaspoon crumbled
    rosemary

Soak artichoke hearts in water briefly and drain. Sprinkle chicken generously with salt, pepper and paprika. In a pan, brown chicken on all sides in 4 Tablespoons butter. Transfer chicken to casserole. Arrange artichokes among chicken. Add remaining butter to drippings in frying pan. Add onions and mushrooms and sauté until tender. Sprinkle with flour and add broth, wines and rosemary. Stir until liquid is blended and slightly thickened. Pour over chicken. Cover and bake 40 minutes or until tender.

Baked Almond Chicken Casserole

350 degrees, preheated
6 × 10 baking dish
Yield: 4 to 6 servings

3   cups chopped cooked
    chicken
1   cup sliced celery
½   to 1 cup salad dressing
½   cup slivered almonds,
    toasted
1   cup (4 ounces) finely
    chopped Swiss cheese
¼   cup chopped onion
2   Tablespoons chopped
    pimiento
1   teaspoon salt
⅛   teaspoon black pepper
1   tomato, cut in wedges

Combine first 9 ingredients and mix lightly. Place in 6 × 10 baking dish. Sprinkle with additional almonds. Bake 25 minutes. Top with tomato wedges and continue baking 5 minutes.

Delightfully Different Divan

350 degrees, preheated
9 × 13 baking dish, buttered
Yield: 6 to 8 servings

1   7-ounce package sage
    stuffing mix
2   cups white wine, divided
½   to ¾ cup water
1   pound fresh mushrooms,
    sliced
1   onion, chopped
2   Tablespoons butter
¼   teaspoon garlic powder
2   10-ounce packages frozen
    broccoli spears, cooked
    and drained
6 to 8 boneless chicken
    breasts, cooked in
    seasoned water
2   10¾-ounce cans cream of
    chicken soup
1   10¾-ounce can cream of
    mushroom soup
1½ cups mayonnaise
Juice of 1 lemon
¼   teaspoon curry powder
8   ounces Cheddar cheese,
    grated

Combine stuffing mix, ½ cup wine and ½ to ¾ cup water. Layer stuffing mix in 9 × 13 buttered baking dish. Sauté mushrooms and onion in butter. While cooking, season with garlic powder and ⅓ cup wine. Cook until liquid is diminished. Pour over stuffing. Line casserole with cooked broccoli. Slice each chicken breast into thirds lengthwise. Place in center of casserole. Combine soups, mayonnaise, lemon juice, curry powder and remaining wine. Pour over top of casserole, covering chicken and broccoli. Top with cheese. Bake for 30 to 40 minutes.

Golden Chicken Rolls

Advance Preparation
Time Required
350 degrees, preheated
Yield: 8 to 10 servings

¼ cup chopped onion
¼ cup chopped bell pepper
¼ cup margarine, melted
¼ cup flour
1½ teaspoons salt
¼ teaspoon black pepper
1 cup chicken broth
3 cups cooked, chopped
   chicken
2 cups cooked rice
3 Tablespoons grated
   Parmesan cheese
1 cup cornflake crumbs
3 Tablespoons margarine

Sauté onion and bell pepper in melted margarine. Blend in flour, salt and pepper. Add chicken broth. Cook, stirring constantly, until it boils and thickens. Let cool. Combine chicken, rice, cheese and sauce. Shape into small loaves. Combine cornflake crumbs with 3 Tablespoons margarine. Coat loaves in crumbs. Chill overnight. Bake for 40 minutes.

Stuffed Cornish Hens

450 degrees, preheated
Deep baking dish
Yield: 4 servings

1 box wild rice
1 small onion, chopped
5 shallots, chopped
1 cup chopped celery
¼ to ½ cup butter
1 egg
1 cup bread crumbs
2 cups chicken broth
¼ teaspoon thyme
¼ teaspoon sage
Salt and pepper to taste
4 cornish hens
4 slices bacon

Prepare the wild rice according to package directions. Sauté onions, shallots and celery in butter. Combine wild rice, sautéed onions, shallots, celery, egg, bread crumbs, chicken broth and seasonings to form stuffing. Clean cornish hens and stuff each with prepared stuffing. Wrap each hen in bacon and put into a baking dish. Put into a preheated oven and immediately lower oven temperature to 350 degrees. Bake for 1 hour.

Smothered Quail

350 degrees, preheated
Covered baking dish
Yield: 4 to 6 servings

12 quail
6   Tablespoons butter
3   Tablespoons flour
2   cups chicken broth
½   cup sherry
Salt and pepper to taste

Season quail liberally. In a heavy skillet, brown quail in butter. Remove quail to baking dish. Add flour to butter in skillet and stir well. Slowly add chicken broth, sherry, salt and pepper. Blend well and pour over quail. Cover and bake for 1 hour.

Skillet Quail

Heavy skillet
Yield: 4 servings

Salt and black pepper to taste
8 to 10 quail, cleaned
Flour
½   cup margarine
1½ cups milk

Salt and pepper quail and roll in flour. Melt margarine in large, heavy skillet and brown birds. Remove quail from skillet and add 3 Tablespoons or more flour, salt and pepper to taste. Brown flour lightly and slowly stir in milk to make a smooth gravy. Return quail to skillet and roll in gravy. Cover and simmer on low for 30 to 45 minutes, basting occasionally.

Quail in Wine

Yield: 3 to 4 servings

Salt and black pepper to taste
6   quail
Flour
½   cup butter
1   clove garlic, pressed
¾   cup chopped celery
¾   cup chopped onion
½   cup boiling water
1½ cups white wine
½   cup mushrooms
Cooked rice

Salt and pepper birds and dust them with flour. Melt butter in skillet and sauté birds until brown. Add garlic, celery and onion. Add water, cover and simmer for 30 minutes. Add 1 cup of wine and mushrooms and simmer 30 minutes. Add the other ½ cup of wine if needed. Serve with rice.

Quail in Wine Sauce

Large skillet
Yield: 4 servings

6 to 8 quail
½ cup vegetable oil
2   small onions, chopped
2   cloves garlic, pressed
2   whole cloves
1   teaspoon whole black
    peppercorns
½ bay leaf
2   cups dry white wine
½ teaspoon salt
⅛ teaspoon cayenne or red
    pepper
1   teaspoon chives
2   cups whipping cream

Brown quail in oil and remove. Add onions, garlic and seasonings and sauté for several minutes. Add wine, salt, cayenne pepper and chives. Add browned quail and simmer for 30 minutes. Remove quail and strain sauce. Return sauce to pan and add cream. Cook until thickened and pour over quail.

Baked Dove

325 degrees, preheated
Covered baking dish
Yield: 4 servings

12 doves
3   Tablespoons margarine
Salt and black pepper to taste
Garlic salt
Juice of ½ lemon
2   teaspoons liquid smoke
1   Tablespoon
    Worcestershire sauce
4   strips bacon
¼ cup sherry
¼ cup water

Brown doves in margarine. Salt and pepper while browning. Remove doves to baking dish. Sprinkle with garlic salt, lemon juice, liquid smoke and Worcestershire sauce. Cover with bacon. Deglaze skillet with sherry and water and pour this mixture over doves. Cover and bake for 1 hour 30 minutes.

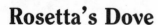

Rosetta's Dove

Iron skillet
Yield: 3 to 4 servings

8   doves, seasoned
Dash of onion flakes
Flour
Sage
Salt to taste
½   cup vegetable oil
½   cup red wine

Boil doves in just enough water to cover birds. Add a dash of onion flakes. Cook until tender. Remove doves and reserve stock. Coat each bird in flour seasoned with sage and salt. In an iron skillet, brown birds in hot oil. When brown, pour off excess oil. Mix ½ cup of stock and the red wine and pour over hot birds. Let them marinate in sauce for a few minutes. Leaving birds in the marinade, bring to a boil for 8 to 10 minutes. Have broiler hot. Broil until skin begins to bubble. Remove and serve.

Sherried Doves

350 degrees
Dutch oven
Yield: 8 servings

1   clove garlic, pressed
1   cup chopped celery
1   cup chopped onion
3   Tablespoons chopped
     parsley
½   cup butter
8   ounces fresh mushrooms,
     sliced
16 doves
Salt, cayenne or red pepper,
     and black pepper, mixed
     to taste
8   slices bacon, halved
1   10-ounce can consommé
½   cup sherry
1   bay leaf
2   Tablespoons browned
     flour

Sauté in Dutch oven, garlic, celery, onion and parsley in butter, until crisp tender. Add mushrooms and continue to sauté briefly. Rub birds inside and out with mixed seasoning. Place ½ slice bacon in each bird. Place birds in Dutch oven. Pour in consommé and sherry. Add bay leaf. Cover and bake for 2 hours 30 minutes or until birds are tender. Remove birds to heated serving dish. Thicken gravy with browned flour.

To brown flour, place quantity of flour desired in iron or heavy skillet over medium heat and stir constantly until browned.

Deer Stroganoff

Large skillet
Yield: 4 to 6 servings

1½ pounds deer ham, cubed
3   Tablespoons butter
1   onion, chopped
2   Tablespoons flour
½   teaspoon salt
1   teaspoon dry mustard
1   teaspoon black pepper
1½ teaspoons Worcestershire
     sauce
½   pound fresh mushrooms
Butter
1   cup sour cream

Brown deer in 1 Tablespoon of butter. Remove from skillet. In the same skillet, melt the remaining 2 Tablespoons of butter and brown onion for 10 minutes. Add flour, salt, mustard, pepper and Worcestershire sauce. Brown mushrooms in separate pan in additional butter. Stir meat, mushrooms and sour cream into skillet with onion mixture. Let simmer 15 to 20 minutes.

Venison Backstrap, Chicken Fried

Advance Preparation
Time Required
Large skillet

Frozen venison backstrap
1   13-ounce can evaporated
     milk
Flour
Salt and black pepper to taste
Vegetable oil

Put frozen backstrap in a Pyrex dish. Cover with milk and 1 can of water. Thaw overnight. If you do not cook the next morning, refrigerate in marinade until ready to cook. Remove backstrap when ready to fry. Cut in slices about ¾-inch thick. Tenderize with a meat hammer. In a paper sack, combine flour, salt and pepper. Place backstrap in sack and shake to coat thoroughly. Fry in hot oil, about ½ inch deep, browning both sides. Drain on paper towels.

Venison Scallopini

375 degrees, preheated
Large covered, ovenproof skillet
Yield: 4 to 6 servings

1½ pounds venison steak
Salt and black pepper to taste
Flour
1 egg, beaten
⅓ cup half and half
1 cup fine cracker crumbs
1 cup grated Parmesan
    cheese
¼ cup minced parsley
¼ cup butter
1 clove garlic, pressed
½ cup sherry or Marsala
    wine
½ cup venison broth or
    water

Slice venison into serving pieces and pound thoroughly. Sprinkle meat with salt and pepper, then dredge in flour. Combine egg and cream. Combine cracker crumbs, cheese and parsley. Dip each meat slice into egg mixture and then into cracker crumb mixture. Melt butter and garlic in a heavy ovenproof skillet with a cover. Brown prepared meat on both sides in butter. Pour in wine and broth. Cover skillet and bake for 45 minutes to 1 hour.

Excellent with wild rice.

Crab au Gratin

350 degrees, preheated
Individual au gratin
dishes or large casserole
Yield: 4 servings

⅛ cup finely chopped green onions
⅛ cup finely chopped celery
¼ pound fresh mushrooms
½ cup butter
1 Tablespoon parsley
1 Tablespoon chives
¼ cup flour
1 cup half and half
1 pound white lump crabmeat
½ cup grated cheese (American or medium Cheddar)
½ cup sherry
Grated cheese to top

Sauté onions, celery and mushrooms in butter until bubbling. Stir in parsley and chives. Over medium heat, gradually add flour and stir until smooth and bubbly. Add half and half, stirring constantly. Add crabmeat, cheese and sherry. Pour into individual au gratin dishes or a large casserole. Top with grated cheese and bake for about 15 minutes. Serve immediately.

Crab Casserole

350 degrees, preheated
2-quart casserole, buttered
Yield: 8 servings

1 pound crabmeat, cooked
1 pound shrimp, cooked
1 4-ounce can mushrooms, drained
½ cup chopped bell pepper
½ cup chopped onion
1 2-ounce jar chopped pimiento
1 cup chopped celery
1 cup mayonnaise
½ teaspoon salt
1 cup milk
⅛ teaspoon black pepper
1 Tablespoon Worcestershire sauce
2 cups cooked rice
Bread crumbs

Mix all ingredients. Place in a 2-quart buttered casserole. Top with bread crumbs. Bake for 30 minutes.

Shrimp Creole

Yield: 6 to 8 servings

3   Tablespoons bacon
    drippings
¼   cup chopped onion
½   medium bell pepper, cut
    into strips
¾   cup chopped celery
1   4-ounce can mushroom
    stems and pieces,
    reserving liquid
1   16-ounce can sliced and
    stewed tomatoes
1   clove garlic, pressed
1   beef bouillon cube
1   8-ounce can tomato sauce
1   6-ounce can tomato paste
1   sprig parsley, chopped
1   small bay leaf
3 or 4 dashes thyme
3 or 4 dashes basil
Salt and black pepper to taste
Dash of cayenne or red pepper
1½ to 2 pounds clean raw
    shrimp

Sauté first 5 ingredients until limp. Add the rest of the ingredients except shrimp. Simmer for 45 minutes. Add hot water if it gets too thick. Add shrimp and cook for 15 minutes. Serve over rice.

Shrimp Elegánt

Large skillet
Yield: 6 to 8 servings

3   Tablespoons butter
1   pound shrimp, peeled and
    veined
8   ounces mushrooms, sliced
¼   cup butter
¼   cup flour
¼   teaspoon dry mustard
2   cups half and half
3   Tablespoons sherry
¼   cup grated Parmesan
    cheese
Salt to taste

Melt 3 Tablespoons butter in a skillet. Add shrimp and mushrooms. Cook over medium heat for 5 minutes, stirring frequently, until tender. Remove from skillet. Add ¼ cup butter to skillet and melt. Add flour and seasonings. Stir in cream and cook, stirring constantly, until mixture thickens. Add shrimp and mushrooms to the sauce. Heat 2 to 3 minutes. Stir in sherry, cheese and salt. Serve over rice or parsley rice.

Shrimp Victoria

Dutch oven
Yield: 4 to 6 servings

1   pound shrimp, peeled and
    veined
1   onion, chopped
¼   cup butter
1   6-ounce can mushrooms
1   Tablespoon flour
¼   teaspoon salt
Dash of cayenne or red pepper
1   cup sour cream

Sauté shrimp and onion in butter for 10 minutes or until shrimp are tender. Add mushrooms and cook 5 minutes. Sprinkle in flour, salt and pepper. Stir in sour cream and simmer for 10 minutes, being careful not to boil. Serve over rice.

New Orleans Jambalaya

Dutch oven
Yield: 8 to 10 servings

1   pound smoked sausage,
    cut in ½ inch rounds
½   cup vegetable oil
2   onions, chopped
1   bunch green onions,
    chopped
½   cup chopped celery
1   bell pepper, chopped
¼   teaspoon thyme
2   bay leaves
2 to 4 cloves garlic, pressed
½   teaspoon salt
¼   teaspoon cayenne or red
    pepper
2   pounds shrimp, peeled
    and veined
2   16-ounce cans tomatoes
1   6-ounce can tomato paste
Thin slice of lemon
3   cups cooked rice

Brown sausage in oil. Add onions, celery, bell pepper, thyme, bay leaves, garlic, salt and pepper. Cook 3 minutes. Add shrimp, tomatoes, tomato paste and lemon. Simmer slowly, uncovered, tossing often with a fork, until shrimp are pink. Remove bay leaves and lemon. Stir in rice.

Shrimp Gumbo

Dutch oven
Yield: 8 to 10 servings

4 slices bacon
2 cloves garlic, pressed
1 cup chopped celery
1 bell pepper, chopped
1 onion, chopped
2 to 3 bay leaves
1 teaspoon sugar
1 6-ounce can tomato paste
1 teaspoon lemon juice
2 teaspoons chili powder
Dash of Worcestershire sauce
Dash of Tabasco sauce
Salt and black pepper to taste
8 cups water
1 16-ounce package frozen okra
2 pounds shrimp, peeled and veined
1 teaspoon gumbo filé

In a Dutch oven, fry bacon, drain and crumble. In bacon drippings, sauté garlic, celery, bell pepper, onion and bay leaves until tender. Sprinkle sugar over vegetables. Add tomato paste, lemon juice, chili powder, Worcestershire sauce, Tabasco sauce, salt and pepper. Add water and boil gently. Add okra and simmer for 2 hours. Add shrimp and cook until shrimp are pink, 30 to 45 minutes. Add filé just before serving. Serve over rice.

Shrimp and Rice Casserole

350 degrees, preheated
9 × 13 baking dish
Yield: 12 to 14 servings

2 cups uncooked rice
4 10¾-ounce cans cream of mushroom soup
¼ cup chopped green onions
5 pounds shrimp, cooked
3 cloves garlic, pressed
4 teaspoons lemon juice
2 teaspoons black pepper
1 teaspoon salt
8 Tablespoons butter
4 teaspoons chopped parsley
4 10-ounce packages sharp cheese, grated and divided
3 to 4 bell peppers, cut in rings and parboiled

Cook rice according to package directions. Add remaining ingredients, reserving enough cheese to top casserole and reserving bell peppers. Place in a 9 × 13 casserole. Top with cheese and bell pepper rings. Bake for 1 hour.

Salmon Loaf Supreme with Creamy Pea Sauce

375 degrees, preheated
Loaf pan, greased
Yield: 4 to 8 servings

2　cups fresh bread crumbs
　　(about 5 slices white
　　bread, grated)
½　cup milk
2　eggs, well beaten
½　teaspoon salt
¼　teaspoon Tabasco sauce
¼　teaspoon poultry
　　seasoning
1　16-ounce can red salmon,
　　drained and crumbled

Creamy Pea Sauce:
2　Tablespoons butter
2　Tablespoons flour
Salt and black pepper to taste
2　cups milk
1　16-ounce package frozen
　　peas, cooked and drained
⅓　cup chopped green onion

In large mixing bowl, with fork combine bread crumbs, milk, eggs, salt, Tabasco and poultry seasoning. Add salmon. Mix thoroughly. Turn into greased loaf pan. Bake for 45 minutes or until firm.

Creamy Pea Sauce:
In saucepan over low heat, melt butter. Stir in flour. Add salt and pepper until blended and smooth. Slowly add milk. Stir until thickened. Stir in peas and green onion. Serve hot over Salmon Loaf.

Bass Filets with Crabmeat Sauce

350 degrees, preheated
Cookie sheet, greased
Yield: 6 servings

½　cup finely chopped green
　　onions
2　Tablespoons butter
3　Tablespoons flour
½　cup milk
1　cup sour cream
1　pound lump crabmeat
6　6-ounce bass filets
¼　cup butter, melted
Salt and black pepper to taste

Sauté onions in 2 Tablespoons butter until soft. Stir in flour, stirring until smooth. Slowly stir in milk, stirring constantly. Add sour cream and crabmeat. Remove from heat. Brush filets with ¼ cup melted butter and place on a greased cookie sheet. Spoon crabmeat sauce over each filet. Bake for 30 minutes.

Red Snapper Veracruzana

400 degrees, preheated
9 × 13 casserole
Yield: 6 servings

¼   cup margarine
1   onion, chopped
1   bell pepper, chopped
1   clove garlic, pressed
1   tomato, chopped
1   Tablespoon beef extract or
    1 bouillon cube
2   Tablespoons lemon juice
½   teaspoon thyme
½   teaspoon black pepper
½   teaspoon salt
3   Tablespoons chili sauce
6   drops Tabasco sauce
1   Tablespoon chopped
    parsley
2   Tablespoons capers
½   cup sliced mushrooms,
    sautéed in butter
½   cup small shrimp
¼   cup white wine
6   red snapper filets

Mix together all ingredients except red snapper. Spoon this mixture over red snapper. Bake for 15 to 25 minutes or until flesh separates easily when pierced with fork. Serve with rice.

Broiled Red Snapper

Broiler pan, buttered
Yield: 8 servings

8   Red Snapper filets
Salt and cayenne or red
    pepper to taste
Lemon Juice
Olive oil

Sauce:
¼   cup butter, melted
¼   cup lemon juice
½   cup dry sherry
1   Tablespoon minced
    parsley

Sprinkle filets with salt and pepper, then rub with lemon juice and olive oil. Place fish on a buttered broiler pan and broil quickly under a hot broiler, 6 to 8 minutes until brown. Place on serving dish.

Sauce:
Combine sauce ingredients in a saucepan and boil. Pour over filets and serve immediately.

Seafood Stuffed Bell Peppers

350 degrees, preheated
Baking pan
Yield: 4 servings

8   bell peppers
½   cup butter
½   cup chopped onions
½   cup chopped celery
1   teaspoon tomato paste
½   pound shrimp, peeled and
    veined
1   cup cooked rice
1   5-ounce can crabmeat or
    lobster
Salt and black pepper to taste
Cayenne or red pepper to taste
½   cup bread crumbs
Melted butter

Cut off tops and remove seeds from bell peppers. Place peppers in a saucepan and cover with water. Boil for 10 minutes and drain. Sauté onions, celery and tomato paste in butter, until vegetables are soft. Add shrimp and cook for 6 minutes. Add rice, crabmeat or lobster and season to taste. Mix well. Fill each pepper with stuffing mixture. Top with bread crumbs and brush lightly with melted butter. Place in a baking pan and bake for 15 minutes.

Hot Tuna-Olive Casserole

350 degrees, preheated
1½ to 2-quart casserole
Yield: 6 to 8 servings

3   cups cooked elbow
    macaroni
½   cup sliced stuffed olives
2   6½-ounce cans tuna,
    drained
1   8-ounce can sliced
    mushrooms, drained
½   cup chopped celery
½   cup salted peanuts
1   cup mayonnaise
½   teaspoon black pepper
¼   teaspoon salt
¼   teaspoon oregano
1   cup grated Cheddar
    cheese

Combine all ingredients in a 1½ to 2-quart casserole. Sprinkle with cheese and bake for 25 minutes.

Trout Amandine

Skillet
Yield: 6 servings

8 to 12 trout filets (or any
    white fish)
Milk to cover
2   teaspoons salt, divided
4   drops Tabasco sauce
1½ cups flour
1   teaspoon white pepper
½ cup butter
2   Tablespoons vegetable oil

Sauce:
1   cup butter
½ cup sliced almonds
2   Tablespoons lemon juice
1   teaspoon Worcestershire
   sauce
1   teaspoon salt
¼ cup chopped parsley

Soak filets in milk, 1 teaspoon salt and Tabasco sauce for 30 minutes. In a shallow bowl combine flour, remaining salt and pepper. Coat soaked filets with flour mixture. In a skillet melt butter and add oil. Fry filets in oil. Add more butter and oil if needed. Place fried filets on a warm platter. Drain and wipe out skillet.

Sauce:
Prepare sauce in same skillet. Melt butter and lightly brown almonds. Add remaining ingredients and heat well. Pour over filets and serve.

Monterey Fondue Bake

350 degrees, preheated
8 × 8 baking dish
Yield: 8 servings

Margarine
6   slices firm-textured bread
4   eggs, beaten
2½ cups milk
1   teaspoon salt
1   teaspoon Tabasco sauce
1½ cups (12-ounces) grated
   Monterey Jack cheese
   with jalapeño peppers
1   12-ounce can Mexican
   style corn

Butter bread lightly, cut into ½-inch cubes and set aside. In a large bowl, combine eggs, milk, salt and Tabasco sauce. Stir in bread cubes, cheese and corn. Pour into baking dish and let stand 1 hour at room temperature. Bake for 55 to 60 minutes or until knife inserted comes out clean.

Good for breakfast. Bread can be buttered and cubed the night before, then assembled in the morning.

Chiles Relleños

350 degrees, preheated
Baking dish
Yield: 6 servings

3 4-ounce cans whole green
   chiles, drained
6 ounces Monterey Jack
   cheese
4 eggs, separated
Salt and black pepper to taste
Flour
Vegetable oil
1 16-ounce can stewed
   tomatoes

Carefully rinse chiles, remove seeds and drain on paper towels. Cut cheese into strips and carefully place into chiles. Sometimes the chiles might tear, but hold them together and it will work. Beat egg yolks with salt and pepper. Beat egg whites until stiff and fold yolk mixture into beaten whites. Heat a small amount of oil in a small skillet. Dip chiles in flour, then in egg mixture. Brown in hot oil on both sides. Drain on paper towels. Place in a shallow baking dish and pour tomatoes over chiles. Bake for 30 minutes.

Spinach Timballs

300 degrees, preheated
Muffin tin, greased
Yield: 12 servings

2 cups cooked, chopped
   spinach or 1 10-ounce
   package frozen spinach
2 Tablespoons butter
3 eggs
1 cup milk
Salt and black pepper to taste
Juice of 1 lemon
1 Tablespoon chopped
   onion
Dash of nutmeg
2 teaspoons vinegar
12 bread rounds or 6 English
   muffins, halved
Butter
12 tomato slices
Blender Hollandaise Sauce
   (see page 113)
Paprika or cayenne pepper

Mix first 9 ingredients and pour into greased muffin tins. Fill to about 1 inch deep. Bake for about 25 minutes or until firm. Butter bread round or ½ English muffin, add spinach cup and top with Hollandaise sauce. Garnish with paprika or cayenne pepper.

Mexican Cream Tortillas

250 degrees, preheated
9 × 13 baking dish
Yield: 8 to 10 servings

1   clove garlic, pressed
2   medium onions, chopped
2   Tablespoons bacon
    drippings
1   16-ounce can stewed
    tomatoes
Salt and black pepper to taste
3   cups grated Cheddar
    cheese
1   cup sour cream
18 corn tortillas
Vegetable oil

Brown garlic and onions in bacon drippings. Add stewed tomatoes, salt and pepper. Stir in cheese and cook until cheese melts. Over low heat, add sour cream and stir well. Fry tortillas by dipping them in hot oil until soft. Place 3 tortillas in the bottom of a 9 × 13 baking dish. Cover with small amount of sauce. Repeat layers ending with sauce. Bake for 45 minutes.

Tex-Mex Quiche

350 degrees, preheated
9-inch pie pan
Yield: 4 to 6 servings

Crust:
½   of an 11-ounce piecrust
    mix
1   teaspoon chili powder
2   Tablespoons cold water

Filling:
¾   cup grated Cheddar
    cheese
½   cup grated Monterey Jack
    cheese
3   large eggs, slightly beaten
1   teaspoon salt
¼   teaspoon white pepper
1½ cups half and half
1   4-ounce can diced green
    chiles
¼   cup sliced ripe olives
2   Tablespoons finely
    chopped green onions

Crust:
Blend pie crust mix and chili powder. Add water and mix with fork until dough holds together. With hands, form into smooth ball. Roll out on floured surface until 1½ inches larger than 9-inch pie pan. Ease into pan and flute edges.

Filling:
Mix cheeses together and spread on bottom of pie shell. Combine remaining ingredients and pour over cheeses. Bake for 40 to 45 minutes or until knife inserted in center comes out clean. Serve at once.

Serve as hors d'oeuvres or main course.

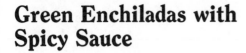

Green Enchiladas with Spicy Sauce

425 degrees, preheated
11½ × 7½ × 1¼ baking dish
Yield: 6 to 8 servings

Enchiladas:
12 corn tortillas
½ cup vegetable oil
2 cups grated Monterey
   Jack cheese
¾ cup chopped onion
¼ cup butter
¼ cup flour
2 cups chicken broth
1 cup sour cream
1 4-ounce can jalapeño
   peppers, seeded and
   chopped

Spicy Sauce:
1 medium tomato, finely
   chopped
½ cup finely chopped onion
2 jalapeño peppers, with
   seeds, finely chopped or 1
   4-ounce can green chiles
¼ cup tomato juice
½ teaspoon salt

Enchiladas:
In a skillet, cook tortillas one at a time in hot oil for 15 seconds on each side. Don't overcook or they won't roll. Place 2 Tablespoons cheese and 1 Tablespoon onion on each tortilla and roll up. Lay seam side down on baking dish. In saucepan, melt butter; blend in flour. Add chicken broth; cook, stirring constantly, until mixture thickens and bubbles. Stir in sour cream and jalapeño peppers; cook until thoroughly heated, but do not boil. Pour over tortillas and bake for 20 minutes. Sprinkle remaining cheese on top and cook for an additional 5 minutes or until cheese melts. Serve with Spicy Sauce.

Spicy Sauce:
In mixing bowl, combine all ingredients and mix well. Serve over enchiladas.

Fritata

Large ovenproof skillet
Yield: 6 servings

4 or 5 slices bacon
1 cup frozen hash brown
   potatoes
6 green onions, chopped
½ onion, chopped
½ cup chopped bell pepper
1 cup chopped mushrooms
4 eggs, beaten
¼ cup milk
1 cup grated cheese

Fry bacon, drain well and crumble. In bacon drippings, brown potatoes. Add onions, bell pepper and mushrooms. Beat eggs and milk together and add to potato mixture. Top with crumbled bacon. Cook over low heat for 5 to 6 minutes. Stir in cheese. Place under a broiler to set and brown slightly.

Casserole Quiche

400 degrees, preheated,
reduce to 350 degrees
9 × 13 casserole
Yield: 10 to 12 servings

1	cup butter
10	eggs
1½	cups flour
1	teaspoon baking powder
1	teaspoon salt
2	4-ounce cans green chiles, chopped
2	cups cottage cheese
1	pound Monterey Jack cheese, grated

Melt butter in 9 × 13 casserole. Beat eggs in a large bowl until fluffy. Add flour, baking powder and salt. Beat until smooth. Add green chiles, cottage cheese and Monterey Jack cheese to egg mixture. Stir well. Pour into casserole and bake for 15 minutes. Reduce temperature and bake an additional 35 minutes or until toothpick comes out clean.

Spinach and Ricotta Pie

425 degrees, preheated,
reduce to 350 degrees
9-inch pie pan
Yield: 6 to 8 servings

1	10-ounce package frozen chopped spinach, thawed and drained well
2	cups ricotta cheese or cottage cheese
¼	pound mushrooms, chopped
½	cup grated Swiss cheese
½	cup grated Parmesan cheese
¼	pound pepperoni, thinly sliced
¼	cup chopped onion
½	teaspoon oregano leaves
2	teaspoons prepared mustard
¼	teaspoon salt
1	egg, slightly beaten
Pastry for 2	9-inch pie crusts

Press out moisture from spinach. Combine ricotta, mushrooms, cheeses, pepperoni, onion, oregano, mustard and salt. Blend well. Stir in egg. Spread filling in pastry-lined pie pan. Cover with top crust and flute edges, pricking top with fork. Bake for 10 minutes. Reduce temperature and bake for an additional 20 minutes.

Spinach Pie

400 degrees, preheated
reduce to 350 degrees
9-inch pie plate
Yield: 6 to 8 servings

1 9-inch deep dish pie shell
½ onion, chopped
3 cloves garlic, pressed
¼ cup butter
2 10-ounce packages frozen
   chopped spinach, cooked
   and drained
3 eggs, well beaten
¾ teaspoon dried dill weed
½ pound Swiss cheese,
   sliced or grated
½ pound Cheddar cheese,
   sliced or grated
½ pound bulk sausage,
   browned
1 4-ounce can sliced
   mushrooms

Bake pie crust for 10 minutes or until dry but not brown. Brown onions and garlic in butter. Remove from heat. In a bowl, combine spinach, eggs, onion mixture and dill. Alternate layers of spinach and Swiss cheese in the pie shell. Then layer Cheddar cheese, sausage and mushrooms. Bake at 350 degrees for 30 minutes.

Onion Pie

350 degrees, preheated
8-inch pie pan
Yield: 6 to 8 servings

1 cup finely crushed cracker
   crumbs
¼ cup butter, melted
2 cups thinly sliced onions
2 Tablespoons butter
¾ cup milk
2 eggs, slightly beaten
¾ teaspoon salt
Dash of black pepper
¼ cup grated sharp Cheddar
   cheese
Paprika

Mix cracker crumbs with ¼ cup melted butter. Press into bottom and sides of pie pan. Cook onion in the 2 Tablespoons butter, stirring to separate in rings. Cook until onion rings are tender but not brown. Place in pie pan. Combine milk, eggs, salt and pepper. Pour over onions. Sprinkle with cheese and a dash of paprika. Bake for 30 minutes.

Can be served as an appetizer.

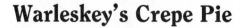

Warleskey's Crepe Pie

375 degrees, preheated
9 × 13 × 2 baking dish, buttered
Yield: 16 to 20 servings

Swiss Cheese Sauce:
½   cup butter
½   cup plus 2 Tablespoons
     flour
5½ cups milk
1   teaspoon salt
¼   teaspoon black pepper
½   teaspoon nutmeg
½   cup whipping cream
2   cups grated Swiss cheese
3   Tablespoons grated
     Parmesan cheese

Swiss Cheese Sauce:
Melt butter in heavy saucepan over low heat; blend in flour and cook one minute. Gradually add milk; cook over medium heat, stirring constantly until thick and bubbly. Add seasonings to white sauce. Add cream, stirring constantly. Add cheeses, stirring until melted.

Spinach Filling:
3   10-ounce packages frozen
     chopped spinach
½   cup Swiss cheese sauce

Spinach Filling:
Cook spinach according to package directions; drain well. Combine spinach and sauce, mixing well.

Mushroom Filling:
2   cups fresh diced
     mushrooms
¼   cup minced green onion
2   Tablespoons butter,
     melted
2   8-ounce packages cream
     cheese
2   eggs, beaten
1   cup Swiss cheese sauce

Mushroom Filling:
Sauté mushrooms and onion in butter until tender. Combine cream cheese and eggs in blender and blend thoroughly. In a large bowl, add mushroom mixture and cheese sauce to cream cheese mixture, mixing well.

16 crepes (See Basic Crepe
     Recipe, page 183)
2   cups grated Swiss cheese
Paprika

Place 2 crepes side by side in a 9 × 13 × 2 inch baking dish. Spread 2 Tablespoons spinach filling evenly over each crepe. Top each crepe with another crepe. Spread 2 Tablespoons mushroom filling evenly over each crepe. Repeat procedure with remaining crepes, spinach filling and mushroom filling, ending with crepes. Top with remaining Swiss cheese sauce, 2 cups grated Swiss cheese and paprika. Bake for 20 to 25 minutes or until bubbly and lightly brown. To serve, cut into wedges.

Egg Casserole

350 degrees, preheated
9 × 13 casserole
Yield: 8 to 10 servings

12   eggs
1   pound ham, chopped or 1 pound cooked sausage
2   bell peppers, chopped
1   pound Velveeta cheese, cubed
¼   cup butter, melted
1   cup sour cream
1   14½-ounce can stewed tomatoes

Beat eggs well. Add remaining ingredients and mix. Pour into a 9 × 13 casserole dish. Bake for 45 minutes to 1 hour, until brown and firm. Cool slightly.

Can mix and refrigerate before cooking.

Eggs au Gratin

11½ × 7½ × 1½ baking dish
Yield: 6 servings

2   large onions, thinly sliced
2   Tablespoons margarine
6   hard-boiled eggs, sliced
¾   cup mayonnaise
¼   cup milk
3   Tablespoons Parmesan cheese
1   teaspoon mustard
¼   teaspoon salt
⅛   teaspoon cayenne or red pepper

In a large skillet, sauté onions in margarine. Layer onions and eggs in a baking dish. Stir together the remaining ingredients and spread over the egg and onion mixture. Broil 3 minutes or until brown and bubbly. If prepared ahead, heat gently in oven, then broil for browning.

Eggs Mimosa

Yield: 6 servings

6   hard-boiled eggs, peeled
    and cut in half cross-wise
12 rolled anchovies
1   cup whipping cream,
    whipped
2   cups mayonnaise
Lemon juice
Salt and black pepper to taste
Fresh parsley, finely chopped

Remove and reserve hard-boiled egg yolks. Cut a thin slice from the bottom of the egg halves to make them stand upright. Place 1 anchovy in each egg half. Placed filled eggs on serving dish. Combine whipped cream and mayonnaise. Season to taste with lemon juice, salt and pepper. Spoon over eggs. Chop yolks and scatter over eggs. Garnish with chopped parsley. Serve cold.

Variation:
Optional fillings include deviled ham, chopped ham, pimiento cheese or any other cold sandwich fillings.

Party Breakfast Casserole

350 degrees, preheated
9 × 13 casserole, buttered
Yield: 8 servings

6   slices bread, crust
    removed and buttered
1   pound breakfast sausage,
    browned
6   ounces Cheddar cheese,
    grated
5   eggs
2   cups half and half
1   teaspoon dry mustard
1   teaspoon salt

Place bread on bottom of a 9 × 13 buttered casserole dish. Add a layer of sausage and cheese. Beat together eggs, half and half, salt and mustard. Pour mixture over the cheese layer. Refrigerate for at least 2 to 3 hours. Bake for 40 minutes.

Grains and Pasta

Italian Baked Rice

375 degrees, preheated
1½-quart casserole, greased
Yield: 6 to 8 servings

¼   cup butter
1   onion, chopped
8   ounces fresh mushrooms,
    sliced
1   pound bulk sausage
1   9-ounce package frozen
    artichokes or 1 14-ounce
    can artichokes
1   10-ounce package frozen
    peas
1   10½-ounce can beef
    bouillon, divided
3   cups cooked rice
½   cup grated Parmesan
    cheese

Sauté onion, mushrooms and sausage in butter until lightly brown. Add artichokes, peas and ½ cup bouillon and simmer uncovered for 10 minutes. Stir in rice and remaining bouillon. Toss lightly. Pour into a greased 1½-quart casserole. Sprinkle with cheese and bake for 15 to 20 minutes or until browned.

Parsley Rice

350 degrees, preheated
2-quart baking dish
Yield: 6 to 8 servings

⅔   cup finely chopped fresh
    parsley
⅔   cup finely chopped bell
    pepper
2   cloves garlic, finely
    chopped
8   ounces sharp cheese,
    grated
1½ cups milk
2   cups cooked rice
⅓   cup vegetable oil

Cook parsley and bell pepper in a small amount of water. Mix all ingredients together and bake in a covered dish for 1 hour.

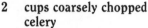

Rice Pilaf

Yield: 6 to 8 servings

2   cups coarsely chopped
     celery
1   cup coarsely chopped
     onion
1   cup coarsely chopped bell
     pepper
3   Tablespoons butter
1   10-ounce can beef
     bouillon
¼   teaspoon garlic salt
1½   teaspoons parsley flakes
2   teaspoons Worcestershire
     sauce
Salt and black pepper to taste
3   dashes Tabasco sauce
1   cup uncooked rice
1   4½-ounce jar sliced
     mushrooms, drained

Sauté celery, onion and bell pepper in butter until glossy. Add enough water to bouillon to make 2 cups liquid and add to sautéed mixture. Add remaining ingredients, except rice and mushrooms and bring to a boil. Add rice and bring to a boil again. Cover and simmer for 30 minutes. Add mushrooms before serving.

Variation:
Chicken broth may be substituted for beef bouillon.

Spanish Rice

Yield: 6 to 8 servings

2   cups quick cooking rice,
     uncooked
¼   cup vegetable oil
¼   cup chopped bell pepper
¼   cup chopped onion
1   clove garlic, pressed
8   ounces tomato sauce
1   teaspoon salt
½   teaspoon black pepper
1½   teaspoon chili powder
     (optional)

Brown rice in oil. Add bell pepper, onion and garlic and cook until onion is transparent. Add tomato sauce and 1 tomato sauce can of water, salt, pepper and chili powder. Bring to a boil and cover. Lower heat and cook until rice is almost dry.

South of the Border Rice

350 degrees, preheated
2-quart buttered casserole
Yield: 6 servings

¾ cup uncooked rice
2   cups sour cream
Salt to taste
8   ounces Monterey Jack
     cheese, cut in strips
1   3-ounce can chopped
     jalapeño peppers or 1 4-
     ounce can green chiles
½ cup grated Monterey Jack
     cheese

Cook and drain rice. Add the sour cream and salt. Arrange half the rice mixture in a buttered casserole. Place half the cheese strips on top and add half the green chiles or peppers. Repeat rice, cheese and chiles. Cover all with the grated cheese. Bake for 30 minutes.

Wonderfully hot!

Tomato and Basil Fettuccine

Yield: 4 generous
servings

¼ cup onion, chopped
1   clove garlic, pressed
¼ cup olive oil
3½ cups canned tomatoes,
     chopped, reserving liquid
1   Tablespoon basil
½ to 1 teaspoon salt
½ teaspoon black pepper
Homemade fettuccine, freshly
     cooked
Parmesan cheese

Sauté onion and garlic in olive oil. Add tomatoes. Spice with basil, salt and pepper. Add 1 cup reserved liquid. Bring to a boil. Simmer uncovered for 15 to 20 minutes. Toss with homemade fettuccine. Garnish with Parmesan cheese.

Linguine with Clam Sauce

Yield: 4 to 6 servings

¼ cup oil
3 Tablespoons chopped
   parsley
2 cloves garlic, pressed
3 medium tomatoes,
   chopped
¼ teaspoon salt
⅛ teaspoon black pepper
¼ teaspoon oregano
1 6½-ounce can minced
   clams
8 ounces cooked linguine

Heat oil. Add parsley, garlic, tomatoes, salt, pepper and oregano. Simmer for 15 to 20 minutes. Add clams with juice and simmer 5 more minutes. Pour over linguine in individual servings.

Variations:
Canned tomatoes may be substituted for fresh ones. Tuna may be substituted for clams. Spaghetti may be substituted for linguine.

Deluxe Macaroni and Cheese

350 degrees, preheated
9 × 9 × 2 greased baking dish
Yield: 6 to 8 servings

1 7-ounce package elbow
   macaroni
2 cups small curd cream
   cottage cheese
1 cup sour cream
1 egg, slightly beaten
¾ teaspoon salt
Dash of black pepper
8 ounces Cheddar cheese,
   grated
Paprika

Cook macaroni according to package directions; drain well. Combine cottage cheese, sour cream, egg, salt and pepper. Add Cheddar cheese, mixing well. Stir in cooked macaroni. Turn into a greased baking dish. Sprinkle with paprika. Bake for 40 to 45 minutes.

Basic Noodles

Yield: 4 to 6 servings

2   eggs, beaten
1   teaspoon salt
½   teaspoon black pepper
1½ cups flour

Beat together the eggs, salt and pepper. Begin beating in flour ¼ cup at a time until 1¼ cups have been added. Knead the resulting dough and add remaining flour as you knead. Roll out dough on floured surface. Cut into strips and allow to dry for 30 minutes. Boil in broth (chicken or beef) until tender (4 to 8 minutes).

Vegetables

Asparagus Soufflé

375 degrees, preheated
2-quart soufflé dish, buttered
Yield: 4 to 6 servings

4   eggs, separated
¼   teaspoon cream of tartar
¼   cup butter
¼   cup flour
½   teaspoon thyme
½   teaspoon Tabasco sauce
¼   teaspoon salt
1¼ cups milk (warmed)
¾   cup Parmesan cheese
2   15-ounce cans asparagus,
    sliced in ¾-inch pieces

Beat egg whites with cream of tartar. Melt butter in a saucepan. Add flour and cook until bubbly. Add seasonings and stir. Add milk and stir with a whisk until thick. Add egg yolks, Parmesan cheese and asparagus. Mix well. Fold egg whites into asparagus mixture. Pour into the soufflé dish. Bake for 40 to 45 minutes.

Mushroom Asparagus Casserole

350 degrees, preheated
1½-quart casserole
Yield: 8 to 10 servings

4   cups fresh mushrooms,
    halved
1   cup chopped onion
4   Tablespoons butter
2   Tablespoons flour
1   teaspoon instant chicken
    bouillon granules
½   teaspoon salt
Dash of black pepper
½   teaspoon nutmeg
1   cup milk
2   8-ounce packages frozen
    cut asparagus, cooked and
    drained
¼   cup chopped pimiento
1½ teaspoons lemon juice
¾   cup soft bread crumbs
1   Tablespoon butter, melted

Cook mushrooms and onions, covered, in 4 Tablespoons butter until tender (about 10 minutes). Remove vegetables; set aside, leaving butter in skillet. Blend in flour, bouillon granules, salt, pepper and nutmeg. Add milk. Cook and stir until bubbly. Stir in mushroom and onions, cooked asparagus, pimiento and lemon juice. Turn into 1½-quart casserole. Combine crumbs, melted butter and sprinkle over top. Bake for 35 to 40 minutes.

Green Beans with Zucchini

Yield: 6 servings

4 slices bacon
1 small onion, chopped
1 9-ounce package frozen
   cut green beans
2 medium zucchini, sliced
   ¼-inch thick
¾ teaspoon salt
Dash of black pepper

In a large skillet, fry bacon until crisp. Drain and crumble; set aside. Sauté onion in drippings until tender. Over medium heat add frozen green beans. Stir fry for 2 minutes, add zucchini slices and cook until tender, stirring occasionally (about 4 minutes). Stir in bacon, salt and pepper and heat through. Be careful not to overcook.

Argo's Pressure Cooker Pinto Beans

Yield: 4 to 6 servings

1 pound pinto beans,
   washed (no need to soak)
3 quarts water
4 or 5 beef bouillon cubes
3 to 5 dashes Tabasco sauce
7 dashes soy sauce
7 dashes Worcestershire
   sauce
2 to 3 large onions, chopped
Salt to taste
1 teaspoon Kitchen Bouquet
¾ pound bacon, cut into 1-
   inch pieces

Add all ingredients to water in pressure cooker. Cook for 1 hour 10 minutes. For a thicker pot liquor, cook another 15 to 20 minutes without pressure.

Variation:
Blackeyed peas may be substituted for pinto beans.

Pinto Beans for Mexican Dinner

Large pot
Yield: 10 to 12 servings

2 pounds dry pinto beans
½ cup sugar
Salt to taste
4 to 6 slices bacon
3 to 4 Tablespoons bacon
   drippings

Wash and sort beans. Add enough water so that beans will float. Add remaining ingredients and cook slowly, 3 to 4 hours, until beans are very tender.

Green Vegetable Casserole

300 degrees, preheated
3-quart casserole
Yield: 10 to 12 servings

1   10-ounce package frozen
    baby lima beans
1   10-ounce package frozen
    green peas
2   10-ounce packages frozen
    green beans
Salt to taste
½   cup chopped onion
¼   cup chopped bell pepper
¼   cup butter
1   cup whipping cream
1   cup mayonnaise
Parmesan cheese

Cook each vegetable separately according to package directions. Vegetables should be crisp-tender. Add salt to taste and mix vegetables together. Sauté onion and bell pepper in butter until limp. Whip cream and fold in mayonnaise. Put vegetables in large casserole, add sautéed items and mayonnaise mixture, and sprinkle liberally with Parmesan cheese. Bake for 30 minutes or until hot and bubbly.

Broccoli Puff

350 degrees, preheated
9-inch square baking dish, buttered
Yield: approximately 9 servings

2   10-ounce packages
    chopped broccoli
3   eggs, separated
1   Tablespoon flour
Pinch of nutmeg
1   cup mayonnaise
1   Tablespoon margarine,
    softened
¼   teaspoon salt
¼   teaspoon black pepper
¼   cup and 1 Tablespoon
    grated Parmesan cheese

Cook broccoli by package directions, drain well. Beat egg yolks while adding flour and mix well. Stir in next 6 ingredients. Add broccoli, mixing lightly. Beat egg whites until stiff but not dry. Gently fold into broccoli mixture. Pour into lightly buttered 9-inch square baking dish. Bake for 30 minutes. Cut into squares and serve.

Especially good buffet item!

Carrot Casserole

350 degrees, preheated
9 × 13 baking dish
Yield: 8 to 10 servings

1	white onion, chopped
½	cup chopped celery
¼	cup margarine
¼	cup flour
1	teaspoon salt
¼	teaspoon dry mustard
¼	teaspoon black pepper
2	cups milk
12	sliced cooked carrots
8	ounces sharp cheese, sliced
2	cups buttered bread crumbs

Cook onion and celery in margarine. Stir in flour, salt, mustard and pepper. Reduce heat and add milk. Stir and cook until it thickens. In baking dish, add carrots and cheese slices in layers, beginning and ending with carrots. Pour sauce over carrots and top with bread crumbs. Bake 20 to 25 minutes until bread crumbs are brown.

Carrots in Orange Marmalade

Yield: 6 to 8 servings

6	cups carrots, sliced thinly on the diagonal
2	Tablespoons butter
¼	cup chicken stock
½	teaspoon salt
½	teaspoon black pepper
1	cup orange marmalade

Dash of Grand Marnier (optional)

Put carrots, butter and stock in pan and cook, covered, on high for 3 minutes. Add remaining ingredients and cook, uncovered, over low heat until carrots are tender and sauce is a thick glaze. Stir often.

Cauliflower Crown

Yield: 4 to 6 servings

1 head cauliflower
½ cup mayonnaise
1 teaspoon mustard
¼ teaspoon dried minced onion
½ cup grated Cheddar cheese
Parsley to garnish

Wash and core cauliflower. Cook head whole in microwave on high for 8 to 10 minutes. Spread top with mayonnaise, mustard and minced onion mixture. Top with grated cheese. Heat until melted. Place on platter and garnish with parsley.

Corn Pudding

325 degrees, preheated
1½-quart baking dish
Yield: 8 to 10 servings

4 eggs
1 5.33-ounce can evaporated milk, with enough fresh milk to make 1 cup
6 Tablespoons butter, melted
½ bell pepper, finely diced
1 2-ounce jar diced pimiento
¼ cup sugar (optional when using canned corn)
10 large ears of corn, cut and scraped or 1 16-ounce can of yellow cream corn
Salt and black pepper to taste

Beat eggs and add to milk. Add rest of ingredients. Pour into baking dish and cook slowly for 1 hour. Bake until knife inserted in center comes out clean.

Barbecued Tomatoes

Yield: 4 to 8 servings

Salt and black pepper to taste
4 tomatoes, halved
⅓ cup bread crumbs
1 cup grated Cheddar cheese
4 Tablespoons butter, melted

Salt and pepper the tomato halves. Combine bread crumbs and cheese then pour butter over this and mix well. Top tomatoes with cheese mixture. Wrap tomatoes in heavy foil and seal edges. Grill over hot coals 8 to 10 minutes or until tomatoes are heated and cheese is melted.

Cream Corn

Yield: 6 to 8 servings

6 ears corn
2 cups milk, divided
2 Tablespoons butter
⅓ cup chopped onion
3 Tablespoons flour
2 eggs, beaten
1 teaspoon salt
1 teaspoon white pepper
Cheese (to taste)
Paprika

Cut kernels from ears of corn. Put in saucepan with ½ cup milk, butter and onion. Bring to a boil and cook until bubbly. In a bowl, mix together flour and remaining milk. Pour into corn mixture and cook until thick. Bring to a boil. Add eggs and season with salt and pepper. Garnish with cheese and paprika to taste.

Variation:
May also pour corn mixture into a casserole and bake at 350 degrees for 15 to 20 minutes with cheese on top.

Eggplant Dressing

350 degrees, preheated
Large casserole, buttered
Yield: 8 to 10 servings

1 medium eggplant, boiled and mashed
1 16-ounce loaf bread (can substitute biscuits or rolls)
1 13-ounce can evaporated milk
1 cup chopped onions
½ cup chopped celery
½ cup chopped bell pepper
1 Tablespoon vegetable oil
1 10¾-ounce can cream of mushroom soup
3 eggs
2 teaspoons pimiento
Salt and black pepper to taste
½ cup grated cheese

Boil and mash eggplant. Soak bread in canned milk. Sauté onions, celery and bell pepper in oil. Add soup, eggs, pimiento, salt, pepper, bread and mashed eggplant. Pour into buttered casserole dish. Top with grated cheese. Bake for 20 minutes.

Eggplant Supreme

350 degrees, preheated
Casserole dish
Yield: 4 to 6 servings

1   medium eggplant
1   egg, beaten
2   Tablespoons milk
1   cup bread crumbs
½   cup vegetable oil
1   8-ounce can tomato sauce
1   teaspoon salt
½   teaspoon black pepper
1   garlic clove, pressed
1   cup grated Cheddar
    cheese

Peel and slice eggplant (¼-inch slices). Dip in beaten egg and milk mixture and then dip in bread crumbs. Fry until brown in skillet with oil. Place slices in casserole dish. In saucepan, heat tomato sauce, salt, pepper and garlic. Pour over eggplant and sprinkle with cheese. Bake for 30 minutes.

Good even if you don't like eggplant!

Garden Fresh Casserole

400 degrees, preheated
9 × 12 casserole, greased
Yield: 6 to 8 servings

1   large eggplant, thinly
    sliced
1   large onion, thinly sliced
3   or 4 large, fresh tomatoes,
    thinly sliced
2   bell peppers, chopped
1½ teaspoons salt
1   teaspoon black pepper
½   teaspoon garlic powder
1   cup grated cheese for
    topping (Cheddar,
    Monterey Jack, Parmesan)

Layer ingredients in a casserole beginning with eggplant and ending with cheese. Do not add water. Bake for 15 minutes, then reduce heat to 350 degrees for 45 minutes more.

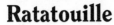

Ratatouille

Yield: 6 to 8 servings

1   pound zucchini, cubed
1   small eggplant, cubed
1   onion, sliced
¼   cup butter
1   clove garlic, pressed
2   tomatoes, peeled and
     chopped
1   bell pepper, chopped
1   teaspoon salt
⅛   teaspoon black pepper
¼   teaspoon basil leaves,
     crumbled
¼   teaspoon thyme leaves,
     crumbled

Cut zucchini and eggplant into ½-inch cubes. In large skillet, sauté zucchini, eggplant and onion in butter. Stir in garlic, tomatoes, bell pepper, salt, pepper, basil and thyme. Cook, covered, on medium heat 10 to 15 minutes or until vegetables are tender.

Very colorful!

Swiss Mushrooms

375 degrees, preheated
Medium casserole
Yield: 10 to 12 servings

1   pound fresh mushrooms
2   to 3 Tablespoons butter
⅓ to ½ cup sour cream
¼ to ½ teaspoon garlic salt
2   dashes black pepper
1   Tablespoon flour
¾   cup grated Swiss cheese

Wash and drain mushrooms carefully. Slice large ones into thirds and small ones in half. Sauté in butter until slightly brown. In bowl, blend sour cream, garlic salt, pepper and flour. Add to mushrooms. Cook over medium to low heat until bubbly. Remove from heat and pour into a casserole. Sprinkle with cheese. Heat uncovered for 15 to 20 minutes.

Onion Casserole

350 degrees, preheated
Baking dish
Yield: 6 to 8 servings

3   medium onions, chopped
    in large pieces (about 3
    cups)
½   cup chopped celery
Water
½   cup pimiento, chopped
1   cup mushrooms
¼   cup sherry
¼   teaspoon thyme
2   cups medium white sauce
1   cup Cheddar cheese
Cracker crumbs

Cook onions and celery in small amount of water until tender. Drain well. Add pimientos, mushrooms, sherry and thyme. Add white sauce and cheese. Cover with cracker crumbs. Bake 30 minutes.

Medium white sauce:
4   Tablespoons butter
4   Tablespoons flour
½   teaspoon salt
¼   teaspoon black pepper
2   cups milk

White sauce:
Melt butter over low heat. Blend in flour, salt and pepper. Cook over low heat, stirring until mixture is smooth and bubbly. Remove from heat. Stir in milk. Heat to boiling, stirring constantly. Boil and stir 1 minute. Yield: 2 cups

Oven-Fried Potatoes

375 degrees, preheated
9 × 13 baking dish
Yield: 4 to 6 servings

3   medium potatoes, cut into
    ⅛-inch wedges
¼   cup vegetable oil
1   Tablespoon grated
    Parmesan cheese
½   teaspoon salt
¼   teaspoon garlic powder
¼   teaspoon paprika
¼   teaspoon black pepper

Place potato wedges slightly overlapping in a single layer in a 9 × 13 inch baking pan. Combine remaining ingredients and baste potatoes with one half of mixture. Baste occasionally during cooking with remaining mixture. Bake uncovered for 45 minutes.

Swiss Potatoes

425 degrees, preheated
3-quart oven baking dish, buttered
Yield: 8 to 10 servings

10   Tablespoons butter
2 to 3 cups thinly sliced
     onions
12 to 16 medium potatoes,
     peeled and thinly sliced
Salt and freshly ground black
     pepper to taste
1½ cups grated Swiss cheese,
     or ¾ cup each grated
     Swiss and Cheddar cheese
2 to 3 cups chicken broth

Sauté onions in 4 Tablespoons butter until soft but not browned. Alternate layers of potatoes seasoned lightly with salt and pepper, sautéed onions, and cheese, ending with cheese. Dot with butter. Pour in enough chicken broth to cover half the layers in the dish. Bake uncovered for 30 to 40 minutes, or until potatoes are tender and top cheese and onions are dark golden brown.

Almond Broccoli

350 degrees, preheated
8 × 12 baking dish
Yield: 8 servings

3   cups chopped broccoli,
    cooked and drained
4   Tablespoons butter
4   Tablespoons flour
1   cup cream or half and half
1   cup hot water
1   cube beef boullion
3   Tablespoons dry sherry
2   Tablespoons lemon juice
Pepper to taste
¼   cup grated Parmesan
    cheese
¼   cup slivered almonds,
    toasted

Arrange broccoli in baking dish. In a saucepan, melt butter and add flour. Cook over medium heat until flour is browned. Slowly add cream, stirring until smooth. Dissolve boullion cube in hot water and slowly add to the cream mixture. Stir until mixture thickens. Add sherry, lemon juice and pepper and stir until blended. Pour sauce over broccoli and then top with Parmesan and almonds. Bake 20 minutes or until bubbling.

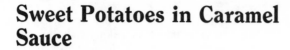

Sweet Potatoes in Caramel Sauce

350 degrees, preheated
9 × 13 casserole
Yield: 8 to 10 servings

6   medium to large sweet
     potatoes
1   cup brown sugar
1   teaspoon salt
1   Tablespoon flour
1   teaspoon allspice
2   teaspoons cinnamon
Pats of margarine or butter to
     taste
1   cup evaporated milk
1   or 2 cups miniature
     marshmallows

Scrub sweet potatoes and cut in 1½ to 2-inch round slices. Boil until fairly tender. Drain and cool until these are easy to handle. Peel potato slices and lay in casserole. Combine sugar, salt, flour and spices. Sprinkle over potatoes. Dot with desired amount of butter. Pour milk over this and bake for 35 minutes. Sprinkle marshmallows over top and bake until marshmallows are brown. Serve immediately.

Sweet Potato Mountains

375 degrees, preheated
Baking sheet
Yield: 6 to 8 servings

2   16-ounce cans whole
     sweet potatoes or yams,
     drained
8   slices canned pineapple,
     drained, liquid reserved
¼   cup butter, softened
¼   cup lightly packed brown
     sugar
1   teaspoon cinnamon
½   teaspoon nutmeg
½   cup chopped pecans
Miniature marshmallows, at
     least 36
Orange marmalade

Empty yams and reserved pineapple juice into a saucepan and heat to boil; simmer 5 minutes. Drain. Add butter and brown sugar; beat until well mashed. Add cinnamon, nutmeg and pecans. Arrange pineapple slices on a baking sheet. Make a mountain of about ½ cup mixture on top of each slice. Arrange marshmallows around top of mountain (as many as desired). Add 1 teaspoon marmalade to top of marshmallows. Bake 15 to 20 minutes or until marshmallows brown.

Variation:
3½ to 4 cups mashed fresh sweet potatoes may be substituted for canned sweet potatoes.

Spinach Casserole (or Dip)

350 degrees, preheated
Large baking dish
Yield: 10 to 12 servings

4   10-ounce packages frozen
    chopped spinach
2   bunches green onions and
    tops, chopped
1   cup butter
1   6-ounce roll garlic cheese
2   Tablespoons Parmesan
    cheese
1   clove garlic, pressed
1   pound crabmeat (fresh if
    possible)
Salt and black pepper to taste
Tabasco sauce to taste

Cook spinach and drain well. Sauté onions in butter. Add garlic cheese and melt. Add remaining ingredients. Place in baking dish and heat.

Spinach Madeleine

350 degrees, preheated
Large baking dish, buttered
Yield: 4 to 6 servings

2   10-ounce packages frozen
    chopped spinach
2   Tablespoons chopped
    onion
4   Tablespoons butter
2   Tablespoons flour
½   cup evaporated milk
½   cup reserved liquid from
    spinach
1   6-ounce roll jalapeño
    cheese, chopped
½   teaspoon black pepper
¾   teaspoon celery salt
½   teaspoon garlic salt
1   teaspoon Worcestershire
    sauce
3   to 4 drops Tabasco sauce
1   cup cracker crumbs

Cook spinach according to package directions. Drain well reserving ½ cup vegetable liquid. Sauté onion in butter, then stir in flour. Add liquids and cheese and heat, but do not boil. Remove from heat and stir in all seasonings, stirring until cheese is completely melted. Add spinach. Pour mixture in casserole and top with cracker crumbs. Heat until bubbly.

Acorn Squash

350 degrees, preheated
Baking dish
Yield: 8 servings

4 small acorn squash, cut in
   half lengthwise, seeds
   removed
Salt to taste
Melted butter
1 cup fresh cranberries,
   chopped
1 large orange, peeled and
   diced
2 Tablespoons butter,
   melted
2 Tablespoons dark brown
   sugar

Place squash halves, cut side down, on flat dish and bake for 25 minutes. Sprinkle cavities with salt. Brush cavities with melted butter to prevent drying. Mix cranberries, orange and butter and fill squash with fruit mixture. Bake 25 minutes or until squash is tender. Sprinkle with brown sugar and broil until bubbly.

Bacon Flavored Squash

350 degrees, preheated
2-quart casserole, greased
Yield: 6 servings

4 slices bacon
4 large yellow squash, sliced
1 medium yellow onion,
   chopped
1 egg, beaten
½ cup sour cream
½ cup grated Swiss cheese
¾ cup grated Cheddar
   cheese

Cook bacon in large skillet until crisp; drain, crumble and set aside, reserving drippings. Sauté squash and onion in drippings 8 to 10 minutes. Combine egg and sour cream and add to squash mixture. Stir in half the bacon. Spoon half the squash mixture into a shallow casserole. Sprinkle Swiss cheese over the top. Spoon remaining squash over cheese. Sprinkle Cheddar cheese over surface and top with remaining bacon. Bake for 20 minutes or until bubbly.

Squash Casserole

350 degrees, preheated
3-quart casserole
Yield: 6 to 8 servings

1   pound yellow squash,
     sliced
1   pound zucchini, sliced
½   cup chopped onion
¾   cup grated carrot
6   Tablespoons butter,
     divided
2½   cups herb stuffing, divided
1   10¾-ounce can cream of
     chicken soup
½   cup sour cream

Cook squash and zucchini and drain. Brown onion and carrot in 3 Tablespoons butter. Stir in 1¼ cups stuffing. Add soup, sour cream, squash and zucchini and put in casserole dish. Melt 3 Tablespoons butter; add remainder of stuffing and use it to top casserole. Bake, uncovered, 30 to 40 minutes or until bubbly.

Cheese Stuffed Zucchini

450 degrees, preheated
Yield: 2 to 3 servings

2   medium zucchini squash
¼   cup minced onion
1   Tablespoon butter
⅛   cup fine bread crumbs
Salt and black pepper to taste
2   Tablespoons grated
     Parmesan cheese
Chopped fresh parsley
     (optional)

Wash zucchini and cut off ends. Drop into boiling water to cover for 10 minutes. Drain and slice zucchini lengthwise. Scoop out pulp to make zucchini boats. Finely chop pulp. Sauté onion in a small amount of butter until golden. Add zucchini pulp, bread crumbs, salt, pepper and Parmesan cheese. Cook until soft and some of moisture has evaporated. Fill zucchini boats with bread crumb mixture, dot with butter and sprinkle top with additional Parmesan cheese. Bake 10 to 15 minutes or until golden. If desired, sprinkle with parsley.

Zucchini and Mushrooms

350 degrees, preheated
9 × 11 casserole
Yield: 6 to 8 servings

1   pound whole mushrooms
1   box whole cherry
    tomatoes
½   pound zucchini, cut in
    ½-inch rounds
1   teaspoon Italian seasoning
1   teaspoon onion powder
1   teaspoon salt
¼   teaspoon garlic powder
⅛   teaspoon black pepper
3   Tablespoons olive oil
2   Tablespoons margarine,
    melted

In a 9 × 11 casserole, combine mushrooms, tomatoes and zucchini. In small bowl, combine remaining ingredients and mix well. Pour seasoning mix over vegetables. Double wrap foil around the casserole dish. Bake 25 minutes.

Spanish Summer Squash

350 degrees, preheated
3-quart casserole
Yield: 16 servings

8   summer squash, boiled
    whole until tender but
    firm
1   cup grated cheese
1   Tablespoon chopped
    onion
2   Tablespoons chopped
    pimiento
1   Tablespoon vinegar
1   Tablespoon sugar
2   Tablespoons chopped bell
    pepper (optional)
4   teaspoons butter
Paprika

Slice squash in half lengthwise and scoop out centers. In a mixing bowl, combine cheese, onion, pimiento, vinegar, sugar and bell pepper. Arrange squash shells in casserole. Fill shells with cheese mixture and dot tops with butter. Sprinkle with paprika. Bake for 10 to 15 minutes until cheese melts and bubbles.

Breads

Sweet White Bread

350 degrees, preheated
8 loaf pans
Yield: 8 loaves

5   pounds flour
7   teaspoons salt
2   cups sugar
2½ cups shortening
2   packages dry yeast
5   cups warm water (105-115 degrees)

Sift dry ingredients. Cut in shortening. Add yeast dissolved in water. Work into dough. Knead 10 to 12 minutes or until smooth and elastic. Cover and let rise at room temperature overnight. Knead again. Separate into 8 loaves. Place in loaf pans and let rise until double in bulk. Bake 45 minutes to 1 hour.

Granny's White Bread (Adapted for Food Processor)

375 degrees, preheated
2   9 × 5 loaf pans, greased
Yield: 2 loaves

1   egg, beaten
1½ cups warm milk (105 to 115 degrees)
1   package yeast
3   Tablespoons sugar
1½ teaspoons salt
4   cups flour (bread flour preferred)
¼   cup butter

In a small bowl, combine egg and milk. Sprinkle yeast over egg and milk mixture and stir to dissolve. In a large food processor, mix sugar, salt, flour and butter. Process until butter is dissolved. Add liquid mixture and process until dough forms a ball (1 to 1½ minutes). Remove dough from bowl and shape into a smooth ball. Place dough into a greased bowl, turning to coat top. Cover and let rise in a warm place for 1 hour or until double in bulk. Punch down and divide dough in half. Roll each half into an 11 × 8-inch rectangle, using as little flour as possible. Roll each rectangle into an 8-inch loaf. Place in 2 well greased loaf pans. Cover and let rise 1 hour to 1 hour 30 minutes or until double in bulk. Bake for 35 to 40 minutes.

Dill Bread

350 degrees, preheated
2 large loaf pans

2   packages yeast
½ cup water
2   Tablespoons sugar
2   cups cottage cheese
2   Tablespoons dried minced
    onion
4   Tablespoons dill weed
2   Tablespoons margarine
4   Tablespoons sugar
2   teaspoons salt
½ teaspoon baking soda
2   eggs
4½ cups flour

Dissolve yeast in water and 2 Tablespoons sugar. Heat until warm, all ingredients except the flour. Beat in 4 cups of the flour. Knead 5 to 7 minutes. Cover and let rise until double in size. Work in the remaining ½ cup flour. Form 2 loaves. Put into loaf pans and let rise again. Bake for 35 minutes. Serve warm with butter.

Pita (Pocket Bread)

500 degrees, preheated
Cookie sheet, ungreased
Yield: 12 servings

1   package yeast
1⅓ cups warm water (105 to
    115 degrees)
1   teaspoon salt
¼ teaspoon sugar
1   Tablespoon vegetable oil
3 to 3½ cups flour
Cornmeal

Dissolve yeast in warm water. In a medium bowl, combine salt, sugar and oil. Add yeast to oil mixture. Add 1½ cups flour and beat until smooth. Gradually add remaining flour until dough is easy to handle. Turn onto floured surface and knead until smooth and elastic (about 10 minutes). Place in a greased bowl, turning once so that greased side is up. Cover and let rise in a warm place for 1 hour or until double in bulk. Punch down and divide into 6 equal parts. Shape into balls and let rise 30 minutes. Sprinkle ungreased cookie sheet with cornmeal. Roll balls into ⅛-inch thick circles. Place on cookie sheet and let rise 30 minutes. Bake for 10 minutes or until puffed and brown. Cut in half and fill with favorite filling.

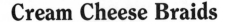

Cream Cheese Braids

Advance preparation
time required
350 degrees, not preheated
Cookie sheets, greased
Yield: 4 loaves

Braids:
1   cup sour cream, scalded
½   cup granulated sugar
½   cup butter, melted
1   teaspoon salt
2   packages yeast
½   cup warm water (105 to 115 degrees)
2   eggs, beaten
4   cups flour

Braids:
Combine scalded sour cream, sugar, butter and salt. Mix well and let cool to lukewarm. In a medium bowl, combine yeast and warm water. Stir in sour cream mixture and eggs. Gradually add flour (dough will be soft). Cover tightly and chill overnight.

Divide dough into 4 equal parts. On a floured surface, knead each part 4 or 5 times. Roll each part into a 12 × 8-inch rectangle. Spread ¼ filling over each rectangle, leaving ½ inch margins. Carefully roll up jelly roll fashion beginning at the long side. Firmly pinch edge and ends to seal. Carefully place rolls, seam side down, on greased baking sheets. Make 6 equally spaced, small, X-shaped cuts, across the top of each loaf. Cover and let rise in a warm place (85 degrees), free from drafts, for at least 1 hour or until double in bulk. Place in cold oven; bake for 15 to 20 minutes. Spread warm loaves with glaze while warm.

Filling:
2   8-ounce packages cream cheese, softened
¾   cup granulated sugar
1   egg, beaten
⅛   teaspoon salt
2   teaspoons vanilla

Filling:
Combine all ingredients. Process in food processor or electric mixer until well blended.

Glaze:
2   cups sifted powdered sugar
¼   cup milk
2   teaspoons vanilla

Glaze:
Combine all ingredients, mixing well.

Raisin Easter Egg Nests

350 degrees, preheated
Cookie sheet, greased
Yield: 12 servings

6 to 6½ cups flour, divided
¾   cup sugar
1   teaspoon salt
2   packages yeast
1   cup milk
¼   cup water
¼   cup butter
2   teaspoons grated orange
     rind
1   teaspoon nutmeg
4   eggs
1   cup raisins
12   uncooked eggs in shells,
     tinted as desired

In a large bowl, combine 2 cups flour, sugar, salt and yeast. In a small saucepan, over low heat, combine milk, water, butter, orange rind and nutmeg. Heat to 120 to 130 degrees. Stir milk mixture into flour mixture and beat at medium speed for 2 minutes. Add 3 eggs and 1 cup flour and beat at high speed for 3 minutes. Stir in raisins and remaining flour to make soft dough. Turn out on a floured surface and knead 8 to 10 minutes. Form a ball and place in a greased bowl. Cover and let rise 1 hour 30 minutes or until double in bulk. Punch down and divide into 12 equal pieces. Roll each piece of dough into a rope 8 inches long and 1½ inches thick. Wrap around tinted egg to form a nest. Moisten ends of ropes with water and pinch together to seal. Place on greased cookie sheet and let rise until double in bulk. Beat remaining egg and brush dough portion of each nest. Bake for about 20 minutes or until golden brown. Cool on a rack.

Variation:
Tinted eggs may be omitted and bread shaped into four braids. Let rise and bake as instructed. After baking, top braids with a powdered sugar glaze of 1 cup powdered sugar, 3 Tablespoons milk and ½ teaspoon orange extract or undiluted frozen orange juice concentrate.

Quick Bread

400 degrees, preheated
Bundt pan, greased

3   cups flour
1   package yeast
½   cup vegetable oil
¼   cup sugar
½   cup water
½   cup milk
1   teaspoon salt
2   eggs

Stir together flour and yeast. Heat oil, sugar, water, milk and salt to lukewarm. Add the heated mixture to flour and yeast. Stir well. Add the eggs and mix well. Pour the batter into a greased bundt or tube pan. Cover with a cloth and let rise until doubled in size (approximately 1 hour). Bake for 25 to 30 minutes.

Refrigerator Rolls

400 degrees, preheated
9 × 13 cookie sheet
Yield: 36 rolls

1   cup shortening
1   cup sugar
2   cups water, divided
2   packages yeast
6   cups flour
2   teaspoons salt
2   eggs, beaten

In a saucepan, combine shortening, sugar and 1 cup water. Heat over low heat until sugar and shortening are dissolved. In a small bowl, dissolve yeast in 1 cup warm water (105 to 115 degrees). Stir flour and salt together. In a large bowl, combine shortening mixture, yeast, dry ingredients and eggs. Mix well. Cover bowl and refrigerate at least 2 hours or until double in bulk. (Dough may be stored in refrigerator several days.) Make rolls into desired shapes (parkerhouse, cloverleaf, or pocketbook). Brush with melted butter, if desired. Cover and let rise in a warm place for at least 1 hour. Bake for 10 to 15 minutes or until golden brown.

Orange Butter for Rolls

Yield: enough spread for 48 rolls

¼   cup frozen orange juice concentrate (thawed, undiluted)
¾   cup butter
1   1-pound box (or 4 cups) powdered sugar

Cream all ingredients. Spread on warm rolls. Keep refrigerated in covered container.

Sour Cream Twists

375 degrees, preheated
Cookie sheet, ungreased
Yield: 36 twists

4   cups flour
1   teaspoon salt
1   cup shortening
1   package yeast
¼   cup warm water (105 to 115 degrees)
1   egg
2   egg yolks
1   cup sour cream
1   teaspoon vanilla
½   teaspoon grated lemon rind (optional)
1   cup raisins
⅔   cup sugar
Cinnamon

In a bowl, sift flour and salt; cut in shortening with a pastry blender. In another bowl, dissolve yeast in warm water. Beat egg and egg yolks together until light. Add sour cream, yeast mixture, vanilla, lemon rind and raisins. Stir into pastry mixture and mix well. Let rise in refrigerator for 2 hours. Sprinkle some of the sugar lightly over a bread board. Place dough on board and sprinkle sugar very lightly over it. Roll dough into a 12-inch square. Fold dough from each side to the middle, making 3 layers. Roll out again and repeat folding process, using a little more sugar on dough and board to prevent sticking. Cut into strips 1 inch wide and 4 inches long. Twist each 3 or 4 times. Place on ungreased baking sheet several inches apart. Sprinkle with remaining sugar or a cinnamon-sugar mixture. Bake for 18 minutes or until light brown.

Rich and divine!

All Bran Rolls

350 degrees, preheated
Cookie sheet
Yield: 48 rolls

1   cup All Bran
¾   cup sugar
1½   teaspoons salt
1   cup shortening
1   cup boiling water
1   cup warm water (105 to 115 degrees)
2   packages yeast
6   cups flour, divided
2   eggs, beaten
Melted butter

In a large bowl, combine bran, sugar, salt and shortening. Add 1 cup boiling water and stir. Let cool. Dissolve yeast in 1 cup warm water. Add yeast to bran mixture. Stir in 3 cups flour, then eggs. Add remaining flour and mix well. On a floured surface, roll out dough to ¼-inch thickness. Cut with a biscuit cutter. Dip rolls on one side in melted butter. Fold rolls over (butter side in) and place on a cookie sheet. Cover and let rise for 1 hour 30 minutes. Bake for 20 to 30 minutes.

Crescent Rolls

400 degrees, preheated
Yield: 24 rolls

7 Tablespoons sugar
3 eggs
1 teaspoon salt
1 cup milk
7 Tablespoons shortening
2 cakes yeast, crumbled
2 teaspoons sugar
4½ cups sifted flour
Melted butter

Combine sugar, eggs and salt together and beat well. Scald milk and shortening and let cool. Add to egg mixture. Combine yeast and 2 teaspoons sugar and stir into batter. Stir in flour. Beat dough for 5 minutes. Place in covered bowl in refrigerator overnight. Take out 3 hours before using. Divide dough into 2 equal parts and roll each into a circle. Spread with melted butter. Cut into pie-shaped wedges. Roll up starting at large end. Put in a greased pan and let rise for 3 hours. Bake for 15 to 20 minutes or until golden brown.

Easy Dinner Rolls with Food Processor

400 degrees, preheated
Yield: 12 to 18 rolls

3½ cups flour (bread flour preferred)
¾ teaspoon salt
2 Tablespoons margarine
3 Tablespoons sugar
1 egg, beaten
1 cup warm water
1 package yeast

In food processor bowl, mix flour, salt, margarine and sugar until margarine is dissolved. In a separate container, add warm water to the beaten egg. Dissolve yeast in egg and water mixture. Once the yeast is dissolved, pour liquid into the flour mixture. Process for about 1 minute. Dough should be soft but not sticky. (If sticky, add flour, but no more than ½ cup.) Process again for about 30 seconds. Remove dough and place in an oiled bowl, turning to coat top with oil. Cover and let rise in a warm place until double in size. Roll out and shape into dinner rolls. Let rise for 1½ to 2 hours. Bake for 12 to 15 minutes.

Caramel Pecan Rolls

400 degrees, preheated
2 9 × 13 baking pans, greased
Yield: 18 rolls

Rolls:
2   packages yeast
1   Tablespoon granulated
    sugar
1   cup warm water (105 to
    115 degrees)
1   cup milk, scalded
½   cup granulated sugar
6   Tablespoons shortening
1   teaspoon salt
7   cups flour, divided
3   eggs, beaten
½   teaspoon mace
Melted butter
½   cup granulated sugar
3   Tablespoons cinnamon

Caramel Topping:
¼   cup melted butter
½   cup brown sugar
⅛   cup light corn syrup
1½ Tablespoons water
½   cup chopped pecans

Rolls:
Dissolve yeast and 1 Tablespoon sugar in warm water. Combine scalded milk, ½ cup sugar, shortening and salt. Cool to lukewarm. Add 2 cups flour to make a batter. Add yeast mixture and eggs, beat well. Add remaining flour and mace. Knead lightly and place in a greased bowl. Cover and let rise in a warm place for 2 hours or until double in bulk. Roll dough to about ⅓-inch thick. Brush with melted butter and sprinkle with combined sugar and cinnamon. Roll up jelly roll fashion, pinching seams along edge. Cut into ½ to 1-inch slices, flattening with palm of hand.

Caramel Topping:
To prepare each pan: melt butter in 9 × 13 baking pan so that butter covers entire bottom. Sprinkle with brown sugar. Drizzle syrup over sugar. Sprinkle with water and cover with pecans. Place rolls in prepared pan and let rise until double in bulk. Bake for 20 minutes or until brown. Let rolls stand a few minutes. Turn out onto wax paper.

Refrigerator Breakfast Rolls

*Advance preparation
time required*
400 degrees, preheated
Cookie sheet, greased
Yield: 36 rolls

Rolls:
¼ cup warm water (105 to 115 degrees)
1 teaspoon sugar
1 package yeast
4 cups flour
1 teaspoon salt
1 teaspoon grated lemon or orange rind
¼ cup sugar
1 cup butter, softened
1 cup milk
2 eggs, beaten
½ cup butter, melted
1 cup sugar
1 Tablespoon cinnamon

Rolls:
In a small bowl, combine warm water and 1 teaspoon sugar. Sprinkle in yeast and stir until dissolved. In a large bowl, combine flour, salt, lemon or orange rind and ¼ cup sugar. Cut in butter. Scald 1 cup milk and cool to lukewarm. Add eggs and yeast mixture to cooled milk. Add milk mixture to flour mixture and mix lightly. Cover tightly and refrigerate overnight. Divide dough in half. On a floured surface, roll each part into an 18 × 12 inch rectangle. Brush each rectangle with butter. Combine 1 cup sugar and cinnamon and sprinkle over each rectangle. Roll up jelly roll fashion, beginning with large end. Cut each roll into 1-inch slices. Place on greased cookie sheets. Flatten slices slightly. Bake for 12 minutes or until golden brown.

Glaze:
1 cup sifted powdered sugar
3 Tablespoons milk
½ teaspoon extract of choice (vanilla, lemon or almond)

Glaze:
Combine ingredients and frost rolls.

Batter for Frying Vegetables or Chicken

Yield: 1½ to 2 cups

¾ cup cornstarch
¼ cup flour
1 teaspoon baking powder
½ teaspoon salt
¼ teaspoon black pepper
½ cup water
1 egg, slightly beaten

Mix all ingredients well. Dip prepared vegetables or chicken into mixture. Deep fry in hot oil.

Basic Crepes

6- to 7-inch crepe pan
Yield: 18 crepes

1 cup flour
3 eggs, beaten
1½ cups milk
¼ cup vegetable oil

Beat flour and eggs until smooth. Gradually stir in milk to make a thin batter. Cover and refrigerate for 1 hour. Heat crepe pan or small skillet until it begins to smoke. Brush pan lightly with oil before making each crepe. Pour ⅛ cup batter into the center of the pan. Tilt pan to spread batter evenly. Cook over medium heat for about 1 minute or until top of crepe is dry and bottom is lightly brown. Turn crepe and cook about 15 seconds. Repeat for each crepe.

Betsy Bread

400 degrees, preheated
8 × 8 baking pan
Yield: 6 to 8 servings

2 cups cornmeal
1 cup flour
½ cup sugar
2 cups buttermilk
3 Tablespoons vegetable oil
1 teaspoon salt
1 teaspoon baking soda

Combine all ingredients, mixing well. Pour into an 8 × 8 baking pan. Bake for 40 minutes. This may also be baked in a 9½ × 5½ loaf pan at 350 degrees for 1 hour.

Hot Water Cornbread

Skillet
Yield: 8 servings

2 cups yellow cornmeal
½ teaspoon salt
½ teaspoon baking powder
1 Tablespoon bacon
   drippings
1 to 2 cups boiling water
Pinch of sugar (optional)
Garlic powder to taste
   (optional)
Bacon drippings for frying

Mix dry ingredients together. Add bacon drippings and mix well. Gradually add boiling water until batter is consistency to pat into thin patties. Dip hands into cool water and shape batter into a 3-inch flat patty. Drop in hot bacon drippings and fry until golden brown, turning once. Drain on paper towels. Keep warm in the oven until serving time.

Serve with fried fish or chili.

Skillet Corn Bread

450 degrees, preheated
11½ to 12-inch iron
skillet, greased
Yield: 16   2-inch servings

1   cup white cornmeal
½   cup flour
1   teaspoon salt
1   Tablespoon sugar
½   teaspoon baking soda
1   Tablespoon baking
     powder
1   cup buttermilk
½   cup sweet milk
1   egg
½   cup vegetable oil

Place a greased 11½ to 12-inch iron skillet in the oven until hot. Mix together all dry ingredients. In a separate bowl, combine buttermilk, sweet milk, egg and oil. Refrigerate until ready to use. Mix together dry ingredients and liquid ingredients. Pour into hot skillet. Bake for about 20 minutes or until brown.

Yeast Cornbread

375 degrees, preheated
Loaf pans, greased and floured
Yield: 12 to 14 servings

1   cup milk
6   Tablespoons sugar
2   teaspoons salt
½   cup margarine
1   cup warm water
2   packages yeast
2   eggs, beaten
3½   cups flour
1¾   cups cornmeal

Scald milk. Stir in sugar, salt and margarine. Cool until lukewarm. Measure warm water into large warm bowl. Sprinkle in yeast and stir until dissolved. Add lukewarm milk mixture, eggs, flour and cornmeal to yeast mixture and stir well. Turn into either 2 large or 3 medium loaf pans that have been greased and floured. Cover with wet cloth. Let rise in warm place, free from draft, until double in bulk (about 1 hour). Bake for 30 to 35 minutes.

Yam Biscuits

450 degrees, preheated
Cookie sheet, greased
Yield: 18 biscuits

2 cups sifted flour
3 teaspoons baking powder
1 teaspoon salt
¼ cup shortening
½ cup grated raw yams
Milk

Sift together flour, baking powder and salt. Cut in shortening; add yams and mix lightly. Add enough milk to make a soft (not sticky) dough. Turn out and knead for 30 seconds. Lightly roll out to ½-inch thickness and cut into small squares. Bake on greased cookie sheet 1 inch apart for 12 minutes.

Good with mustard and ham slices.

Apple Bread

350 degrees, preheated
2 8-inch loaf pans, greased

1½ cups brown sugar
⅔ cup vegetable oil
1 egg
1 teaspoon baking soda
1 teaspoon salt
1 teaspoon cinnamon
1 cup buttermilk
2½ cups flour
1½ cups chopped apples
½ cup chopped nuts

Stir together ingredients in the order listed, beginning with brown sugar and ending with nuts. Bake in 2 greased 8-inch loaf pans for 1 hour.

Almond Butter for Sweet Breads   Yield: 8 to 10 servings

½ cup butter
½ teaspoon almond extract
3 Tablespoons sugar, or more to taste

Cream butter until fluffy. Beat in extract and sugar. Serve with any fruit bread, especially with Apricot Nut Bread.

Apricot Nut Bread

350 degrees, preheated
8½ × 4½ × 2½ loaf pan, greased

1½ cups sifted flour
2 teaspoons baking powder
½ teaspoon baking soda
1 teaspoon salt
½ cup sugar
1 cup old-fashioned oats
1 cup chopped dried
   apricots
½ cup chopped pecans
2 eggs, beaten
⅓ cup vegetable oil
1¼ cups milk

Sift together flour, baking powder, baking soda, salt and sugar. Stir in oats, apricots and nuts. Add eggs, oil and milk. Stir only until dry ingredients are moistened. Pour into a greased 8½ × 4½ × 2½ loaf pan. Bake for 1 hour. Cool slightly; remove from pan and cool on rack.

Banana Nut Bread

350 degrees, preheated
9½ × 5½ loaf pan or
2 7½ × 3½ loaf pans
Yield: 1 large or 2 small loaves

3 ripe bananas, mashed
1½ cups sugar
2 eggs
⅓ cup shortening or butter,
   softened
1 teaspoon vanilla
½ teaspoon salt
2 cups flour
1 teaspoon baking soda
1 cup buttermilk
1 cup chopped pecans

Cream bananas, sugar, eggs, shortening or butter and vanilla. Combine salt and flour. Combine baking soda and buttermilk. Add flour mixture to creamed mixture, mixing alternately with buttermilk mixture. Mix well. Stir in pecans. Pour into loaf pans and bake for 1 hour 10 minutes for 1 large loaf. Bake for 45 minutes for 2 small loaves.

Tangy Glazed Lemon Bread

325 degrees, preheated
2 8 × 4 loaf pans,
greased and floured
Yield: 2 loaves

½ cup butter, softened
2 cups sugar
4 eggs
1 cup milk
3 Tablespoons grated lemon rind or grated rind from 2 lemons
3 cups flour
2 teaspoons baking powder
1 teaspoon salt

Cream butter and sugar. Beat in eggs, milk and lemon rind. Sift together dry ingredients; combine with creamed mixture. Bake in 2 greased and floured loaf pans for 60 minutes or until done.

Glaze:
Juice of 2 lemons
1 cup of sugar

Glaze:
Mix together lemon juice and sugar. Pour over bread while hot. Let cool completely before removing bread from pan.

A very good sweet bread for breakfast or with afternoon coffee.

Spicy Pumpkin Bread

350 degrees, preheated
2 loaf pans, greased and floured
Yield: 2 loaves

¾ cup butter
2½ cups sugar
4 eggs
1 16-ounce can pumpkin
⅔ cup water
3½ cups unbleached flour
2 teaspoons baking soda
1½ teaspoons salt
1½ teaspoons baking powder
1 teaspoon cinnamon
1 teaspoon ground cloves
⅔ cup chopped nuts
½ cup chopped maraschino
   cherries (optional)

Cream butter and sugar in a large bowl. Add eggs, one at a time, beating thoroughly. Mix in pumpkin and water. In a separate bowl, combine remaining ingredients (except cherries) and mix well. Stir dry ingredients into pumpkin mixture a little at a time, and continue to stir until batter is thoroughly blended. If cherries are used (mainly for color), stir them in now. Bake in 2 greased and floured loaf pans for 1 hour 10 minutes. Cool 15 minutes before removing from pan. Spread cooled bread slices with whipped cream cheese or butter; good served with separate bowls of butter, nuts, fresh apples and spiked cider.

Bread is spicier if made a day ahead.

Pumpkin Bread

350 degrees, preheated
3 1-pound coffee cans,
greased and floured
Yield: 3 loaves

3 cups flour
3 cups sugar
½ teaspoon salt
1 teaspoon baking powder
1 teaspoon cinnamon
1 teaspoon allspice
1 teaspoon nutmeg
1 cup vegetable oil
3 eggs
1 16-ounce can pumpkin
1 teaspoon vanilla
⅔ cup chopped pecans

Combine dry ingredients. Add oil and eggs; mix well. Stir in pumpkin and vanilla. Add pecans. Divide batter into 3 coffee cans. Bake for 1 hour 15 minutes.

Zucchini Bread

375 degrees, preheated
2 loaf pans, greased and floured
Yield: 2 loaves

3   eggs
1   cup vegetable oil
1½ cups sugar
2   cups grated and unpeeled
    zucchini
3   teaspoons vanilla
3   cups flour
1   teaspoon salt
1   teaspoon baking soda
2   teaspoons baking powder
2   teaspoons cinnamon
1   cup raisins

Beat eggs until foamy; add oil, sugar, zucchini and vanilla. Sift together flour, salt, baking soda, baking powder and cinnamon. With a wooden spoon stir into egg mixture. Add raisins and mix until blended. Bake for 1 hour in 2 greased and floured loaf pans.

Tastes like banana bread!

Banana Bran Muffins

425 degrees, preheated
Muffin tins, greased
Yield: 24 to 30 muffins

3   cups bran flakes
1   cup boiling water
2   eggs, beaten
1¾ cups buttermilk
½   cup vegetable oil
½   cup raisins
½   cup dates (or use 1 cup
    raisins and omit dates)
1   banana, mashed
2½ teaspoons baking soda
½   teaspoon salt
1   cup brown sugar
2½ cups unsifted white pastry
    flour

Combine bran flakes and boiling water in a large bowl and moisten evenly. Cool. Add eggs, buttermilk, oil and fruit. Blend well. Sift together dry ingredients and stir gently into bran mixture. Bake now or refrigerate batter in a tightly covered container (up to 2 weeks). Fill greased muffin cups ⅔ full. Bake for 20 minutes or until done.

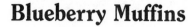

Blueberry Muffins

375 degrees, preheated
Muffin tins, greased
Yield: 36 muffins

⅔ cup shortening
1   cup sugar
3   eggs
2½ cups flour
½   cup wheat germ
2   heaping teaspoons baking
    powder
1   teaspoon salt
1   cup milk
1   16-ounce can blueberries
    (drained) or 1 cup fresh
    blueberries

Cream shortening and sugar together. Add eggs, one at a time, beating well after each addition. Add dry ingredients alternately with milk to the creamed mixture, stirring well after each addition. Fold in blueberries and fill muffin tins ½ to ⅔ full. Bake for 15 to 20 minutes. Batter can be stored in a covered container in the refrigerator for at least 2 weeks.

For sweeter muffins use 1¼ cups sugar.

Date Nut Muffins

400 degrees, preheated
Miniature muffin tins,
greased and floured
Yield: 36 muffins

¾ cup sugar
1   8-ounce package dates,
    chopped
1   cup chopped pecans
2   heaping Tablespoons
    flour
3   eggs, slightly beaten
1   teaspoon vanilla

In a medium bowl, mix all the ingredients. Bake in greased and floured miniature muffin tins for 15 minutes.

Optional topping:
1   Tablespoon lemon juice
1   cup sifted powdered sugar

Optional Topping:
Combine lemon juice and powdered sugar. Spread on muffins immediately upon removal from oven.

Quick Parmesan Muffins

400 degrees, preheated
Muffin tins, greased or
8-inch cake pan, greased
Yield: 12 muffins

2   cups biscuit mix
½   teaspoon oregano
¼   cup butter, melted
½   cup Chablis, or other light
    white wine
1   egg
¼   cup milk
¼   cup Parmesan cheese
Parmesan to sprinkle

Combine ingredients and mix well. Drop by spoon into 12 greased muffin cups or bake in a greased 8-inch round cake pan. Sprinkle with Parmesan cheese. Bake for 20 to 25 minutes or until lightly browned. Serve hot with butter.

Apple-Cornbread Dressing

325 degrees, preheated
1½-quart baking dish
Yield: 6 servings

¾   cup chopped onion
½   cup chopped celery
3   Tablespoons butter
2   cups unpeeled chopped
    apple
¼   cup chopped parsley
½   cup herb dressing mix
1 to 2 cups crumbled stale
    cornbread
1   teaspoon salt
1   teaspoon thyme leaves
½   teaspoon sage
¼   teaspoon black pepper
½   cup hot water or chicken
    broth

Sauté onion and celery in butter. Stir in the remaining ingredients and toss with the hot water. Bake in a 1½-quart baking dish for 25 to 30 minutes. Serve with chicken or pork. Will stuff an 8-pound turkey.

Scones

400 degrees, preheated
Cookie sheet, floured
Yield: 4 to 5 dozen

4   cups flour
1   teaspoon salt
6   teaspoons baking powder
¾   cup sugar
½   cup margarine
1   cup currants
1   egg, beaten
¼ to ½ cup milk
Milk

Cut the dry ingredients into the margarine until the mixture resembles coarse meal. Add the currants. Make a well in the center of the mixture and add the egg and enough milk so that dough is spongy. Turn onto a floured surface and knead lightly. Roll out to a 1-inch thickness and cut in rounds. Brush tops with milk. Bake for 10 to 12 minutes.

Louisiana Banana Toast

Yield: 4 to 5 servings

2   small over-ripe bananas
2   eggs
1   teaspoon vanilla
3   Tablespoons sugar
⅓   cup milk
4 to 5 bread slices
Butter (not margarine or oil)
   for frying

Mash bananas in flat pan; mix well with eggs, vanilla and sugar. Add milk and mix. Dip both sides of bread slices in mixture and fry slowly in butter. Serve at breakfast.

Southern Hushpuppy Olympics

This section of *According to Taste* salutes the annual Southern Hushpuppy Olympics.

Begun in 1972 by the Angelina County Chamber of Commerce and the City of Lufkin, the Olympics spotlights hushpuppy chefs from across the country who compete in a Championship Cook-off to determine the best hushpuppy in the South, and perhaps in the world. Part of a two-day event called the Forest Festival, the Olympics boosts tourism in Lufkin and raises funds which are divided among local charitable organizations, including the Museum of East Texas.

The winning recipes from the first thirteen years of the Southern Hushpuppy Olympics are featured in the following pages. We hope the recipes inspire you to, in the words of one of the winners, "cook some prizewinners"!

1972 Winner

Cecil Davis
Wichita Falls, Texas

1   cup flour
1   cup yellow cornmeal
1½   Tablespoons baking
     powder
1   Tablespoon salt
1   well-beaten egg
¾   cup milk
4   small chopped jalapeño
     peppers with seeds
4   Tablespoons chili meat
½   cup chopped onions
Several chopped boiled shrimp

Mix dry ingredients, add liquid, then seasonings. Mix well. Drop from Tablespoon into hot fat (about 350 degrees) and fry until golden brown. (Davis dries his own chili meat and since this item may be difficult to secure, you may substitute dried bacon bits or crisp beef crumbles.)

1973-1974 Winner

Virgil Tullos
Longview, Texas

Slightly less than 2 cups of
     cornmeal
2   Tablespoons flour
4   teaspoons baking powder
1   teaspoon salt
½   teaspoon baking soda
1   slightly beaten egg
1   cup buttermilk
¼   cup finely chopped young
     onion blades
1   finely chopped clove garlic
1   finely chopped jalapeño
     pepper

Drop 1 Tablespoon of flour in each cup of meal to fill the cup. Mix meal and flour well. Mix in other dry ingredients, add liquids, and then pour in seasonings. Whip batter well. Drop from Tablespoon into hot grease and fry until golden brown.

1975 Winner

Parker Folse's
"Pretzel Hushpuppies"

¾ cup yellow cornmeal
¼ cup flour
½ teaspoon salt
2 teaspoons baking powder
1 whole egg
1 cup milk
2 Tablespoons chopped green onion
2 Tablespoons chopped fresh parsley
1 clove chopped garlic
¼ teaspoon cayenne or red pepper
2 Tablespoons chopped pimiento
1 Tablespoon minced shrimp
1 Tablespoon minced crabmeat

Mix all ingredients thoroughly and place in a pastry bag filled with ⅜-inch star tube. Swirl batter onto surface of cooking oil heated to 360 degrees. Turn once and cook until slightly brown. Salt and serve.

1976 Winner

Parker Folse, Jr.
Dallas, Texas

1 packet Light Crust hushpuppy mix or other
1 egg
½ cup milk
¼ teaspoon cayenne or red pepper
¼ teaspoon jalapeño pepper
½ teaspoon chopped garlic
1 Tablespoon chopped parsley
1 Tablespoon chopped shrimp
1 Tablespoon cooked crabmeat
1 Tablespoon chopped green onion
½ teaspoon ground coriander

Blend all ingredients together and place into a pastry bag fitted with a large star tube. Heat cooking oil to 365 degrees and swirl batter onto the surface of hot oil. Cook until golden brown, turning once. Drain onto paper towels. Salt lightly and serve while hot.

1977 Winner

The Kadlecek Family
New Braunfels, Texas

¾ cup cornmeal
¼ cup flour
2 teaspoons baking powder
½ teaspoon salt
1 Tablespoon sugar
1 whole egg
2 Tablespoons chopped
   green onion
2 Tablespoons chopped
   fresh parsley
1 clove chopped garlic
6 Tablespoons pre-cooked
   New Braunfels Wurst
   (Sausage)
1 cup whole milk

Mix all ingredients together very thoroughly. Using a spoon or a cake decorator with a ½-inch diameter opening, put small bits of the batter into cooking oil heating to at least 350 degrees, but not more than 360 degrees. Turn until lightly browned on both sides.

1978, 1982 Winner

O.O. "Shotgun" Wright
Dallas, Texas

1 cup flour
1 cup yellow cornmeal
1 teaspoon baking powder
½ teaspoon salt
½ cup Trical flour
1 teaspoon hot pepper
1 teaspoon mild cherry
   pepper
1 teaspoon garlic
1 Tablespoon green onion
1 Tablespoon pimiento
   pepper
3 Tablespoons cream style
   corn
¼ cup sweet milk
2 eggs

Mix dry ingredients, add liquids, then seasonings and mix well. Heat grease to 365 degrees and cook some prizewinners.

1979 Winner

Parker Folse
Dallas, Texas

1 Package Light Crust or
   any other hushpuppy mix
1 egg
½ cup milk
½ teaspoon garlic powder
¼ teaspoon cayenne or red
   pepper
½ teaspoon coriander
½ teaspoon chili powder
1 heaping Tablespoon
   chopped parsley
1 heaping Tablespoon
   chopped green onion
1 heaping Tablespoon
   chopped fresh shrimp
1 heaping Tablespoon
   chopped lump crabmeat
1 heaping Tablespoon
   chopped fresh crawfish
   tails

Stir all ingredients together and place in a pastry bag fitted with a large star tube. Swirl onto cooking oil heated to 365 degrees. Turn once. Cook until golden. Remove and drain on paper towels. Salt to taste before serving. Makes 12 large hushpuppies. This recipe can be doubled.

1980 Winner

Parker Folse
Dallas, Texas

½ cup flour
½ cup cornmeal
1 teaspoon sugar
½ teaspoon garlic powder
½ teaspoon cayenne or red pepper
½ teaspoon coriander
½ teaspoon creole seasoning or chili powder
1 heaping Tablespoon chopped parsley
1 heaping Tablespoon chopped green onion
1 heaping Tablespoon chopped pimiento
1 heaping Tablespoon chopped boiled shrimp
1 heaping Tablespoon chopped lump crabmeat
1 heaping Tablespoon chopped fresh crayfish tails
1 egg
½ cup milk

Stir all ingredients together in a bowl adding enough milk to moisten batter. Place in pastry bag fitted with a large star-shaped tip and then swirl batter onto 365 degrees cooking oil. Turn hushpuppies once and cook until golden color. Remove, drain and salt to taste. The recipe, which can be doubled, makes 12 large hushpuppies.

1981 Winner

Linnette Scagliola and
Clarkie Brown
Lufkin, Texas

1 Tablespoon black pepper
2 Tablespoon onion
½ cup meal
3 Tablespoons flour
½ teaspoon salt
2 teaspoons baking powder
2 egg whites
Bacon chips to taste
Buttermilk (for right consistency)

Mix all ingredients together; drop by teaspoons into hot grease. Drain on paper towels.

1983 Winner

Boyd McGaugh
Meredian, Mississippi

2   cups white cornmeal mix
2   Tablespoons flour
3   eggs
Salt and black pepper to taste
1   bunch green onions
     (about 6 stalks), chopped
1   whole white onion,
     chopped
1   Tablespoon jalapeño
     peppers, chopped

Mix cornmeal, flour and eggs. Add onions and mix well with whole milk until tacky. Add jalapeño peppers. Heat Crisco shortening. Fry a few pieces of catfish in the shortening, then add the hushpuppy batter, using a round butter scoop for an even shape. Cook until golden brown.

1984 Winner

Jim Alexander and
David McNeese
Huntington, Texas

1   cup cornmeal
½   cup flour
1   teaspoon baking soda
1   Tablespoon baking
     powder
½   teaspoon creole seasoning
1   teaspoon chicken base
2   Tablespoons sugar
1½ teaspoons onion powder
1   teaspoon black pepper
1   teaspoon parsley
2   teaspoons garlic powder
1   egg
⅓   cup buttermilk

Combine all ingredients and mix well. Cook in boiling oil.

Desserts

Apple Cake

325 degrees, preheated
Tube pan or bundt pan,
greased and floured

Cake:
2 cups granulated sugar
1½ cups vegetable oil
2 Tablespoons vanilla
2 eggs, beaten
½ teaspoon lemon juice
3 cups flour
1¼ teaspoons baking soda
1 teaspoon salt
3 cups chopped apples
1½ cups chopped pecans,
toasted

Glaze:
1 cup granulated sugar
1 cup brown sugar
¼ cup margarine
1 teaspoon nutmeg
1 teaspoon cinnamon
1 teaspoon cream of tartar
½ cup milk

Cake:
In a mixing bowl, combine sugar, oil, vanilla, eggs and lemon juice. Sift together the flour, baking soda and salt. Add the dry ingredients to the batter. Fold in the chopped apples and chopped pecans. Pour batter into a greased and floured tube or bundt pan. Bake for 1 hour 30 minutes. Test for doneness with a toothpick.

Glaze:
In the top of a double boiler, combine sugars, margarine, spices and cream of tartar. Add the milk. Blend well and place over boiling water to cook. Stir constantly until the mixture is warm and the sugars dissolved. Pour over cooled cake.

Fresh Apple Raisin Cake

350 degrees, preheated
Tube pan, greased and floured

½ cup shortening or
   margarine
2 cups sugar
2 eggs
2 cups flour
2 teaspoons baking soda
1 teaspoon salt
2 teaspoons cinnamon
½ teaspoon nutmeg
4 cups chopped apples (use
   Winesaps or Jonathans)
1 cup chopped pecans
1 cup raisins

Hot Rum Sauce:
1 cup sugar
½ cup butter
¼ cup water
¼ cup dark rum

Cream the shortening and sugar together. Add the eggs one at a time, mixing well after each. Sift together the flour, soda, salt, cinnamon and nutmeg. Add the dry ingredients to the batter a little at a time, blending well. Fold in the chopped apples, pecans and raisins. Pour cake into a greased and floured tube pan and bake for 1 hour; or use a greased and floured 9 × 13 pan and bake for 45 minutes.

Variation:
The cake slices may be topped with the following hot rum sauce:

Hot Rum Sauce:
Combine all ingredients in a saucepan over medium heat for 2 minutes. Sauce may be served over individual slices or over the entire cake.

Banana Cake

350 degrees, preheated
2   8-inch cake pans,
greased and floured

Cake:
½   cup shortening
1½ cups granulated sugar
2   eggs
4   mashed bananas
2   cups flour
1   teaspoon baking soda
¼   teaspoon salt
4   Tablespoons buttermilk
1   teaspoon vanilla
½   cup chopped nuts

Topping:
4   cups whipping cream
Powdered sugar to taste
3   bananas, sliced
½   cup chopped pecans

Cake:
In a mixing bowl, cream the shortening and sugar together. Add the eggs one at a time, beating well after each addition. Add mashed bananas. Sift together the flour, baking soda and salt. Add dry ingredients to the batter alternately with the buttermilk. Beat well. Stir in vanilla and nuts. Pour the batter into 2 greased and floured 8-inch cake pans. Bake for 25 to 30 minutes. Cool.

Topping:
In a mixing bowl, beat the whipping cream until stiff peaks form. Beat in powdered sugar to sweeten according to taste. Cover 1 cake layer with sliced bananas and spread whipped cream evenly over the bananas. Add the other cake layer, cover it with sliced bananas and top with the rest of the whipped cream. Do not ice the sides of the cake. Sprinkle on chopped nuts.

Must be refrigerated

Cherry Nut Cake

350 degrees, preheated
3   8-inch cake pans,
greased and floured

Cake:
1   cup butter, softened
2   cups sugar
3   eggs, separated
1   cup applesauce
1   10-ounce bottle cherries,
    chopped
3   cups flour
1   teaspoon baking powder
1   teaspoon cinnamon
½   teaspoon salt
1   teaspoon baking soda
1   cup buttermilk
1   cup chopped nuts

Filling:
1   cup butter, softened
2   cups sugar
½   cup flour
1   cup milk
1   8-ounce box dates
1   cup chopped nuts (may
    use pecans, walnuts or
    almonds)

Cake:
Cream butter and sugar together. Add the egg yolks, applesauce and cherries. Blend well. Sift together the flour, baking powder, cinnamon, salt and baking soda. Add the dry ingredients to the batter alternately with the buttermilk. Fold in the nuts. In a mixing bowl, beat the egg whites until stiff peaks form. Fold the egg whites into the batter until well blended. Pour the batter into 3 greased and floured 8-inch pans. Bake for 30 minutes.

Filling:
In a saucepan, combine butter, sugar and flour. Place over medium heat and stir constantly as butter melts. Add the milk and stir constantly until the mixture thickens. Remove from the heat and add the dates and nuts. When the mixture cools spread between the layers and on top of the cake.

Moss Rose Cake

350 degrees, preheated
2   8- or 9-inch cake
pans, greased and floured

Cake:
2   cups sugar
4   eggs
1   cup milk
½   teaspoon almond extract
2   cups flour
2   teaspoons baking powder
½   teaspoon salt

Icing:
1½ cups sugar
2   egg whites
⅓   cup water
Dash of salt
¼   teaspoon cream of tartar
1   teaspoon vanilla
¼   teaspoon almond extract

Topping
2   cups grated coconut
2   Tablespoons sugar
1   orange (pulp, juice and
    grated rind)

Cake:
In a mixing bowl, blend together the sugar and the eggs, breaking eggs one at a time into the sugar and mixing well after each. In a sauce pan, heat the milk to the point of boiling. Remove it from the heat, add almond extract and cool the mixture. Sift the flour, baking powder and salt together. Add the dry ingredients to the egg and sugar mixture. Add the warm milk slowly to the batter and beat well for 2 minutes. Pour the batter into 2 8- or 9-inch cake pans which are greased and floured. Bake for 25 minutes. When the cake is cool, prepare the icing.

Icing:
In the top of a double boiler (before placing it over the boiling water), blend together the sugar, egg whites, water, salt and cream of tartar. Beat well for 2 minutes. Place over the boiling water and continue beating the icing for 7 minutes at high speed of a mixer. Remove from the heat and blend in vanilla and almond extract. Spread the icing evenly over the cake and between the layers.

Topping:
In a mixing bowl, combine the coconut, sugar, orange juice, pulp and grated rind. The coconut and sugar should soak up all of the orange juice. Blend well. Use the topping on top of the cake after the icing has set or hardened.

Christmas Cranberry Coffee Cake

350 degrees, preheated
Bundt pan, greased and floured

Cake:
- ½ cup margarine
- 1 cup granulated sugar
- 2 eggs
- 1 teaspoon baking powder
- 1 teaspoon baking soda
- 2 cups flour
- ½ teaspoon salt
- 1 cup sour cream
- 1 teaspoon almond extract
- 1 16-ounce can whole cranberry sauce
- 1 cup chopped pecans

Topping:
- 1 cup powdered sugar
- 2 Tablespoons warm water
- 2 teaspoons almond extract

Cake:
Cream margarine and sugar. Add eggs. Add dry ingredients alternately with sour cream to creamed mixture. Stir in almond extract. Layer ½ the batter into greased and floured bundt pan; add ½ the cranberry sauce, spreading evenly. Repeat with remaining batter, then remaining cranberry sauce. Sprinkle with pecans. Bake for 55 minutes. Spread topping on while cake is warm.

Topping:
Mix topping ingredients together and spread on warm cake.

To freeze: wrap in foil without the topping. To thaw: let cake sit out overnight, then warm in oven without the topping. After cake is warm spread the topping.

Colonial Seed Cake

350 degrees, preheated
9 × 5 × 3 loaf pan,
greased and floured

- 1 2-ounce jar poppy seeds
- ¾ cup milk
- ¾ cup butter, softened
- 3 eggs, room temperature
- 1¼ cups granulated sugar
- 1 teaspoon vanilla
- 2 teaspoons baking powder
- 2 cups sifted flour

Powdered sugar (optional)

Combine poppy seeds and milk in a large bowl. Let sit for 3 to 4 hours. Add next 6 ingredients and mix well. Bake for 1 hour 15 minutes in a greased and floured 9 × 5 × 3 loaf pan. Cool on rack 5 minutes. Remove and dust with powdered sugar, if desired.

Grand Marnier Cake

350 degrees, preheated
9-inch tube pan,
greased and floured

Cake:
1   cup butter, softened
1   cup sugar
3   eggs, separated
2   cups flour
1   teaspoon baking powder
¼   teaspoon baking soda
¼   cup sour cream
½   cup walnuts, chopped
Zest of 2 oranges (orange part
    of the rind, grated)
1   teaspoon vanilla

Glaze:
¼   cup orange juice
    concentrate
⅓   cup Grand Marnier
½   cup sugar
¼   cup sliced almonds

Cake:
In a mixing bowl, beat butter slowly, adding sugar gradually. Add egg yolks one at a time beating well after each. Sift together the flour, baking powder and baking soda and add the dry ingredients to the batter alternately with the sour cream. Mix well. Add the walnuts, orange zest, and vanilla. In a mixing bowl, beat the egg whites until stiff peaks form. Fold the egg whites into the batter. Pour the batter into a greased and floured 9-inch tube pan. Bake for 45 minutes. Cool and remove the cake from the pan.

Glaze:
In a saucepan, heat orange juice concentrate, Grand Marnier and ½ cup sugar until sugar dissolves. Brush glaze over the cake (the quantity is generous but use it all) and decorate with almonds.

Japanese Fruit Cake

350 degrees, preheated
3   8-inch cake pans,
greased and floured

Cake:
½   cup butter
2   cups sugar
5   eggs
3   cups flour
2   teaspoons baking powder
1   teaspoon cinnamon
1   teaspoon allspice
1   teaspoon nutmeg
1   cup milk
1   teaspoon vanilla
1   cup chopped pecans

Filling:
Boiling water
Juice and grated rind of 1
    orange
Juice and grated rind of 1
    lemon
5   Tablespoons flour
2   cups sugar
1   20-ounce can crushed
    pineapple
2   3½-ounce cans coconut

Cake:
In a mixing bowl, cream together the butter and sugar. Add the eggs one at a time, mixing well after each addition. Sift together the flour, baking powder, cinnamon, allspice and nutmeg. Add the dry ingredients to the batter alternately with the milk. Blend well. Add the vanilla and chopped pecans. Pour the batter into 3 greased and floured 8-inch pans. Bake for 20 to 25 minutes.

Filling:
In a saucepan, combine the juice of 1 orange, juice of 1 lemon, the juice drained from the crushed pineapple and enough boiling water to total 2 cups of liquid. Add the lemon rind and orange rind, flour and sugar. Bring the mixture to a boil and continue cooking until the temperature on a candy thermometer reaches 218 degrees. Add crushed pineapple and coconut and cook until it coats a metal spoon. Divide the filling between the layers and on top of the cake. Do not ice the sides of the cake.

Finest Cheesecake

Advance Preparation
Time Required
350 degrees, preheated
9 × 3 spring form pan, buttered

Crust:
1½ cups graham cracker
    crumbs
3   Tablespoons granulated
    sugar
½   teaspoon cinnamon
¼   cup butter, melted

Filling:
3   8-ounce packages cream
    cheese, at room
    temperature
1¼ cups granulated sugar
6   eggs, separated
2   cups sour cream
⅓   cup flour
2   teaspoons vanilla
Grated rind of 1 lemon
Juice of ½ lemon
½   cup powdered sugar,
    sifted

Crust:
Place a spring form pan greased with butter in the center of a 12-inch square of aluminum foil. Press the foil up around the sides of the pan. In a mixing bowl, combine graham cracker crumbs, sugar, cinnamon and melted butter. Blend well. Press ¾ of the mixture into the bottom and sides of the pan. Reserve remaining crumb mixture for topping. Chill the prepared pan while you make the filling.

Filling:
In a large mixing bowl, beat the softened cream cheese until it is light and fluffy. Gradually beat in the 1¼ cups of sugar. Beat in the egg yolks, one at a time. Stir in the sour cream, flour, vanilla, lemon rind and lemon juice until the mixture is smooth. In a mixing bowl, beat the egg whites until stiff peaks form. Fold the egg whites into the batter until it is well blended. Pour the batter into the prepared pan. Bake for 1 hour 15 minutes or until the top is golden brown. Turn off the heat and allow the cake to cool in the oven for 1 hour. Remove the cake from the oven and cool to room temperature. Sprinkle reserved crumbs on top and chill overnight. Dust the cake with powdered sugar before serving.

Cream Cheese Cake

300 degrees, preheated
10-inch tube pan,
greased and floured

Cake:
3   cups flour
2   cups granulated sugar
1   teaspoon baking soda
1   teaspoon salt
1   teaspoon ground cloves
3   eggs, beaten
1¼ cups vegetable oil
1   teaspoon almond extract
1   8-ounce can crushed
    pineapple, undrained
1   cup chopped toasted
    almonds
2   cups mashed bananas

Cream Cheese Icing:
½   cup butter, softened
1   8-ounce package cream
    cheese, softened
1   16-ounce package
    powdered sugar
1   Tablespoon instant tea

Cake:
Combine first 5 ingredients in a large mixing bowl; add eggs and oil, stirring until dry ingredients are moistened. Do not beat. Stir in almond extract, pineapple, almonds and bananas. Bake for 1 hour 15 minutes in a greased and floured 10-inch tube pan. Cool completely before icing.

Icing:
Cream butter and cream cheese. Gradually add sugar and tea, beating until light and fluffy.

Butter Cake

350 degrees, preheated
9-inch square pan, greased

1½ cups butter, softened
1½ cups sugar
1   egg
3   cups flour, sifted
1½ teaspoons vanilla

Cream together the butter, sugar and egg. Add the flour and vanilla, mixing until well blended. The dough will be stiff. Pour the dough into a greased 9-inch square pan. Bake for 45 minutes. Cool slightly and cut into squares.

Gingerbread

325 degrees, preheated
9 × 13 pan, buttered
Yield: 12 to 15 servings

Gingerbread:
1   cup boiling liquid (may
    use: water, coffee or fruit
    juice such as pineapple,
    orange or lemon - see
    note)
1   cup butter
1   cup white or brown sugar
1   cup dark unsulfured
    molasses, maple syrup,
    honey, or ribbon cane
    syrup (for an East Texas
    flavor)
3 or 4 large eggs
2½ cups flour
1   teaspoon salt
1½ teaspoons baking soda
1   teaspoon cinnamon
1   teaspoon ginger
1   teaspoon allspice
1   teaspoon cocoa (optional)

Sauce:
3   cups milk
2   eggs, separated
1½ cups sugar
¼   teaspoon salt
3   Tablespoons flour
2   Tablespoons butter
½   teaspoon vanilla

Gingerbread:
In a large mixing bowl, pour boiling liquid over
butter, sugar and syrup. Stir until butter is
melted. Cool slightly. Add eggs and beat well.
Sift together dry ingredients and stir into sugar
mixture. Beat until smooth. Pour into buttered
9 × 13 pan and bake 1 hour or until done.

Sauce:
Put milk in a saucepan. Add beaten egg yolks.
Combine the dry ingredients and add to the milk
mixture slowly. Cook over low heat, stirring
constantly, until the mixture thickens. Remove
from the heat and add butter and vanilla. In a
mixing bowl, beat the egg whites to a heavy
froth. Fold egg whites into the hot sauce. (It will
look lumpy.) Serve over warm gingerbread.

Note: If fruit juice is used, add 1 cup moist fine
coconut when adding dry ingredients.

Variation-Gingerbread Muffins:
Substitute 1 cup sour cream or buttermilk for the
boiling liquid. Prepare according to previous
directions. ½ cup raisins and/or ½ cup chopped
pecans may be added. Bake in greased muffin tins
at 350 degrees for 12 to 15 minutes. Yield: 36
servings.

7 Minute Icing

Double boiler
Yield: icing for 2 layer cake

2   egg whites
1½ cups sugar
¼   teaspoon cream of tartar
⅓   cup water
¼   teaspoon salt
1   teaspoon vanilla

In the top of a double boiler, before placing it over the heat, blend together the egg whites, sugar, cream of tartar, water and salt. Beat the mixture for 2 minutes. Place over boiling water and continue beating for 7 minutes more. Remove from the heat and add vanilla. Beat the mixture for 1 minute more.

Grandmother's Chocolate Cake

350 degrees, preheated
3 9-inch cake pans,
greased and lined with wax paper

Cake:
¾   cup butter, softened
2   cups granulated sugar, divided
4   eggs, separated
4   teaspoons vanilla
¾   cup cocoa
1¾ cups flour
1   teaspoon salt
1   cup strong coffee at room temperature
1   teaspoon baking soda dissolved in 2 Tablespoons water

Cake:
Cream butter with 1½ cups sugar (reserve ½ cup for later use). Add egg yolks one at a time, beating well after each addition. Stir in vanilla. Combine cocoa, flour and salt. Add these dry ingredients to the batter alternately with the coffee. Mix well. Add the baking soda mixture. In another bowl, beat the egg whites until stiff peaks form. Continue beating and add the reserved ½ cup of sugar. Fold the egg whites into the batter. Pour the batter into 3 9-inch cake pans which are greased and lined with wax paper. Bake for 20 to 25 minutes.

Icing:
1   cup butter, softened
5   Tablespoons cocoa
2   pounds powdered sugar, sifted
Cool, strong coffee to moisten
2   teaspoons vanilla

Icing:
Cream the butter. Blend in the cocoa. Gradually beat in the powdered sugar alternately with enough cool coffee to moisten. Add vanilla. Mix well. Be sure the cake is completely cooled before you ice it.

Old Fashioned Devil's Food Cake

350 degrees, preheated
3   8-inch cake pans,
greased and floured

Cake:
1   cup shortening
2   cups sugar
2   eggs
3½ cups sifted flour
½   cup cocoa
½   teaspoon cloves
1   teaspoon cinnamon
1   teaspoon allspice
1   cup buttermilk
1   cup boiling water
1   teaspoon baking soda

Cake:
Cream shortening and sugar together. Add eggs one at a time, beating well after each addition. Sift together the flour, cocoa, cloves, cinnamon and allspice. Add the dry ingredients to the batter alternately with the buttermilk. Blend well. Combine boiling water and baking soda and add to the batter. Pour batter into 3 greased and floured 8-inch cake pans. Bake for 20 to 25 minutes.

Icing:
1½ cups sugar
3   Tablespoons cold water
2   egg whites
1   teaspoon vanilla

Icing:
Combine all the ingredients except vanilla in the top of a double boiler. Place over boiling water and beat rapidly for 7 minutes. Remove from the heat and continue beating as vanilla is added. Spread evenly between cake layers and over the cake.

Fudge Cupcakes

350 degrees, preheated
2   12-cup muffin tins, greased
Yield: 24 cupcakes

4   eggs, beaten
2   cups sugar
1½ cups flour
2   squares semi-sweet
     chocolate
1   cup butter
2   teaspoons vanilla
Chocolate chips
Chopped pecans (optional)

In a large mixing bowl, mix eggs and sugar. Add flour and mix well. In a small saucepan, melt chocolate squares and butter over low heat. Add chocolate mixture to egg mixture. Stir in 2 teaspoons vanilla. Pour into greased muffin tins and top with chocolate chips and pecans. Bake for 20 to 25 minutes.

Special Chocolate Cake

350 degrees, preheated
2 8-inch cake pans,
greased and floured
Yield: 1 cake

Cake:
¼ pound butter
1 pound dark brown sugar
1 teaspoon vanilla
1 teaspoon salt
2 eggs
2 squares unsweetened
   chocolate, melted
2½ cups flour
½ cup buttermilk
1 teaspoon baking soda
1 cup warm water

Icing:
1½ cups granulated sugar
1 cup water
1 pound milk chocolate,
   softened
2 Tablespoons butter,
   softened
1 Tablespoon vanilla
3 Tablespoons evaporated
   milk

Cake:
In a mixing bowl, cream together the butter, brown sugar, vanilla and salt. Add the eggs and blend until smooth. Add the melted chocolate and blend again. Sift the flour and add it to the batter alternately with the buttermilk. Dissolve the soda in water and add it to the batter. Beat until smooth. Pour batter into 2 greased and floured 8-inch cake pans. Bake for 30 minutes.

Icing:
In a saucepan, bring sugar and water to a boil and cook to a thin syrup (230 degrees on a candy thermometer). In a mixing bowl, blend together the softened chocolate and margarine. Pour in the hot syrup and beat well until the icing is smooth and syrupy. Add vanilla and evaporated milk and beat again. Allow the icing to cool. If the icing becomes too stiff when it is cool, add a little more milk. Spread evenly between the 2 layers and on the cake.

Sour Cream Pound Cake

350 degrees, preheated
Bundt or tube pan,
greased and floured

1   cup butter, softened
2¾ cups granulated sugar
6   eggs, separated
¼   teaspoon baking soda
½   teaspoon salt
3   cups sifted flour
1   cup sour cream
Powdered sugar for topping
     (optional)

Cream together the butter and sugar. Add the egg yolks, one at a time, mixing well after each. Sift together the soda, salt and flour and add to the batter alternately with sour cream. Mix well. In a mixing bowl, beat the egg whites until stiff peaks form. Fold the beaten whites into the batter. Pour mixture into a greased and floured tube or bundt pan. Bake for 1 hour 15 minutes or until straw inserted into the cake comes out clean. When the cake cools, it may be topped with powdered sugar.

Spice Crumb Cake

350 degrees, preheated
9 × 13 pan, greased and floured

Cake:
2   cups flour
1   cup granulated sugar
1   teaspoon baking soda
1½ teaspoons cinnamon
1   teaspoon cloves
¼   teaspoon allspice
¼   teaspoon salt
½   cup shortening
1   cup buttermilk
1   egg
2   Tablespoons dark
     unsulphured molasses

Topping:
2   Tablespoons butter,
     melted
1   Tablespoon flour
4   Tablespoons powdered
     sugar
¼   teaspoon cinnamon

Cake:
Sift flour, sugar, baking soda and spices into a mixing bowl. Cut in shortening until it is well blended. Add buttermilk and egg to the mixture. Blend well and add molasses. Beat the mixture until it is smooth. Pour into a well greased 9 × 13 pan.

Topping:
In a mixing bowl, blend the topping ingredients together. Crumble onto the top of the cake. Bake for 30 to 40 minutes.

Sugar and Spice Cake

350 degrees, preheated
9 × 9 × 2 pan, greased and floured
Yield: 9 squares

Cake:
¼   cup granulated sugar
2   teaspoons cinnamon
3   Tablespoons water
3   Tablespoons shortening
⅓   cup granulated sugar
2   eggs, separated
⅔   cup milk
1   teaspoon vanilla
1¾ cups flour
2   teaspoons baking powder
½   teaspoon salt

Cake:
In a saucepan, combine ¼ cup sugar, cinnamon and water. Bring to a boil to dissolve the sugar to a syrup. Remove from heat and set aside. In a mixing bowl, cream together the shortening, ⅓ cup sugar and egg yolks. Beat well until mixture is fluffy. Combine milk and vanilla and add to the batter alternately with flour, baking powder and salt which should be sifted together. Mix well. In a mixing bowl, beat the 2 egg whites until stiff peaks form. Fold the egg whites into the batter. Pour the mixture into a greased and floured 9 × 9 × 2 pan. Drizzle the cinnamon syrup over the batter and swirl through the batter with a knife. Bake for 40 minutes. Serve with cinnamon topping.

Topping:
¾   cup whipping cream
3   Tablespoons powdered
     sugar
½   teaspoon vanilla
¼   teaspoon cinnamon

Topping:
In a mixing bowl, whip the cream until it is thick. Beat in powdered sugar, vanilla and cinnamon. Use mixture to top cake squares.

Vanilla Wafer Cake

275 degrees, preheated
Tube pan, greased and floured

1   12-ounce box of vanilla
     wafers
1   cup butter, softened
2   cups sugar
6   eggs
½   cup milk
1   7-ounce package coconut
1   cup chopped nuts

Crush the vanilla wafers with a rolling pin and set them aside. In a mixing bowl, cream butter and sugar together. Add the eggs one at a time, beating well after each. Add the crushed vanilla wafers alternately with the milk. Stir in the coconut and pecans and mix the batter well. Pour the batter into a greased and floured tube pan. Bake for 1 hour 15 minutes.

Lemon Buttermilk Pound Cake

300 degrees, preheated
Tube pan, greased and floured

Cake:
½   cup butter, softened
1   cup shortening
2½ cups sugar
4   eggs
1   Tablespoon lemon extract
1   teaspoon butter flavoring
1   Tablespoon boiling water
3½ cups flour
½   teaspoon baking soda
1   cup buttermilk
1   cup finely chopped pecans
(optional)

Cake:
Cream together the butter, shortening and sugar. Add the eggs one at a time, mixing well after each. Add the flavorings and water to the batter. Sift the flour and baking soda together and add to the batter alternately with the buttermilk. Add optional pecans. Blend well. Pour into a greased and floured tube pan. Bake for 1 hour 15 minutes. While still hot, brush with glaze.

Glaze:
Juice of 2 lemons
½   cup sugar
½   teaspoon lemon extract

Glaze:
In a saucepan, over medium heat bring the lemon juice and sugar to a boil until the sugar dissolves. Remove from the heat and add lemon extract.

Pound Cake

325 degrees, preheated
Large tube pan, greased and floured

2   cups butter, softened
3   cups sugar
9   eggs
1   teaspoon baking powder
Dash of salt
4½ cups flour
1   cup milk
Juice of 1 lemon
1   teaspoon vanilla

In a mixing bowl, cream together the butter and sugar. Add eggs one at a time, beating well after each addition. Sift the baking powder, salt and flour together and add to the batter alternately with the milk, blending well. Add lemon juice and vanilla. Pour batter into a greased and floured tube pan. Bake for 1 hour 15 minutes or until a straw inserted in the cake comes out clean.

Brown Sugar Pound Cake

325 degrees, preheated
Tube pan, greased and floured

1½ cups butter, softened
2¼ cups packed dark brown
    sugar
6   eggs
5   teaspoons vanilla
1½ teaspoons lemon juice
2½ cups sifted flour
Powdered sugar for topping
    (optional)

Variation:
½   cup butter
2   cups light brown sugar
2   teaspoons vanilla
3 to 4 Tablespoons hot tap
    water

In a mixing bowl, beat butter until it is creamy and fluffy. Add the brown sugar a few Tablespoons at a time, beating constantly. Beat in eggs one at a time and continue beating about 5 minutes, until the batter is light and fluffy. Add vanilla and lemon juice. Gradually blend in flour. When well mixed, pour into a greased and floured tube pan. Bake 1 hour 20 minutes. When the cake cools, the top may be dusted with powdered sugar.

Variation:
Rather than topping with powdered sugar, this glaze may be substituted. In a saucepan over medium heat, brown the butter. Remove from the heat and stir in brown sugar and vanilla. Use enough hot tap water to bring the glaze to a spreading consistency. Pour over a warm cake.

Coconut Pound Cake

350 degrees, preheated
Tube pan, greased and floured

Cake:
1   cup shortening
2   cups sugar
5   eggs
2   cups flour
1½ teaspoons baking powder
Pinch of salt
½   cup milk
1   teaspoon coconut
    flavoring
1   cup coconut

Glaze:
1   cup sugar
½   cup water
1   teaspoon coconut
    flavoring
2   Tablespoons coconut for
    topping (optional)

Cake:
Cream together the shortening and sugar. Add the eggs one at a time, mixing well after each. Sift together the flour, baking powder and salt. Add dry ingredients to the batter alternately with the milk. Add coconut flavoring and mix well. Fold in the coconut. Pour the batter into a greased and floured tube pan. Bake for 45 minutes. Spread glaze over the warm cake.

Glaze:
In a saucepan, bring water and sugar to a boil and cook until sugar dissolves. Remove from the heat and add coconut flavoring. Pour over warm cake. Coconut may be sprinkled over the top.

Cream Cheese Pound Cake

Do Not Preheat Oven
10-inch bundt pan,
greased and floured

1   cup butter, softened
1   8-ounce package cream
    cheese, softened
3   cups sugar
6   eggs
3   cups sifted cake flour
2   teaspoons vanilla

Combine butter and cream cheese. Gradually add sugar and continue beating until light and fluffy. Add eggs, one at a time, beating well after each addition. Mix in flour, 1 cup at a time; then add vanilla. Place in a COLD oven and bake at 325 degrees for 1 hour 20 minutes in a greased and floured 10-inch bundt pan. Cool cake 15 to 20 minutes before removing from pan.

Fried Apple Pie

Yield: approximately 16 fried pies

Filling:
1   6 or 8-ounce package
    dried apples
2   cups water
½   cup sugar
2   Tablespoons butter
½   teaspoon cinnamon

Pastry:
2   cups flour
2½   teaspoons baking powder
1   teaspoon salt
4   Tablespoons shortening
⅔   cup milk

Filling:
Chop apples; place in medium saucepan with water. Bring to a boil. Lower heat and simmer, stirring occasionally, until liquid is almost absorbed. Stir in sugar, butter and cinnamon. Cook until apples are tender. Cool.

Pastry:
Mix flour, baking powder and salt in a large bowl. Cut in shortening, then mix in milk. Roll the dough into ½-inch balls and place them on a floured surface. Roll out each to about ¼-inch thickness. If the dough is sticky, sprinkle with flour. Place a rounded Tablespoon of apples in each pie. Fold the pastry over and press the edges down with a fork. Fry in hot oil until browned. Serve hot.

Derby Pie

325 degrees, preheated
9-inch pie pan

½   cup flour
1   cup sugar
2   eggs, slightly beaten
½   cup butter, melted and
    cooled
1   cup semi-sweet chocolate
    chips
1   cup pecans, crushed or
    very finely chopped
1   teaspoon vanilla
1   9-inch unbaked pie shell

Mix flour and sugar, add eggs and beat well. Add butter and mix. Add chocolate chips, nuts and vanilla. Pour into pie shell. Bake 1 hour.

Buttermilk Pie

350 degrees, preheated
9-inch pie pan

½   cup butter
1⅔ to 2 cups sugar
3   eggs
2   rounded teaspoons flour
1   cup buttermilk
1   teaspoon vanilla
½   teaspoon nutmeg
1   9-inch unbaked pie shell

Cream butter and sugar. Add eggs and flour. Beat well. Add buttermilk, vanilla and nutmeg. Pour into pie shell. Bake for approximately 45 minutes.

Sugar amount may be varied according to the sweetness desired in the pie.

Favorite Coconut Chess Pie

450 degrees, preheated
9-inch pie pan

4   Tablespoons flour
1½ cups sugar
2   eggs, beaten
2   teaspoons vanilla
½   cup butter, melted
1   cup flaked coconut
1   cup milk
1   9-inch unbaked pie shell

Mix flour and sugar; add beaten eggs. Stir in vanilla. Add melted butter. Fold in coconut. Add milk and mix well. Pour into pie shell. Bake for 10 minutes; reduce heat to 350 degrees and bake for 30 to 40 additional minutes or until a wooden pick inserted near the center comes out clean.

Fudge Pie

350 degrees, preheated
9-inch pie pan, greased and floured

2   eggs
1   cup sugar
2   heaping Tablespoons
    flour
½   cup butter, melted
⅔   bar German's Sweet
    Chocolate, melted
1   cup chopped nuts
1   teaspoon vanilla
Whipped cream (optional)

Mix eggs, sugar and flour together. Beat for 3 minutes. Add butter and chocolate, then nuts and vanilla. Pour into prepared pie pan. Bake for 30 minutes. Cool and top with whipped cream to serve.

Chocolate Angel Pie

300 degrees, preheated
9-inch pie pan, buttered

3   egg whites
⅛   teaspoon cream of tartar
¼   teaspoon salt
¼   cup sifted granulated
     sugar
¾   cup finely chopped pecans
½   teaspoon vanilla
4   ounces German's Sweet
     Chocolate
3   Tablespoons strong black
     coffee
½   teaspoon vanilla
1   cup whipping cream,
     whipped

Beat egg whites until foamy. Add cream of tartar and salt. Beat until soft peaks form. Gradually add sugar, pecans and vanilla. Mold inside of pie pan to form a shell. Bake for 50 to 55 minutes. Cool. Over low heat, stir chocolate and coffee together in a small saucepan until melted and smooth. Cool. Stir in vanilla. Fold into whipped cream. Spread into meringue shell. Chill at least 2 hours.

Chocolate Fudge Pie

350 degrees, preheated
9-inch pie pan

½   cup butter
3   1-ounce squares
     unsweetened chocolate
1½ cups sugar
4   eggs
3   Tablespoons light corn
     syrup
¼   teaspoon salt
1   teaspoon vanilla
1   9-inch unbaked pie shell
1   quart vanilla or
     peppermint ice cream

In a saucepan, melt butter and chocolate together over very low heat. With mixer, beat in sugar, eggs, corn syrup, salt and vanilla until barely blended. Pour into pie shell. Bake 30 to 35 minutes. A knife inserted near the center should come out clean, but pie should not be completely firm. Do not overbake. Cool. Serve with ice cream.

Variation:
Add ½ cup flaked coconut and ½ cup chopped pecans to batter before pouring into pie shell. Bake as directed allowing about 5 extra minutes at end of cooking time.

Lemon Cheese Pie

9-inch pie

¾ cup sugar
3 Tablespoons cornstarch
1 cup water
1 teaspoon grated lemon
   peel
⅓ cup lemon juice
2 egg yolks, slightly beaten
3 ounces cream cheese,
   softened
1 9-inch baked pie shell
Whipped, sweetened cream

Combine the first 6 ingredients in a saucepan and beat with an electric mixer until well blended. Cook over medium heat until thick, stirring constantly. Remove from heat. Add cream cheese and stir until blended. Cool. Spoon into a pie shell and chill at least 2 hours. Top with whipped cream when serving.

Lemon Luscious Pie

9-inch pie

1 cup sugar
3 Tablespoons cornstarch
¼ cup butter, softened
1 Tablespoon grated lemon
   rind
¼ cup lemon juice
3 egg yolks, unbeaten
1 cup milk
1 cup sour cream
1 9-inch baked pie shell
1 cup whipping cream,
   whipped, sweetened and
   flavored (for topping)

Combine sugar and cornstarch in a saucepan. Add the butter, lemon rind, lemon juice and egg yolks. Stir in milk. Cook over medium heat until thick, stirring constantly. Cool. Fold in sour cream and pour into pie shell. Cover with whipped cream and chill several hours before serving.

Osgood Pie
9-inch pie pan

4   eggs, separated
2   cups sugar
1   teaspoon cinnamon
2   Tablespoons cornstarch
½   cup butter
1½   cups milk
1   cup chopped dates
1   cup raisins
1   cup chopped nuts
1   9-inch baked pie shell

Mix egg yolks, sugar, cinnamon, cornstarch, butter and milk in a saucepan. Add dates and raisins. Cook until thick, stirring often. Add nuts and cook a few minutes longer, then pour into a baked pie shell. Top with meringue.

See recipe entitled "Creamy Meringue" on page 229 for instructions and ingredients for meringue.

Peppermint Ice Cream Pie
400 degrees, preheated
(only to brown meringue)
9-inch pie pan

1   9-inch baked pie shell
1   pint pink peppermint ice
     cream

Spread peppermint ice cream in baked pie shell and freeze.

Chocolate filling:
2   Tablespoons butter
2   1-ounce squares
     unsweetened chocolate
1   cup sugar
1   5-ounce can evaporated
     milk
1   teaspoon vanilla

Chocolate filling:
Cook and stir butter, chocolate, sugar and milk until thickened. Remove from heat and add vanilla. Pour chocolate mixture over ice cream layer and freeze.

Meringue:
3   egg whites
6   Tablespoons sugar
½   teaspoon cream of tartar
3   Tablespoons crushed
     peppermint candy

Meringue:
Beat egg whites until foamy; gradually add sugar and cream of tartar and beat until stiff peaks form. Spread over frozen pie and top with crushed candy. Place in hot oven only until meringue is lightly brown. Serve immediately or return to freezer.

Pineapple-Coconut Pie

350 degrees, preheated
2   9-inch pie pans
Yield: 2   9-inch pies

2   cups sugar
2   Tablespoons flour
Pinch of salt
2   Tablespoons cornmeal
4   eggs, well beaten
½   cup butter, melted
1   8-ounce can crushed
    pineapple, drained
1   cup flaked coconut
2   9-inch unbaked pie shells
Melted butter

Mix sugar, flour, salt, cornmeal and eggs. Stir in melted butter, then add pineapple and coconut. Brush pie shells with melted butter. Pour coconut mixture into shells. Bake for 40 minutes.

Pumpkin Praline Pie

450 degrees, preheated
10-inch pie pan

Pie Shell:
1   10-inch baked pie shell
⅓   cup butter
⅓   cup brown sugar
⅓   cup chopped nuts

Filling:
¾   cup granulated sugar
1   envelope gelatin
1½ teaspoons pumpkin pie
    spice
¾   cup milk
½   teaspoon salt
4   egg yolks, reserve whites
1   16-ounce can pumpkin
½   cup granulated sugar
1   cup whipping cream,
    whipped and sweetened
Chopped nuts

Pie Shell:
Mix butter, brown sugar and nuts. Press on pastry shell. Bake for 5 to 10 minutes.

Filling:
Cook first 7 ingredients in a double boiler for 15 minutes. Chill until mixture begins to set. Beat egg whites until stiff. Add ½ cup sugar slowly. Beat chilled pumpkin mixture until light and fluffy. Fold egg whites and sugar into pumpkin. Fill pastry shell with mixture and top with whipped cream and nuts.

Sweet Potato Pie

325 degrees, preheated
9-inch pie pan

Filling:
3   medium sweet potatoes
Water to cover potatoes
½   cup butter
1½ cups sugar
1   5 (or 5.33)-ounce can
     evaporated milk
3   eggs
½   teaspoon nutmeg
½   teaspoon vanilla
1   9-inch unbaked pie shell

Filling:
Peel and cut up potatoes. Boil gently in water with a dash of salt until tender. Drain and mash potatoes; add butter, sugar, milk, eggs, nutmeg and vanilla. Mix well with an electric mixer on medium speed. Pour into unbaked pie shell and bake for 45 to 50 minutes.

Crust:
1½ cups flour
½   teaspoon baking powder
1   teaspoon salt
¾   cup shortening
1   egg, slightly beaten
2 to 4 Tablespoons cold water

Crust:
Sift flour, baking powder and salt together. Cut in shortening. Add egg and mix; then add water and mix. Roll out or press into 9-inch pie pan.

French Lemon Pie

325 degrees, preheated
9-inch pie pan

½   cup butter
1½ cups sugar
4   eggs, separated
Juice and grated rind of 1½
     lemons
1   9-inch unbaked pie shell

Cream butter, sugar, egg yolks, lemon juice and rind. Beat egg whites until stiff. Fold into butter mixture. Pour into pie shell and bake for 1 hour 30 minutes.

Easy Pie Crust

400 degrees, preheated
9-inch pie pan

1½ cups flour
1   teaspoon salt
3   Tablespoons milk
3   Tablespoons sugar
    (optional)
Scant ½ cup vegetable oil

Mix all ingredients. Roll into a ball and press into a pie pan. If baked without a filling, prick several times with a fork and bake until golden brown.

Fool Proof Crust

375 degrees, preheated
Yield: 3 single pie shells
or 2 double crusts

4   cups flour (not sifted, but
    lightly spooned into
    measuring cups)
1   Tablespoon sugar
2   teaspoons salt
1¾ cups shortening
½   cup water
1   Tablespoon vinegar
1   large egg

Mix flour, sugar and salt. Cut in shortening until mixture resembles cornmeal. Beat water, vinegar and egg together and add to flour mixture. Stir until well blended. Chill at least ½ hour before rolling. If baked before filling, prick several times with a fork before baking, then bake until lightly browned. The dough will keep a week in the refrigerator.

Perfect Pastry

425 degrees, preheated
Yield: 3 single pie shells
or 2 double shells

1   cup shortening
¼   cup butter
3   cups flour
1   teaspoon salt
1   teaspoon lemon juice
½   cup *cold* water

Cream the shortening and butter. Sift the flour and salt together. Cut the shortening into the dry ingredients with a pastry cutter until the mixture looks like fine crumbs. Mix the lemon juice with the water and stir into the dry mixture with a fork. The pastry will be a little sticky. Roll out. Bake for 8 to 12 minutes. After rolling out, the dough may be frozen.

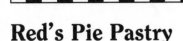

Red's Pie Pastry

375 degrees, preheated
2   9-inch pie pans
Yield: 2   9-inch pie shells

2   cups flour
2   Tablespoons powdered
    sugar
⅛   teaspoon salt
⅔   cup shortening
½   cup unwhipped whipping
    cream

Mix dry ingredients together. Cut shortening into dry ingredients until crumbly. Add whipping cream, a little at a time, until dough forms a ball. It is better not to use quite all the cream, but sometimes the entire ½ cup is needed. Shape into two balls. Wrap in wax paper and chill for several hours until ready to roll out. Bake until lightly brown.

Creamy Meringue

350 degrees, preheated
Yield: meringue for 1 9-inch pie

3   egg whites, at room
    temperature
Dash of cream of tartar
Dash of salt
1   7-ounce jar marshmallow
    cream
Dash of flavoring if desired
    (vanilla, lemon or almond
    extract for example)

Beat egg whites with cream of tartar and salt until soft peaks form. Beat in marshmallow cream gradually, beating until stiff peaks form. A dash of flavoring may be added to complement pie filling. Spread on top of desired pie filling. Bake for 10 to 15 minutes or until meringue is browned.

Marshmallow Brownies

350 degrees, preheated
9 × 13 baking pan,
greased and floured
Yield: 36 to 48

Brownies:
1   cup butter
½   cup cocoa
4   eggs
2   cups granulated sugar
1½ cups flour
½   teaspoon salt
1   teaspoon vanilla
1   cup chopped nuts
15 to 20 large marshmallows,
      cut in half

Icing:
½   cup butter
3   squares unsweetened
      chocolate
1   16-ounce box powdered
      sugar
⅓   cup milk, scalded and
      cooled
2   teaspoons vanilla

Brownies:
Melt butter and stir in cocoa. Cool. In a mixing bowl, beat eggs and slowly add sugar. Fold in flour and salt. Fold in cocoa mixture. Stir in vanilla and nuts. Pour onto a greased and floured 9 × 13 inch baking pan. Bake about 25 to 30 minutes. While hot, cover with marshmallows (cut side down). Bake for an additional 5 minutes. Cool and spread with icing. Refrigerate and cut into squares when ready to serve.

Icing:
Melt butter and chocolate. Add remaining ingredients and mix well. Pour onto brownies.

Butter Cookies

Advance Preparation
Time Required
350 degrees, preheated
Cookie sheet, ungreased
Yield: 60 to 72

2   cups butter
½   cup sugar
2   Tablespoons whiskey
½   teaspoon almond extract
4   cups flour

In a mixing bowl, cream butter and sugar. Add whiskey and almond extract and mix well. Stir in the flour. Chill for several hours then roll out dough to ¼-inch thickness and cut into desired shapes. Bake on a cookie sheet to a light brown, about 10 minutes.

Fudge Squares

350 degrees, preheated
12 × 14 pan, greased and floured
Yield: 24 servings

Squares:
¾ cup butter
1 6-ounce package chocolate chips
2 cups sugar
1½ cups flour
¼ teaspoon salt
4 eggs
1 teaspoon vanilla
1 cup chopped pecans

Icing:
½ cup butter
1 1-ounce square unsweetened chocolate
1 teaspoon vanilla
1 16-ounce box powdered sugar
Evaporated milk (enough to make icing spread easily)

Squares:
Melt butter and chocolate chips in a saucepan. Mix sugar, flour, salt, eggs and vanilla. Add butter mixture, chocolate mixture and pecans. Bake in prepared pan for 15 to 20 minutes.

Icing:
Melt butter and chocolate square. Add remaining ingredients and ice fudge squares while still hot.

Very Best Sugar Cookies

350 degrees, preheated
Cookie sheet, ungreased
Yield: 24 to 36 cookies

1 cup margarine
2 cups sugar
3 egg yolks
1 teaspoon vanilla
2½ cups flour
1 teaspoon baking soda
1 teaspoon cream of tartar
¼ teaspoon salt

Mix all ingredients until thoroughly blended. Roll into 1-inch balls and bake on ungreased cookie sheet for 8 minutes.

Double Fudge Brownies

350 degrees, preheated
12 × 8 pan, greased lightly
Yield: 25 to 30 small servings

Duncan Hines Brownie
    Mix—Family Size
½ cup butter, softened
3 Tablespoons milk
2 Tablespoons instant
    vanilla pudding (dry)
2 cups powdered sugar
1 cup granulated sugar
¼ cup cocoa
¼ cup milk
½ cup butter

Prepare the brownies according to package directions for the chewy style. Let cool. Mix ½ cup butter, 3 Tablespoons milk, vanilla pudding and powdered sugar. Spread over the cooled brownies. Refrigerate for at least 1 hour. Combine granulated sugar, cocoa and remaining milk and butter in a saucepan. Let mixture boil until it thickens like fudge. Pour over second layer and chill.

Gumdrop Cookie Bars

325 degrees, preheated
15 × 10 jelly roll pan,
greased and floured
Yield: 48 bars

Bars:
2 cups flour
3 eggs
1 cup dark brown sugar
1 cup granulated sugar
2 Tablespoons cold water
½ teaspoon salt
1 teaspoon cinnamon
1½ cups gumdrops or orange
    slices, chopped
1½ cups chopped pecans

Bars:
Mix first 7 ingredients together well. Stir in gumdrops and pecans. Spread in a greased and floured jelly roll pan. Bake for 30 minutes. Cut into bars to serve.

Icing:
3 Tablespoons butter
2 Tablespoons orange juice
1 cup sifted powdered sugar

Icing:
Mix all ingredients together. Spread on bars while warm.

Glazed Cinnamon Squares

325 degrees, preheated
15 × 10 × 1 cookie sheet, greased
Yield: 48 squares

Squares:
1 cup granulated sugar
¾ cup vegetable oil
¼ cup honey
1 egg
2 cups flour
¼ teaspoon salt
1 teaspoon baking soda
1 teaspoon cinnamon
1 cup chopped pecans

Squares:
Combine sugar, oil and honey; mix well. Add remaining ingredients. Spread mixture into a greased 15 × 10 × 1 cookie sheet. Bake for 20 to 30 minutes.

Glaze:
1 cup powdered sugar
½ teaspoon vanilla
1 Tablespoon water
2 Tablespoons salad dressing

Glaze:
Combine all ingredients and mix well. Pour onto squares while they are still hot.

Cinnamon Pecan Crisps

275 degrees, preheated
15 × 10 jelly roll pan, greased
Yield: 48 squares

1 cup butter
1 cup sugar
1 egg, separated
1 teaspoon cinnamon
1 teaspoon vanilla
2 cups flour
1 Tablespoon sugar
1 cup finely chopped pecans

In a mixing bowl, cream butter and 1 cup sugar together. Add egg yolk, cinnamon, vanilla and flour and blend well. Pour mixture into jelly roll pan and spread evenly over pan. Whip the egg white in a mixing bowl with 1 Tablespoon sugar. Brush egg white mixture over the top of the dough and sprinkle with chopped pecans. Pat the pecans down into the dough. Bake for 1 hour. Cut into squares while still hot.

Pecan Fingers

350 degrees, preheated
9 × 13 pan, ungreased
Yield: 36 bars

¾   cup shortening (half
    butter, half shortening, if
    desired)
¾   cup powdered sugar
1½ cups flour
2   eggs
1   cup brown sugar
2   Tablespoons flour
½   teaspoon baking powder
½   teaspoon salt
½   teaspoon vanilla
1   cup chopped pecans

Cream shortening and powdered sugar. Blend in flour. Press in baking pan and bake for 12 to 15 minutes. Mix remaining ingredients. Spread over hot baked layer and bake 20 minutes longer. Cool and cut into bars.

Ginger Cookies

350 degrees, preheated
Cookie sheet, greased
Yield: 24 to 36 cookies

¾   cup shortening
1   cup sugar
1   egg
¼   cup molasses plus 1
    teaspoon
2   cups flour
2   teaspoons baking soda
1   teaspoon cinnamon
1   teaspoon ginger
½   teaspoon cloves

Cream shortening and sugar. Add egg and molasses and mix. Sift dry ingredients together and add, mixing well. Roll in balls and flatten with a fork dipped in sugar. Bake for 10 to 12 minutes.

Polvarones

300 degees, preheated
Cookie sheet, greased
Yield: 36 cookies

Cookies:
1   cup butter
2   cups flour
¾   cup granulated sugar
1½ teaspoons cinnamon

Topping:
2   cups powdered sugar
1   Tablespoon cinnamon

Cookies:
Cream butter in a mixing bowl. Add flour, sugar and cinnamon and blend well. Roll dough into 1-inch balls. Place on a cookie sheet and bake for 25 minutes.

Topping:
When the cookies are done and still warm, sift over them the powdered sugar and cinnamon mixed together.

Farina Bonbons

300 degrees, preheated
Cookie sheet, ungreased
Yield: 60 to 72

Cookies:
1   cup butter
½   cup powdered sugar
1   Tablespoon vanilla
1¾ cups flour
¼   teaspoon salt
½ to ¾ cup finely chopped
       pecans
¾   cup farina or cream of
       wheat

Icing:
1   16-ounce box powdered
       sugar
Dash of salt
½   cup butter, softened
2   Tablespoons warm milk
½   teaspoon vanilla
Colored sugar decorations

Cookies:
Cream butter and powdered sugar. Add vanilla. In a small bowl, combine remaining ingredients. Add to butter and sugar mixture and mix well. Roll mixture into balls, using about 1 teaspoon of dough. Place on an ungreased cookie sheet and bake for 20 minutes. Top with icing.

Icing:
Combine icing ingredients except for colored sugar decorations, and mix well. Pour on bonbons. Decorate with colored sugar decorations.

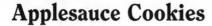

Applesauce Cookies

375 degrees, preheated
Cookie sheet, greased
Yield: 48 servings

Cookies:
½   cup margarine
1   cup brown sugar
1   egg, beaten
1   cup applesauce
1   teaspoon baking soda
2   teaspoons cinnamon
2   teaspoons nutmeg
½   teaspoon cloves
¼   teaspoon salt
2½ cups flour
1   cup raisins
½   cup pecans

Cookies:
Cream margarine and brown sugar. Stir in egg and add applesauce. Add remaining dry ingredients, followed by the raisins and nuts. Drop cookies on greased cookie sheet and bake 10 to 12 minutes.

Frosting:
1   cup powdered sugar
1   Tablespoon butter, softened
1   Tablespoon milk
¼   teaspoon cinnamon
½   teaspoon lemon flavoring
½   teaspoon vanilla

Frosting:
Mix ingredients together and frost warm cookies.

Quick and Easy Oatmeal-Fudge Cookies

Yield: 30 cookies

2   cups sugar
3   Tablespoons cocoa
½   cup margarine
½   cup milk
1   cup coconut
½   cup peanut butter
1   teaspoon vanilla
⅛   teaspoon salt
3   cups oatmeal

Mix first 5 ingredients in a heavy pan and boil for 1 minute. Remove from heat and add peanut butter, vanilla, salt and oatmeal. Mix well and drop by teaspoonful on buttered wax paper. Let cool before removing.

Pumpkin Spice Cookies

350 degrees, preheated
Cookie sheet, ungreased
Yield: 36 cookies

Cookies:
½ cup butter
1½ cups light brown sugar
2 eggs
1¾ cups pumpkin
2¾ cups flour
1 Tablespoon baking
   powder
1 teaspoon cinnamon
½ teaspoon cloves
½ teaspoon nutmeg
½ teaspoon salt
1 cup chopped nuts
1 cup raisins

Icing:
2½ Tablespoons butter,
   softened
1½ cups powdered sugar
1½ Tablespoons milk or
   cream
¾ teaspoon vanilla

Cookies:
In a mixing bowl, cream butter and brown sugar together. Add eggs one at a time, beating after each. Add pumpkin. In a separate bowl, measure and mix dry ingredients. Add dry ingredients to the pumpkin mixture. Stir in nuts and raisins. Drop by teaspoonful on ungreased cookie sheet. Bake for 12 to 15 minutes.

Icing:
Prepare icing by combining all ingredients in mixing bowl. Mix well and frost cookies.

Sand Tarts

325 degrees, preheated
Cookie sheet, ungreased
Yield: 24 to 30 cookies

1 cup butter
1 cup powdered sugar
2 teaspoons vanilla
   (Mexican, if available)
1 Tablespoon water
2 cups flour
1 cup chopped pecans
Powdered sugar to coat tarts

Cream butter and 1 cup powdered sugar. Add vanilla and water. Slowly add flour, mixing well with mixer. Add pecans and form into 1½-inch crescents. Bake on cookie sheet for 30 minutes or until light brown in color. Let cool on newspaper or brown paper. Place cooled cookies in plastic bag with powdered sugar and shake.

Chocolate Drop Cookies

350 degrees, preheated
Cookie sheet, greased
Yield: 36 cookies

Cookies:
1   egg, beaten
1   cup dark brown sugar
1   teaspoon vanilla
½   cup shortening
2   squares unsweetened
     chocolate
1⅔ cups flour
½   teaspoon salt
½   teaspoon baking soda
½   cup milk
½   cup chopped nuts

Cookies:
In a mixing bowl, beat egg and sugar together. Add vanilla. In a saucepan, melt shortening with the chocolate. Add to the egg mixture. Sift flour with the salt and baking soda. Add dry ingredients to the chocolate-egg mixture alternately with milk. Blend well. Add nuts. Drop by teaspoons onto greased cookie sheet. Bake for 10 to 12 minutes.

Icing:
1   cup sifted powdered sugar
2   Tablespoons milk
½   teaspoon vanilla

Icing:
In a mixing bowl, blend sifted powdered sugar with milk and vanilla. Spread evenly over the cookies.

Molasses Sugar Cookies

Advance Preparation
Time Required
350 degrees, preheated
Cookie sheet, greased
Yield: 36 cookies

¾   cup butter-flavored
     shortening
1   cup sugar
¼   cup molasses
1   egg
2   cups flour
1   teaspoon cinnamon
½   teaspoon cloves
½   teaspoon ginger
½   teaspoon salt
Granulated sugar for coating

In a mixing bowl, cream the shortening and sugar. Add molasses and egg. Mix well. Add flour and spices and mix well. Chill the dough for several hours. Roll the dough into 1-inch balls. Roll the balls in granulated sugar to coat and then place them 2 inches apart on a greased cookie sheet. Bake for 10 minutes.

Caramel Popcorn

250 degrees, preheated
9 × 13 baking pan, buttered
Yield: 1 gallon

4   quarts freshly popped
     corn
1   cup firmly packed brown
     sugar
½   cup margarine
½   cup dark corn syrup
½   teaspoon salt
½   teaspoon vanilla
½   teaspoon baking soda

Place popped corn in a large mixing bowl. In a heavy saucepan, combine sugar, margarine, corn syrup and salt. Cook over medium heat, stirring constantly, until boiling. Lower heat and cook without stirring for 5 minutes. Remove from heat and add vanilla. Then add baking soda. Mix well. Pour over popcorn and stir well. Spread coated corn in a buttered 9 × 13-inch baking pan and bake for 1 hour. Cool, break apart and store in an airtight container.

Chewy Caramel Candy

Cookie sheet, greased
Yield: 60 pieces

3   cups sugar
1   cup butter
2   cups whipping cream
1¾   cups light corn syrup
1   teaspoon vanilla
1   cup chopped pecans

Mix together all ingredients except vanilla and pecans. Slowly boil to 260 degrees on a candy thermometer. Remove from heat and slowly add vanilla and pecans. Stir well until evenly blended. Pour onto a greased cookie sheet. When cool, cut into strips and then squares. Wrap each piece individually in wax paper.

Caramel candy can also be dipped in melted chocolate.

Baked Fudge

300 degrees, preheated
8 × 10 × 2 pan
Yield: 8 to 12 servings

½   cup flour
2   cups sugar
½   cup cocoa
4   eggs, well beaten
1   cup butter, melted
2   teaspoons vanilla
1   cup chopped pecans

Sift flour, sugar and cocoa together. Add eggs and stir. Add butter, vanilla and pecans. Pour into pan. Place pan in hot water bath and bake for 45 to 60 minutes or until firm like a baked custard. (Will get firmer as it cools.) Serve with whipped cream.

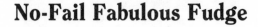

No-Fail Fabulous Fudge

8 × 8 pan, buttered
Yield: 16   2-inch squares

2¼ cups sugar
¾   cup evaporated milk
1   cup marshmallow creme
    or 16 large marshmallows
¼   cup butter
¼   teaspoon salt
1   6-ounce package semi-
    sweet chocolate morsels
1   teaspoon vanilla
1   cup chopped pecans

Mix sugar, milk, marshmallows, butter and salt in a heavy saucepan. Over medium heat, cook stirring constantly, until mixture comes to a boil. Cook an additional 5 minutes, stirring constantly. Remove from heat and stir in chocolate morsels until melted. Stir in vanilla and nuts. Spread in an 8 × 8 buttered pan. Cool and cut into squares.

My Own Peanut Butter Cups

9 × 13 pan
Yield: 50 to 60 pieces

1   cup butter
1¾ cups graham cracker
    crumbs
1   cup smooth peanut butter
2⅓ to 2½ cups powdered
    sugar
2   cups chocolate kisses

Melt butter. Remove from heat and add graham cracker crumbs, peanut butter and powdered sugar. Mix well. Pat into a 9 × 13 pan. Melt kisses and frost top of peanut butter mixture. Refrigerate until chocolate is firm, 30 minutes to 1 hour. Cut into small squares.

Sour Cream Fudge

8-inch square pan, buttered
Yield: 16   2-inch squares

2   cups sugar
1   cup sour cream
2   Tablespoons butter
1   teaspoon vanilla (optional)
½   cup chopped pecans

Mix sugar, sour cream and butter and cook over medium heat to soft ball stage (about 235 to 240 degrees on candy thermometer), stirring occasionally. Remove from heat, add flavoring if desired and let cool until only warm to the touch. Beat with a mixer until gloss begins to disappear. Add pecans and pour into buttered pan.

Variations:
Almond extract or butter rum may be substituted for vanilla. Toasted almonds or walnuts may be substituted for pecans.

Peanut-Oatmeal Candy Bars

350 degrees, preheated
9 × 13 baking pan, greased
Yield: 50 small bars

¾ cup butter
½ cup granulated sugar
½ cup brown sugar
½ cup dark corn syrup
1 Tablespoon vanilla
4 cups quick-cooking oatmeal
⅔ cup crunchy peanut butter
6 ounces semi-sweet chocolate chips

Cream butter and sugars. Beat in corn syrup and vanilla. Stir in oatmeal. Pat mixture into greased baking pan. Bake for 15 to 18 minutes or until slightly browned. Melt peanut butter and chocolate chips. When bar mixture is cooled, spread chocolate mixture over it. Chill to set. Cut into bars. (Will be hard to cut.) Store in refrigerator. Cannot be frozen.

Candy Coated Peanuts

300 degrees, preheated
9 × 13 cookie sheet, greased
Yield: 1 pound

½ cup water
1 cup sugar
2 cups raw peanuts
1 teaspoon vanilla

Combine above ingredients and cook until no liquid remains in pan. Spread on a well-greased cookie sheet making certain peanuts are not touching. Bake for 30 minutes. Cool and store in an airtight container.

Makes a great gift item!

Sugared Nuts

Yield: 12 to 15 servings

1 cup brown sugar
½ cup granulated sugar
½ cup sour cream
1 teaspoon almond extract
3 to 3½ cups nut halves

Cook sugars and sour cream slowly over medium heat stirring continuously. Cook until a little firmer than soft ball stage (about 240 degrees on candy thermometer). Remove from heat and add flavoring. Stir. Add nuts. Mix and separate nuts.

Good at any party!

Pralines

Yield: 60

2   cups granulated sugar
1   13-ounce can evaporated
    milk or 1 cup buttermilk
2   Tablespoons light corn
    syrup or ½ cup sugar,
    caramelized in a small
    skillet over low heat
2 to 8 Tablespoons butter
1   teaspoon baking soda
2   teaspoons vanilla
2   cups pecan halves

Combine first 5 ingredients in a saucepan. Cook over medium heat, stirring constantly, until mixture reaches soft ball stage (235 degrees on a candy thermometer). Remove from heat, add vanilla and pecans. Beat until creamy. Either drop by teaspoon onto wax paper or spread into a buttered platter and cut into squares when cool.

Microwave Pralines

3-quart microwave casserole
Yield: 24

1½ cups firmly packed light
    brown sugar
⅔ cup half and half
⅛ teaspoon salt
2   Tablespoons butter
1½ cups pecan halves

Combine sugar, half and half, and salt in a deep 3-quart microwave casserole, mixing well. Stir in butter. Microwave on high for 7 to 9½ minutes or until mixture reaches 235 degrees; stirring once. Stir in pecans. Cool 1 minute. Beat by hand until mixture is creamy and begins to thicken (about 3 minutes). Drop by Tablespoonsful onto waxed paper. Cool until firm.

Amaretto Freeze

Yield: 6 servings

1   quart vanilla ice cream,
    softened
⅓ cup Amaretto liqueur
⅛ cup Triple Sec
¼ cup Cream de Cocoa
8   Oreo cookies

Combine ice cream, Amaretto, Triple Sec and Cream de Cocoa in mixer or blender until smooth. Place in freezer until time to serve. Grind Oreos in blender or food processor into crumbs. When serving, sprinkle crumbs over ice cream that has been spooned into sherbet glasses.

Amaretto Cheese Spread

300 degrees, preheated
Yield: 8 to 10 servings

1 2½-ounce package sliced
   almonds
1 8-ounce package cream
   cheese at room
   temperature
¼ cup Amaretto
½ teaspoon vanilla
¼ teaspoon almond extract
Assorted sliced fruits—apples,
   oranges, seedless grapes
   or crackers such as Wheat
   Thins

Spread almonds in shallow pan; toast until golden brown, about 6 to 8 minutes. Let cool. Whip softened cream cheese with Amaretto and extracts until it is the consistency of whipped cream. Chill several hours or overnight. Let cream cheese come to room temperature; garnish with toasted almonds and serve with sliced fruit.

The cheese spread can be easily expanded for a party, using the same proportions.

Old Fashioned Apple Cobbler

400 degrees, preheated
9 × 9 glass dish, ungreased
Yield: 4 to 6 servings

Filling:
½ lemon cut into thin slices
½ cup water
¾ cup sugar
2 Tablespoons flour
¼ teaspoon nutmeg
3 cups pared and sliced
   apples
3 Tablespoons butter

Crust:
1 cup sifted flour
¼ teaspoon salt
⅓ cup shortening
2 to 3 Tablespoons cold water

Filling:
Simmer lemon in water until tender (about 5 minutes). Drain water and reserve. In a saucepan combine sugar, flour and nutmeg. Blend in reserved lemon water and cook until thickened, stirring constantly. Arrange apples in a 9 × 9 glass baking dish. Dot with butter and lemon slices. Cover with hot mixture.

Crust:
Sift together flour and salt. Cut in shortening. Add cold water until dough is moist enough to hold together. Roll out on a floured surface and place over filling. Bake for 35 to 45 minutes.

■■■■■■■■■■■■■■■■■■■■■■■■■■■

Apple Dumplings

450 degrees, preheated
9 × 13 baking pan, ungreased
Yield: 6 servings

1   10-inch double crust pie
    pastry
6   small apples, peeled and
    cored
1½ cups sugar, divided
¾   teaspoon cinnamon,
    divided
¼   teaspoon nutmeg
6   Tablespoons butter,
    divided

On a floured surface, roll out pastry to ⅛-inch thickness. Cut into 6 squares. Place whole apple in the center of the pastry square. Combine ½ cup sugar, ½ teaspoon cinnamon, nutmeg and 2 Tablespoons butter. Fill each apple core with sugar mixture. Moisten edges of pastry and seal around apple. Prick pastry with a fork in several places. Chill for 1 hour. In a saucepan, combine remaining sugar, cinnamon and butter and boil for 5 minutes to make a syrup. Place apples in a 9 × 13 baking pan and bake for 10 minutes. Reduce heat to 350 degrees. Pour syrup over apples and bake for 35 minutes more, basting occasionally.

Apricot Delight

Advance Preparation
Time Required
11 × 13-inch pan, buttered
Yield: 20 to 24 servings

1   pound sugar cookies
1   cup butter
1   cup sifted powdered sugar
2   eggs, beaten
1   cup chopped pecans
1   29-ounce can apricot
    halves
2   cups whipping cream,
    whipped

Crush the sugar cookies. Press ⅔'s of the crumbs into a buttered 11 × 13 inch pan. Reserve ⅓ for topping. To make the custard filling, combine butter, powdered sugar, and eggs in the top of a double boiler. Cook until the mixture is thick, stirring constantly. Spread custard on top of the crumb crust. Sprinkle chopped nuts over the custard. Drain the apricots and reserve the liquid. Place the apricot halves with hollow side down on the nut layer. Spread whipped cream layer on next. Pour reserved apricot juice over whipped cream and sprinkle on remaining cookie crumbs. Chill overnight. Cut into squares to serve.

Apricot Tarts

Advance Preparation
Time Required
350 degrees, preheated
Cookie sheet, ungreased
Yield: 48 tarts

Dough:
2   cups flour
Dash of salt
1   8-ounce package cream
    cheese, softened
1   cup butter, softened

Dough:
In a mixing bowl, sift together the flour and salt. Add cream cheese and butter, stirring until the mixture is well blended. Cover and chill several hours. Divide the dough into 4 portions and roll out one portion at a time on a floured board to a thickness of ⅛ inch. Cut the dough into 3-inch squares and place a tablespoon of apricot filling in the center of each square. Fold corners of the dough to the center (over the filling) and pinch to seal. Place tarts on an ungreased cookie sheet 2 inches apart. Bake for 20 minutes. Remove them from the cookie sheet and cool on a wire rack.

Filling:
1   11-ounce package dried
    apricots
¾   cups sugar

Filling:
Chop the apricots into ¼-inch pieces and place in a saucepan. Add enough water to cover the fruit. Cook uncovered over medium heat until apricots are soft and water is absorbed. Remove from the heat and stir in sugar.

Variation:
1   cup sifted powdered sugar
2   Tablespoons milk
½   teaspoon vanilla

Variation:
In a mixing bowl, combine all ingredients. Blend until smooth and use to ice apricot tarts after they have cooled.

Crepes à la Bananas Foster

Crepe pan or skillet
Yield: 6 to 8 servings

Crepes:
4   eggs
1   cup flour
2   Tablespoons granulated
    sugar
1   cup milk
¼   cup water
1   Tablespoon butter, melted

Crepes:
In a medium bowl, beat eggs. Combine flour and sugar. Combine milk and water. Gradually add flour mixture, alternately with milk mixture. Beat until smooth. Add butter. Refrigerate batter for at least 1 hour. Cook in a crepe pan.

Filling:
4   bananas
1   Tablespoon lemon juice
¼   cup butter
½   cup light brown sugar
⅛   teaspoon cinnamon
½   cup rum, warmed
8   crepes
8   small scoops vanilla ice
    cream
¼   cup chopped nuts

Filling:
Peel and slice bananas. Pour lemon juice over bananas. In a skillet, melt butter and sugar. Add bananas and cook until hot. Sprinkle with cinnamon. Remove from heat and pour rum over bananas. Ignite with a long match. Spoon sauce over bananas until flame burns out. Fill crepes with ice cream and top with bananas and sauce. Sprinkle with nuts.

Boiled Custard

Heavy saucepan
Yield: 24 servings

6   eggs, beaten
8   cups milk
1¼   cups sugar
3   teaspoons vanilla

In a heavy saucepan, mix eggs, milk and sugar. Cook on medium heat (185 degrees) until steaming and thickened, stirring constantly. Remove from heat and cool slightly. Add vanilla. May be strained for a smoother texture. Do not overcook or it will curdle.

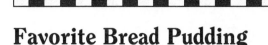

Favorite Bread Pudding

350 degrees, preheateed
9 × 13 baking dish, ungreased
Yield: 12 to 15 servings

4   eggs, separated
4   cups milk
4   cups fresh bread cubes
¾   cups sugar
2   Tablespoons melted butter
1   teaspoon grated lemon
    peel
1   teaspoon vanilla
1   cup strawberry or
    raspberry or apricot
    preserves
½   teaspoon vanilla
¼   teaspoon cream of tartar
½   cup sugar

In a mixing bowl, beat egg yolks slightly and then stir in milk, bread cubes, sugar, butter, lemon peel and vanilla. Beat the mixture until the sugar is dissolved. Pour into an ungreased 9 × 13 inch baking dish. Bake for 40 minutes. Remove from the oven and spread preserves over the hot pudding. In a mixing bowl, beat the egg whites with vanilla and cream of tartar until soft peaks form. Continue beating and gradually add sugar. Beat until stiff peaks form. Spread the egg white mixture over the preserves, sealing to the edges. Return to the oven and bake for 10 to 12 minutes more.

Flan Almendra

350 degrees, preheated
9-inch cake pan, greased
Yield: 6 to 8 servings

½   cup sugar
1⅔ cup sweetened condensed
    milk
1   cup milk
3   eggs
1   teaspoon vanilla
1   cup slivered almonds,
    toasted and coarsely
    ground

Sprinkle the sugar evenly in a 9-inch cake pan and place it over a burner on medium heat. Using oven mitt, caramelize the sugar by shaking the pan occasionally until the sugar is melted and a light brown color. Allow the pan to cool. (The mixture may crack slightly as it cools). Combine the remaining ingredients in the container of an electric blender and blend at high speed for 15 seconds. Pour the mixture over the caramelized sugar. Cover the pan with aluminum foil and place in a larger, shallow pan. Pour about 1 inch of hot water into the larger pan. Bake for 55 minutes or until a knife inserted in the center comes out clean. Flan may be garnished with fresh strawberries.

Demitasse Mousse

Blender
Yield: 4 servings

1   4-ounce bar German's
    Sweet Chocolate
¼   cup semi-sweet chocolate
    morsels
2   eggs
3   Tablespoons strong hot
    coffee
2   Tablespoons Kahlua
¾   cup half and half
Whipped cream
Chocolate syrup for garnish

Combine first 6 ingredients in a blender. Blend at high speed for 2 minutes. Fill demitasse cups ¾ full. Chill. Before serving, fill remainder of cup with whipped cream. Garnish with chocolate syrup drops.

Peach Delight

350 degrees, preheated
9-inch pie pan, greased and floured
Yield: 8 servings

¾   cup flour
1   teaspoon baking powder
½   teaspoon salt
1   3½-ounce package vanilla
    pudding (not instant)
3   Tablespoons margarine
1   egg
½   cup milk
1   15 to 20-ounce can sliced
    peaches
1   8-ounce cream cheese,
    softened
½   cup sugar
3   Tablespoons reserved
    peach juice
1   Tablespoon sugar
½   teaspoon cinnamon

Beat flour, baking powder, salt, pudding, margarine, egg and milk together. Pour into a greased and floured pie pan. Drain peaches well, reserving 3 Tablespoons peach juice. Mix together cream cheese, sugar and peach juice. Fold in peaches. Spread peach mixture on top of the pie mixture, about ¾ inches from the edge of the pan. Combine 1 Tablespoon sugar and cinnamon and sprinkle over top. Bake 30 to 35 minutes. Chill in refrigerator.

Ice Cream Roll With Hot Fudge Sauce

*Advance Preparation
Time Required*
350 degrees, preheated
12 × 15 jelly roll pan
lined with wax paper

Cake:
5   eggs, separated
1½ cups powdered sugar
3   Tablespoons cocoa
1   pint vanilla ice cream, softened

Cake:
In a mixing bowl, beat egg yolks until they are creamy. Add 1 cup of powdered sugar and cocoa. Mix well. In another mixing bowl, beat the egg whites until stiff peaks form. Fold the beaten egg whites into the batter until well blended. Pour the batter into a 12 × 15 jelly roll pan which has been lined with wax paper. Spread the batter evenly in the pan. Bake for 10 to 15 minutes. When the cake is still warm, turn it out onto a towel which has been sprinkled with ½ cup powdered sugar. Remove the wax paper from the cake. Cover the cake with a damp towel and allow the cake to cool. When the cake is cooled, spread softened vanilla ice cream over it evenly at about ¼-to-½-inch thickness. Roll the cake up jelly roll style. Wrap it in foil and freeze for about 2 hours or until you are ready to use it.

Sauce:
2   squares unsweetened chocolate
2   Tablespoons butter
⅔   cup granulated sugar
1   cup half and half

Sauce:
In a saucepan over low heat, melt chocolate and butter together. Add sugar and half and half and stir constantly until the sugar dissolves and the mixture thickens. Cool the sauce. Spoon sauce over slices of ice cream roll when ready to serve.

Hot Fudge Sundae Surprise

350 degrees, preheated
9 × 9 baking pan
Yield: 8 servings

1   cup flour
¾   cup granulated sugar
2   Tablespoons cocoa
2   teaspoons baking powder
¼   teaspoon salt
½   cup milk
2   Tablespoons vegetable oil
1   teaspoon vanilla
1   cup chopped nuts
1   cup dark brown sugar
¼   cup cocoa
1¾ cups hot tap water
Vanilla ice cream
1   11-ounce jar chocolate
    fudge sauce

In a mixing bowl, combine flour, granulated sugar, cocoa, baking powder and salt. Mix well and then put into a 9 × 9 × 2-inch ungreased pan. In the pan, add milk, oil and vanilla to the dry ingredients. Mix well. Stir in nuts and spread the mixture evenly in the pan. Combine the brown sugar and cocoa and sprinkle over the dough mixture. Pour hot tap water into the pan but *do not stir*. Bake for 40 minutes. Let it stand for 15 minutes then spoon mixture into ice cream dishes. Top with vanilla ice cream and spoon fudge sauce on top of ice cream.

Quick Dobosh Torte

Yield: 14 to 16 servings

1   Sara Lee 16-ounce pound
    cake, still frozen or
    partially thawed
1   6-ounce package chocolate
    chips
¼   cup hot, strong coffee
2   Tablespoons powdered
    sugar
4   egg yolks
½   cup butter, softened
1   teaspoon vanilla
Chopped nuts (optional)

Slice cake lengthwise into 6 thin layers with an electric knife. Put half of the chocolate chips into the blender and turn on high for 10 seconds. Then add remaining half of chips, blending them in the same manner. Add hot coffee and mix well. Add remaining ingredients and blend until smooth. Put layers of blended chocolate mixture between layers of cake and frost top and sides. Put chopped nuts on top. Chill.

Lemon Cake-Top Pudding

375 degrees, preheated
8 custard cups
Yield: 8 servings

2 Tablespoons butter
1½ cups sugar
⅓ cup flour
¼ teaspoon salt
½ cup lemon juice
1 teaspoon grated lemon rind
3 eggs, separated
1¼ cups milk

Cream butter and sugar. Add flour, salt, lemon juice and lemon rind. Combine egg yolks and milk and mix well. Stir into flour mixture. Stiffly beat egg whites and fold them into mixture. Pour into 8 custard cups. Set into a pan of water and bake for 45 minutes. Serve hot or cold.

Cold Lemon Soufflé

Spring form pan
Double boiler
Yield: 10 servings

Soufflé
3 lemons, juiced and rind grated
2 envelopes unflavored gelatin
6 eggs, separated
1½ cups sugar
2 cups cream, whipped
24 lady fingers
Juice of 3 oranges

Soufflé:
In a small saucepan, combine lemon juice and gelatin, and heat to soften. In a double boiler, dissolve egg yolks, sugar, and grated lemon rind. Heat for 15 minutes, stirring occasionally. Remove from heat and stir in gelatin mixture. Beat egg whites until stiff. Fold egg whites and whipped cream into egg yolk mixture. Moisten lady fingers in orange juice one by one. Line bottom of spring form pans with lady fingers. Add layer of lemon cream mixture. Continue alternating layers, ending with lady fingers. Freeze for 3 hours and unmold and serve with raspberry pureé.

Raspberry Pureé:
1 10-ounce box frozen raspberries
2 Tablespoons powdered sugar, sifted

Raspberry Purée:
In a food processor or blender, process raspberries until creamy. Strain pureé through a sieve to remove seeds. Stir in powdered sugar. Refrigerate until ready to use.

Poached Dessert Pears in Almond Custard

Double boiler
Yield: 4 servings

Poached Pears:
4   medium-sized ripe pears
¼   cup sugar
1   teaspoon grated orange rind
⅓   cup orange juice
1   Tablespoon lemon juice
⅔   cup water
1   stick cinnamon

Poached Pears:
Peel and core pears from large end, leaving stems intact. In a saucepan, combine remaining ingredients, and boil. Add pears and boil uncovered until pears are tender (8 to 10 minutes). Remove pears. Boil syrup 7 to 10 minutes longer. Pour syrup over pears and refrigerate.

Almond custard:
2½ Tablespoons sugar
1   teaspoon cornstarch
⅛   teaspoon salt
1   cup milk or half and half
2   egg yolks, beaten
½   teaspoon vanilla extract
⅛   teaspoon almond extract

Almond Custard:
In a double boiler, combine sugar, cornstarch and salt. Slowly stir in milk and bring mixture to a boil. Cook 8 to 9 minutes. Add a small amount of milk mixture to egg yolks and mix well. Add eggs to mixture in double boiler and cook an additional 2 to 3 minutes. Remove from heat and add extracts. Pour over chilled pears and refrigerate. Serve chilled.

Easy Homemade Ice Cream

5-quart ice cream freezer
Yield: 10 to 12 servings

6   eggs, beaten
1½ cups sugar
1   14-ounce can sweetened condensed milk
1   13-ounce can evaporated milk
2   Tablespoons vanilla
8   cups milk
Ice
Rock salt

Mix all ingredients until well blended. Pour the mixture into the canister of the ice cream freezer. Alternate layers of ice and salt in the bucket surrounding the canister and freeze until the mixture is thick.

French Vanilla Ice Cream

4-quart ice cream freezer
Yield: 8 servings

4   eggs
2   cups sugar
⅛   teaspoon salt
1   3¾-ounce box instant
     vanilla pudding and pie
     filling
4   cups milk
4   cups half and half
3   teaspoons vanilla extract
Ice
Rock salt

Beat the eggs in a mixing bowl until fluffy. Add the remaining ingredients and continue beating until the sugar and pudding dissolve. Pour the mixture into the canister of the ice cream freezer. Alternate layers of ice and salt in the bucket surrounding the container and freeze until the mixture is thick.

Homemade Vanilla Custard Ice Cream

5-quart ice cream freezer
Yield: 12 servings

8   eggs, slightly beaten
6   Tablespoons vanilla
2½   cups sugar
8   Tablespoons flour
1   teaspoon salt
2   cups milk
2   13-ounce cans evaporated
     milk
2   14-ounce cans sweetened
     condensed milk
Ice
Rock salt

In a saucepan, beat together the eggs, vanilla, sugar, flour and salt. Cook over low heat and add milk. Stir constantly until mixture thickens. Remove from heat and add evaporated milk and sweetened condensed milk. (The mixture may be refrigerated at this point until you are ready to freeze it.) Pour the mixture into the canister of a 5-quart ice cream freezer. Add enough milk for the mixture to reach the "fill line" on the canister. Alternate layers of ice and salt in the bucket surrounding the canister and freeze until the mixture is thick.

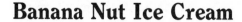

Banana Nut Ice Cream

5-quart ice cream freezer
Yield: 8 servings

1 to 2 cups chopped pecans
   (according to taste)
2   14-ounce cans sweetened
   condensed milk
2   13-ounce cans evaporated
   milk
3   cups sugar
2   teaspoons vanilla
2   cups whipping cream
4 to 6 large bananas, mashed
   and coated with lemon
   juice or "fruit fresh"
Ice
Rock salt

Toast the pecans in a 350 degree oven for about 15 minutes. In a mixing bowl, combine all canned milk with the sugar and vanilla and blend well. Add whipping cream and mix well. Fold in bananas and toasted pecans and pour into the canister of an ice cream freezer. Alternate layers of ice and salt in the bucket surrounding the ice cream canister and freeze until the mixture is thick.

Pistachio Fudge Nut Ice Cream

5-quart ice cream freezer
Yield: 8 to 12 servings

4   eggs
2   cups sugar
¼   teaspoon salt
1   3¾-ounce box instant
   pistachio pudding mix
4   cups milk
4   cups half and half
6   drops green food coloring
2   Tablespoons almond
   extract
1   cup unsalted pistachio
   nuts, chopped
1   11-ounce jar fudge sauce,
   chilled
Ice
Rock salt

In a mixing bowl, beat the eggs until they are fluffy. In a saucepan, combine eggs, sugar, salt, pudding mix, milk and half and half. Heat until the sugar and pudding are dissolved. Remove from heat and add green food coloring and almond extract. Pour the mixture into the freezer canister. Freeze until the mixture is thick and nearly set. Remove from the canister and put ice cream into a freezer tight container. Fold in the nuts and fudge sauce carefully for a rippled effect. Freeze.

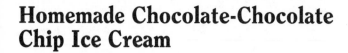

Homemade Chocolate-Chocolate Chip Ice Cream

4-quart ice cream freezer
Yield: 8 servings

1½ cups sugar
6 eggs, beaten
4 cups half and half
4 cups whipping cream
1 16-ounce can chocolate
   syrup
1 1-ounce square of semi-
   sweet chocolate, melted
Ice
Rock salt

Combine the sugar and eggs in a mixing bowl and beat well. Add half and half and whipping cream and continue beating slowly. Add chocolate syrup and melted chocolate square. Beat the mixture until the chocolate is evenly distributed. Pour the mixture into the canister of the ice cream freezer. Alternate layers of ice and salt in the bucket surrounding the ice cream canister and freeze until the mixture is thick.

Homemade Milky Way Ice Cream

Ice cream freezer
Yield: 10 to 15 servings

1 pound Milky Way bars
2 cups milk
6 eggs
1½ cups sugar
2 5.33-ounce cans
   evaporated milk
2 teaspoons vanilla
Ice
Rock salt

In a saucepan over low heat, melt Milky Way bars in milk. Let cool. Beat eggs and sugar. Mix the evaporated milk and the vanilla. Combine all of the ingredients in an ice cream freezer container. (More milk may be needed for your ice cream freezer to meet the fill line.) Pack freezer with ice and rock salt. Churn until frozen.

Chocolate Sauce

Double boiler
Yield: 2 cups

6   ounces semi-sweet
    chocolate
½   cup butter
2   cups sugar
1   13-ounce can evaporated
    milk
1   teaspoon vanilla
¼ to ½ teaspoon salt
    (optional)

Melt chocolate and butter together in a double boiler. Add sugar. Boil a few minutes. Add milk, mixing well. Cook until thick. Add vanilla and blend thoroughly. Keep in refrigerator until ready to use. Warm in a double boiler before serving. May also be used cold.

Great over ice cream or in tart shells.

Fruit Dipping Sauce

Yield: 1 cup

¾   cup apricot preserves
¼   cup orange juice
3   cloves
1   stick cinnamon
1   teaspoon brandy extract

In a saucepan, combine all ingredients and simmer for 10 to 12 minutes. Remove cinnamon stick and cloves. Serve sauce warm with deep fried crepes, angel food cake squares or any kind of fruit.

Deep Fried Crepes:
Cut 18 crepes into 1-inch strips. In a saucepan, heat vegetable oil to 350 degrees and deep fry crepes until golden brown (about 1 minute). Drain strips. While warm, sprinkle with a mixture of 2 Tablespoons cinnamon and 2 Tablespoons sugar.

Hot Buttered Rum Sauce

Medium saucepan
Yield: 10 to 12 servings

2   cups whipping cream
5   Tablespoons butter,
    melted (do not substitute
    margarine)
1   cup sugar
3   Tablespoons light rum

Combine all ingredients in a saucepan and keep warm for a least 2 hours before serving.

Canning and Pickling

Canned Green Beans

Large Dutch oven and
canning equipment
Yield: 4 quarts

1   **gallon green beans,
    snapped**
½   **gallon water**
½   **cup sugar**
½   **cup vinegar**
¼   **cup salt**

Combine all ingredients in a large Dutch oven
and boil for 3 minutes. Seal in sterile canning
jars. When you are ready to cook beans, drain
and rinse several times. Soak overnight in ice
water. Cook like fresh beans.

*This method preserves fresh green beans so
that they are crisp and taste just like fresh
ones when cooked.*

Mustard Beans

Medium saucepan
Yield: 2 cups

1   **cup sugar**
½   **cup cider vinegar**
3   **Tablespoons prepared
    mustard**
½   **teaspoon instant minced
    onion**
¼   **teaspoon salt**
1   **16-ounce can yellow wax
    beans, drained or 1
    9-ounce package frozen
    yellow wax beans, thawed**

Combine first 5 ingredients in medium saucepan.
Bring to a boil, stirring until sugar is dissolved.
Add beans and simmer uncovered for 5 minutes.
Cool. Cover and refrigerate overnight.

Bread and Butter Pickles

Large Dutch oven and
canning equipment
Yield: 6 quarts

8   pounds cucumbers
4   pounds onions
6   banana peppers
½   cup pickling salt
8   cups vinegar
6   cups sugar
2   teaspoons celery seed
2   teaspoons mustard seed
⅛   cup tumeric

Slice cucumbers, onions and peppers and soak for 2 hours in water and pickling salt. Drain and wash well. Make a syrup of remaining ingredients and add to vegetables. Bring to a boil, boil for 5 minutes, stirring occasionally. Seal in sterile canning jars.

Lazy Pickles

Yield: 1 gallon

1   gallon dill or sour pickles
5   pounds sugar
1   2-ounce jar Tabasco sauce
4 to 6 cloves garlic, minced
½ of a 1.25-ounce jar pickling
     spice

Drain juice off pickles. Pour sugar over pickles with the seasonings. Shake and mix well. Keep refrigerated.

This very easy recipe makes a hot and sweet pickle.

Sweet and Crisp Pickles

Advance Preparation
Time Required
Large enamel, crockery
or stainless steel pan
Yield: 5 quarts

7	pounds cucumbers, sliced ¼-inch thick
1	cup pickling lime
Water to cover	
4	cups vinegar
5	pounds sugar
¾	of a 1.25-ounce jar pickling spice

1st Day:
Wash and slice cucumbers. Mix lime with cucumbers in a large crock and cover with water. Soak 24 hours.

2nd Day: Rinse cucumbers thoroughly several times in cold water. Handle cucumbers carefully. Add vinegar, sugar and spices to cucumbers and soak 24 hours.

3rd Day: Sterilize canning jars and lids. Pour cucumbers, vinegar, sugar and spices into a large pan; bring to a boil over medium heat. Begin timing when mixture comes to a boil; simmer 20 minutes, then begin filling clean jars. Continue to simmer while all jars are being filled.

Pickled Okra

Large saucepan and
canning jars
Yield: 4 pints

1	cup water
4	cups vinegar
½	cup salt
1½	pounds okra
2	heads dill
1	clove garlic
1	hot pepper
¼	teaspoon alum

Mix and boil water, vinegar and salt. Wash okra and pack in jars; in the first layer, pack okra stem end down. In the second layer, pack okra stem end up. Add dill, garlic, hot pepper and alum to vinegar; pour hot vinegar solution over okra and seal jars. Date jars and do not use for at least 6 weeks.

Peach Marmalade

Large Dutch oven and
canning equipment
Yield: 13 pints

1 whole orange
12 large peaches, peeled and
mashed
1 cup sugar per cup of
peaches

Peel, seed and remove white membrane from orange, then grind pulp and half of peel. Measure mashed peaches and use 1 cup sugar to each cup of peach pulp. Cook slowly, stirring frequently, until very thick, approximately 1 hour 30 minutes to 2 hours. Seal in sterile canning jars.

Pear Marmalade

Large saucepan and
canning equipment
Yield: 4 pints

1 pound pears
¾ pound sugar
1 lemon slice
1 orange slice
¼ teaspoon powdered ginger
Pinch of salt
1 cup white raisins

Wash and core pears but do not peel. Chop or process until coarsely ground. Place pears (including any juices that have accumulated), sugar, lemon and orange slices, ginger, salt and raisins in a large saucepan. Cook over low heat, stirring occasionally, until pears are transparent. Seal in sterile canning jars.

Jalapeño Pepper Jelly

Dutch oven
Yield: 6½ pints

¾   cup ground sweet bell
     peppers
¼   cup ground jalapeño
     peppers (seeds discarded)
6½ cups sugar
1½ cups apple cider vinegar
1   6-ounce bottle Certo
Green food coloring

Peppers should be cleaned, all seeds discarded, and ground separately, then measured. Accumulating juices should be reserved. To measure peppers, pack solidly into measuring cup and fill with reserved juices. Bring peppers, sugar and vinegar to a hard, rolling boil for 10 minutes. Remove from heat; add Certo and food coloring to the tint desired, stir and seal in sterile canning jars.

Variation:
Increase ground jalapeños to ⅓ cup for hotter jelly.

Caddo Lake Relish

Large Dutch oven
Yield: 6 quarts

1   gallon tender green
     tomatoes
½   gallon small onions
½   gallon bell peppers
9   hot green peppers (for
     medium hot relish; more
     peppers will make relish
     hotter)
6   cups vinegar
4   Tablespoons salt
5   cups sugar
½   teaspoon black pepper
2   teaspoons pickling spice
     (tied in cheesecloth)

Chop first 4 ingredients coarsely and mix in large Dutch oven. Mix remainder of ingredients in a separate container, then pour over vegetables. Bring to a boil and seal into sterile canning jars. Let "ripen" for at least a week before serving.

Damn Hot!

Large Dutch Oven and
canning equipment
Yield: 6½ quarts

1	quart green tomatoes (approximately 5 large)
1	quart cabbage (approximately ½ head)
1	quart onions (approximately 6)
1	quart bell peppers (approximately 5)
1	pint hot peppers (approximately 26), seeded if desired
2	Tablespoons salt
4	cups sugar
1	cup flour
1	quart vinegar
1	quart mustard

Grind vegetables and drain juice. Set aside vegetables. Mix salt, sugar and flour in Dutch oven; slowly add vinegar, stirring constantly to prevent lumping. Add mustard. Cook vinegar mixture until it begins to thicken. Add ground vegetables and cook, stirring constantly, until mixture is fairly thick. Use low heat as mixture scorches easily. Seal in sterile canning jars.

Fresh Tomato Relish

Large Dutch oven and
canning equipment
Yield: 6½ pints

20	large ripe tomatoes, peeled
6	onions, cut up
8 or less	bell peppers, chopped
2	Tablespoons salt
2	cups vinegar
4	Tablespoons red hot peppers
1	teaspoon cinnamon
1	teaspoon ginger
½	teaspoon cloves
1	cup sugar

Cook all ingredients in a large Dutch oven until very thick, about 2 to 4 hours. Seal in sterile canning jars.

This relish is very good served with fresh peas and beans.

Tomato Relish

Medium saucepan and
canning equipment
Yield: 4 to 6 servings

2½ cups canned tomatoes
1   onion, chopped
½   cup vinegar
¾   cup sugar
¼   teaspoon cayenne or red
    pepper
½   teaspoon salt

Combine all ingredients in a medium saucepan.
Bring to a boil, then reduce heat to simmering.
Cook for about 45 minutes to 1 hour, stirring
occasionally. Either seal in sterile canning jars or
refrigerate until used.

Pear Relish

Large Dutch oven or roaster
Yield: 8 quarts

25 medium to large pears
12 bell peppers
4 to 12 jalapeño peppers
10 large onions
3   cups sugar
2   cups white vinegar
2   Tablespoons celery seed
2   Tablespoons salt

Peel and core pears. Cut peppers in half and
remove seeds. Grind pears, peppers and onions in
food processor or put through food chopper.
Place ground vegetables in large pan or roaster;
add remainder of ingredients. Bring to a boil.
Reduce heat and simmer for 40 minutes. Seal in
sterile canning jars.

*This recipe is very typical of East Texas. Relish
is served with locally grown peas and other
vegetables.*

Spiced Cranberry Relish

Large saucepan
Yield: 8 to 10 servings

4 cups fresh cranberries
1½ cups water
½ cup orange juice
3 cups sugar
1½ teaspoons cinnamon
½ teaspoon allspice
½ teaspoon cloves
Pinch of ginger
Peel of 1 orange, with white membrane removed, fresh or dried, cut in small pieces

Wash and drain cranberries; set aside. Bring remaining ingredients to a boil in a large saucepan; add cranberries. Cook over moderate heat until cranberry skins pop; reduce heat and simmer one hour, stirring occasionally. Cool. Chill until ready to serve. This relish may be sealed in sterile canning jars while hot.

Relish may be served instead of cranberry sauce or substituted in recipes calling for whole berry cranberry sauce.

Chili Sauce

Large Dutch oven and
canning equipment
Yield: 7 to 8 pints sauce

1 gallon chopped, peeled ripe tomatoes
2 cups finely chopped onions
2 cups finely chopped red bell peppers
3 Tablespoons salt
1⅔ cups dark brown sugar
2 cups granulated sugar
3 cups vinegar
1 cup finely chopped green bell peppers
1 hot pepper, chopped
1 teaspoon whole cloves
1 teaspoon allspice
2 teaspoons cinnamon
1 teaspoon pickling spice (tied in cheesecloth)

Combine all ingredients in a large Dutch oven and cook for approximately 1 hour over low heat or until sauce is as thick as desired. Seal in sterile canning jars.

Green Tomato Mincemeat

Large Dutch oven and
canning equipment
Yield: 6 pints

3   pounds green tomatoes
3   pounds apples, unpeeled
    and cored
2   pounds raisins
8   cups sugar
2   Tablespoons salt
1   cup butter
Water to equal tomato juice
    discarded after chopping
    tomatoes
1   cup vinegar
2   Tablespoons cinnamon
2   teaspoons cloves
½   teaspoon nutmeg

Process or chop tomatoes coarsely. Put chopped tomatoes in cloth bag and squeeze out juice, measuring juice before discarding. Pour hot water over tomatoes and squeeze again. Repeat. Process or chop apples and raisins. Mix tomatoes, apples, raisins, sugar, salt, butter and water to equal amount of tomato juice discarded; cook until mixture is clear, approximately 40 minutes after it comes to a boil. Stir frequently. Add remaining ingredients and cook until thick. Seal in sterile canning jars.

Equivalents

Table of Equivalent Weights and Measures

Dash = Less than ⅛ teaspoon
1 teaspoon = 60 drops
1 Tablespoon = 3 teaspoons
2 Tablespoons = ⅛ cup
4 Tablespoons = ¼ cup
5 Tablespoons plus 1 teaspoon = ⅓ cup
6 Tablespoons = ⅜ cup
8 Tablespoons = ½ cup
10⅔ Tablespoons = ⅔ cup
12 Tablespoons = ¾ cup
16 Tablespoons = 1 cup or 8 ounces
1 cup = ½ pint
2 cups = 1 pint
1 pint = 16 fluid ounces
1 quart = 2 pints
4 quarts = 1 gallon
4 cups = 1 quart
1 ounce = 2 Tablespoons
4 ounces = ½ cup
8 ounces = 1 cup
16 ounces = 1 pound
2 cups (liquid) = 1 pound

When You Need Approximate Measurements

1 stick butter = ½ cup
4 sticks butter = 1 pound
1 square chocolate = 3 Tablespoons chocolate, grated
8 to 10 egg whites = 1 cup
12 to 14 yolks = 1 cup
1 cup whipping cream = 2 cups whipped cream
1 medium lemon = 1 Tablespoon grated rind = 3 Tablespoons juice
1 medium orange = 2 Tablespoons grated rind = ⅓ cup juice
1 dozen medium oranges = 4 cups juice
1 chopped medium onion = ½ cup pieces
1 pound grated cheese = 4 cups
4 ounces uncooked macaroni = 2½ cups, cooked
7 ounces uncooked spaghetti = 4 cups cooked
4 ounces uncooked noodles = 2 cups, cooked
1 cup uncooked rice = 3 cups cooked
3 cups pared apples = 1 pound, unpared
3 to 4 medium bananas = 2 cups, mashed
1 pound raw unpeeled potatoes = 2 cups, mashed

Make 1 cup of crumbs with:

(a) 28 saltine crackers
(b) 4 slices bread
(c) 14 square graham crackers
(d) 22 vanilla wafers

Emergency Substitutions

1 teaspoon baking powder = ¼ teaspoon baking soda + ½ teaspoon
cream of tartar

1 square chocolate = 3 Tablespoons cocoa + ½ teaspoon butter

1 Tablespoon cornstarch = 2 Tablespoons flour when used for
thickening

1 cup sifted *all-purpose flour* = 1 cup plus 2 Tablespoons sifted cake
flour

1 cup sifted *cake flour* = 1 cup minus 2 Tablespoons all-purpose flour

1 cup milk = ½ cup evaporated milk + ½ cup water OR 4 Tablespoons
dry milk + 1 cup water

1 cup buttermilk = 1⅓ Tablespoons vinegar or lemon juice + 1 cup
milk

1 cup molasses = 1 cup honey

1 cup honey = 1¼ cup sugar + ¼ cup liquid

1 cup canned tomatoes = about ⅓ cup cut-up fresh tomatoes simmered
10 minutes

1 small fresh onion = 1 Tablespoon instant minced onion

1 Tablespoon prepared mustard = 1 teaspoon dry mustard

1 clove garlic = ⅛ teaspoon garlic powder

1 cup tomato juice = ½ cup tomato sauce + ½ cup water

1 cup buttermilk = 1 cup plain yogurt

1 cup sour cream = ½ cup butter + ¾ cup buttermilk

1 teaspoon lemon juice = ½ teaspoon vinegar

Pan and Baking Dish Sizes

4-cup baking dish
9-inch pie plate
8-inch layer cake pan
7⅜ × 3⅝-inch loaf pan

6-cup baking dish
8 or 9-inch layer cake pan
10-inch pie plate
8½ × 3⅝-inch loaf pan

8-cup baking dish
8 × 8-inch square pan
11 × 7-inch baking pan
9 × 5-inch loaf pan

10-cup baking dish
9 × 9-inch square pan
11¾ × 7½-inch baking pan
15 × 10-inch jelly roll pan

12-cup baking dish
13½ × 8½-inch glass baking pan
13 × 9-inch metal baking pan
14 × 10½-inch roasting pan

Oven Temperatures for Baking

Very slow: 250 to 275 degrees
Slow: 300 to 325 degrees
Moderate: 350 to 375 degrees
Hot: 400 to 425 degrees
Very Hot: 450 to 475 degrees

Contributors

The Lufkin Service League would like to thank its members and their friends who contributed so much to this book.

Melissa Patterson Abeldt
June Holton Arnett
Philip Arnett
Mary Jule Shands Baggett
Margaret Kubin Bancroft
Charolotte Brown Barrett
Kathy Twilley Barrett
Suzanne Fitts Barrett
Bobbeye Spivey Bartlett
Mrs. E. L. Bartlett, Sr.
Lynn Stearman Bass
Patty Burrows Bate
Martha Huff Bates
Gertrude Bazine
Pat Coburn Berry
Beth Blevins
Becky Rutherford Bowers
Ann Booth
La June Ivy Bradley
Suzanne Scott Briscoe
Clarkie Mae Brown
Carol Buchanan
Sue Mitchell Burk
Mary Jo Burns
Patricia Mathews Butts
Sally Davis Cain
Betty Camp
Corie Rendleman Camp
Barbara Mazzagatti Carter
Enoma Carter
Ann Sherrill Caskey
Julie Noland Castleberry
Martha Reichert Chandler
Barbara Hogan Corley
Karan Corley
Linda Warner Coward
Dianne Moore Croom
Barbara Brashear Davis
Jill Platt Day
Jan Bybee Deaton
Lena Belle Koch Denman
Annette Corne Domingue
Patti Woods Draper
Joan Norris Duncan
Judy Robicheau Dunn
Mary Leah Poss Duran
Mozelle Durham
Tempe Medford Durham
Jean Hurst English
Barbara Vines Ferguson
Harriett Fleming

Genie Walton Flournoy
Llewellyn Little Fraizer
Andrea Watts Friesen
Cathey Puckett Friesen
Rona Lassiter Friesen
Vicki Wallace Gann
Betty Moss Gardemal
Mary Pinkston Gibbs
Ross Maddox Gibbs
Doran Pelham Gipson
Marcia Stolnacke Griffin
Cathy Gallas Guidi
Vickie Anders Haglund
Barbara Mattiza Haley
Joanne Seals Hallmark
Anne Hunter Halter
Mrs. Patrick H. Hardy
Bonnie Bell Henderson
Joie Honea Henderson
Mary Martha Gardner Henderson
Burtleye Henderson Hicks
Katherine Hicks
Nancy Read Hicks
Susan Hicks
Woddie Lou Trout Hicks
Barbara Price Hill
Ruth Hinchliffe
Becky Loesch Holton
Ginna Bradford Hudgens
Margaret Billingsley Huggins
Sarah Zeagler Hunter
Brenda Widner Jones
Joanna Puckett Jones
Judy Westerman Jordan
Danna Rusk Jumper
Pat Kennaugh
Beverly McLane Kent
Lynda Denton Langston
Pastsy DeFee Lawrence
Paula McMinn Leeves
Sandra Wallen Leinart
Debbie Smith Lloyd
Dottie Lovett
Martha Painter Mahan
Lynda Steele Martin
Georgia Woods Mathews
Susan Rutherford Mathis
Florence Mazzagatti
Cissy Dailey McCarroll
Sharon Spivey McClure
Yvette Durham McManus

John McNeil
Teresa Jackson McNiel
Len Arnett Medford
Jan Matthews Metteauer
Marilyn Allen Miller
Peggy Pedigo Montgomery
Carol Camp Moore
Debra Sedlacek Moore
Holly Newsom Moore
Jan Norris Moore
Nancy DeBerry Moore
Peggy Moore
Virginia Moore
Clem Morrison
Sarah Kesinger Murray
Jo Ann Ricks Nerren
Effie Nini
Margie Norris
Becky Millif Oates
Jan O'Toole
Mary Elizebeth Owens
Gay Roper Parker
Cathy George Pavlic
Annie Mae Peoples
Rudy Pharis
Ladeen Fogel Pluss
Dianne Jones Poland
Madelyn Erwin Porter
Bennie Lowry Prince
Alys Frazier Ray
Janet Bauman Read
Nancy Hopkins Reily
Bobbi Riassetto Robinson
Sue Barber Rolf
Tamesha Lindsey Root
Nancy Ledbetter Roper
Sherry Mathis Roper
Joanne Morton Roquemore
Janice Ann Royle Rowe
Phyllis Moore Royle
Carolin Shands Sanders

Helen Lowe Scott
Cissy Gault Seely
Susie Oviatt Shands
Emily Barbee Shelton
Susan Shands Simpson
Margie Smallwood
Sandra Blackburn Smelley
Donna King Spore
Roschelle Durham Springfield
Libby Love Stapleton
Marian Stapleton
Amanda Harrelson Stover
Susan Gissell Sumners
Carolyn Todd Swan
An Walker Sweeny
Harriet Duncan Tamminga
Cindy Bresie Taylor
Janet Sisk Taylor
Marcia Wolff Thompson
Cathy Culwell Todd
Debbie Moore Todd
Brenda Jackson Walker
Betty Owen Wareing
Lisa Denman Warner
Ann Brown Watson
Mary Jane Medford West
Elizabeth Rowe Westerman
Clarice Alexander Whitaker
Laddie Books Williams
Stacy Williams
Donna Baker Willis
Callie Brown Winston
Pearl Witherell
Barbara Whitaker Wood
Marcelle Mitchell Woods
Ethel Barrett Yates
Marietta "Cookie" Lanier Yeates
Carol Guettler Zbranek
Erin Vanessa Zeagler
Terri Rucker Zeleskey

Index

M

Macaroni
Marmalades
Meat Sauces
Meringue
Mexican
Microwave
Mincemeat
Muffins

Mushrooms
Mustard

N

Noodles
Nuts

O

Oatmeal
Okra
Onions

P

ACCORDING TO TASTE
Lufkin Service League Publications
P.O. Box 1311
Lufkin, Texas 75902-1311

Please send _____ copies at	$11.95 each	$ _____
Plus postage & handling	2.00 each	$ _____
Tax for Texas residents	.61 each	$ _____
Gift wrap per book	1.00 each	$ _____
Enclosed is check Total		$

Please make checks payable to Lufkin Service League Publication.

Name _____

Address _____

City _____ State _____ Zip _____

ACCORDING TO TASTE
Lufkin Service League Publications
P.O. Box 1311
Lufkin, Texas 75902-1311

Please send _____ copies at	$11.95 each	$ _____
Plus postage & handling	2.00 each	$ _____
Tax for Texas residents	.61 each	$ _____
Gift wrap per book	1.00 each	$ _____
Enclosed is check Total		$

Please make checks payable to Lufkin Service League Publication.

Name _____

Address _____

City _____ State _____ Zip _____

ACCORDING TO TASTE
Lufkin Service League Publications
P.O. Box 1311
Lufkin, Texas 75902-1311

Please send _____ copies at	$11.95 each	$ _____
Plus postage & handling	2.00 each	$ _____
Tax for Texas residents	.61 each	$ _____
Gift wrap per book	1.00 each	$ _____
Enclosed is check Total		$

Please make checks payable to Lufkin Service League Publication.

Name _____

Address _____

City _____ State _____ Zip _____

If you would like to see *According to Taste* in your area, please add the names and addresses of your local gift or book stores:

Name   Address

If you would like to see *According to Taste* in your area, please add the names and addresses of your local gift or book stores:

Name   Address

If you would like to see *According to Taste* in your area, please add the names and addresses of your local gift or book stores:

Name   Address